D0561143

The Basic Business Library: Core Resources

The Basic Business Library: Core Resources

2nd Edition

Edited by Bernard S. Schlessinger

Rashelle S. Karp and Virginia S. Vocelli,
Associate Editors

ORYX PRESS
1989

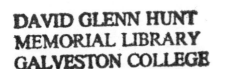

The rare Arabian Oryx is believed to have inspired the myth of the unicorn. This desert antelope became virtually extinct in the early 1960s. At that time several groups of international conservationists arranged to have 9 animals sent to the Phoenix Zoo to be the nucleus of a captive breeding herd. Today the Oryx population is nearly 800, and over 400 have been returned to reserves in the Middle East.

Copyright © 1989 by
The Oryx Press
2214 North Central at Encanto
Phoenix, AZ 85004-1483

Published simultaneously in Canada

Printed and Bound in the United States of America

∞ The paper used in this publication meets the minimum requirements of American National Standard for Information Science—Permanence of Paper for Printed Library Materials, ANSI Z39.48, 1984.

Library of Congress Cataloging-in-Publication Data

The Basic business library : core resources / edited by Bernard S. Schlessinger ; Rashelle S. Karp and Virginia S. Vocelli, associate editors. — 2nd ed.
    p.   cm.
Includes index.
ISBN 0-89774-451-9
    1. Business libraries.   2. Business—Bibliography.   3. Business libraries—Bibliography.   4. Reference books—Business—Bibliography.   I. Schlessinger, Bernard S., 1930- .   II. Karp, Rashelle S.   III. Vocelli, Virginia S.
Z675.B8B37   1989
016.0276'9—dc19   88-37381

Contents

Preface

This second edition of *The Basic Business Library: Core Resources* follows the first edition in its objectives and in its structure, except for changes in the indexes provided. The extensive revision of each section was based on correspondence received from many of the users of the popular first edition.

Part I, "Core List of Printed Business Reference Sources," has been updated and revised as described in the introduction to Part I. Its purpose remains the same, as a checklist of essential business reference tools for smaller to medium-sized libraries to use in collection development. In accordance with user requests, sources for management and for law libraries have been expanded.

To Part II, "The Literature of Business Reference and Business Libraries," has been added the output of the years 1981–1987; the output of the years 1976–1981 has been retained. This section now provides a 11-year overview of a burgeoning field of librarianship for the student and the practitioner.

Part III, the series of state-of-the-art essays, has been significantly expanded to serve student and practitioner as an introduction to the field. As in the first edition, expert practicing librarians were commissioned to write the essays. Some of the essays are titled similarly to their counterparts in the first edition, but have been revised by the original writers. The massive revision of the essay on databases makes it almost totally new. The promotion essay of the first edition has been expanded into a treatment of marketing. Two essays dealing with the area of government documents are new to this edition.

The indexes to the second edition have been restructured, based on comments from users, who found the multiple indexes of the first edition unwieldy. This edition accordingly contains a comprehensive, alphabetical index to the entire book, which we hope will be easier to use.

Two persons assumed especially heavy burdens in the preparation of the book: Virginia Vocelli, who produced Part I, and Rashelle Karp, who produced Part II and supervised the computer composition of all parts of the book. In addition, particular thanks are due to the essayists and to the students in business courses and workshops at Texas Woman's University and Northern Illinois University who served as evaluators of the first edition and provided material for this second edition. Finally, a word of thanks to our editor, Jan Krygier, who cheerfully supplied both editing and prodding.

Any effort of this sort is rewarded with its reception by purchasers and by its use. We hope that the second edition will be as well received as was the first.

Bernard S. Schlessinger

PART I

Core List of Printed Business Reference Sources

Introduction

by Bernard S. Schlessinger

The following core list of business reference sources was originally a selection of sources for small and medium-sized libraries with a total purchase price of below $5,000. It was developed by a small group of public and academic business librarians who attended the Business Reference Workshop at the State University of New York at Albany in the summer of 1975. After editing by the author, the original list was reviewed by all the attendees at the workshop and was distributed on demand for three years. The response prompted the author to revise the original list in 1979 with the help of Helen Jordan, director of the Columbia College Library in Columbia, South Carolina. That revision, plus succeeding revisions and annotations, both in the first edition and this second edition (the latter with the help of Virginia Vocelli, director of the West Hartford Public Library in West Hartford, Connecticut), changed the list from one intended for smaller business libraries to a core list of business reference sources. The attendant increase in cost was unavoidable.

The total assignable cost of the 177 titles in the core list, based on August 1988 prices without discounts, is now close to $29,500. This does not include titles such as the *Area Handbook Series* (in which prices of individual items vary) or *Business Periodicals Index* (which is sold on a service basis) or expensive series like *Predicasts*, which will probably not be purchased by the smaller library, but which are nevertheless included.

There is some duplication of information within these various sources, but such titles have been included deliberately to allow for choice. For example, although there is duplication of the publications on business services, it would be expected that the smaller library would buy selectively.

It is important to note that, in preparing the "Core List" for this second edition, each title in the first edition was reexamined and reevaluated, with all annotations revised and updated. An attempt was made to round out the list by adding some general, business-related items (such as *Letitia Baldrige's Guide to Business Etiquette*), supplementing management- and high-technology-oriented items, and adding law titles of interest to business. The review resulted in 36 sources being dropped from the original list and 57 being added. A newer edition of the same source is provided for 106 items. Only 14 items listed are the same source and same edition as the first book.

The list is arranged alphabetically by titles, with letter-by-letter alphabetization. Data in citations, where applicable, include title, author or editor, edition, publisher and location, date of publication or beginning date, frequency of publication and price. The index provides access to the list by author or editor, by publisher, and by subject.

As noted in the preface, this book is aimed at students and business reference practitioners. For the student, this core list will become meaningful only as the items are used. As with all reference tools, successful use transforms a lifeless title into an old friend. The student should use the list to become familiar with basic helpers in the area of business reference. The business reference practitioner will recognize many of the titles but should find the core list helpful in three other ways: (1) as a checklist for essential business reference tools, which may be used to test the completeness of the business reference collection and to expand it, if funds permit; (2) for smaller libraries beginning a business reference collection, as a core list from which to choose in building the best collection possible within any budget limitations; and (3) for referral, i.e., to identify sources rarely needed and the libraries that own them, to whom requesting patrons can be referred. Although the readers will find that the majority of the tools included in the list are recommended for all (or almost all) librarians, it is unrealistic to assume that budget limitations will not be a factor in purchasing decisions. As a checklist and as a core list, this volume should help in the efficient use of funds, but the individual librarian will know best what is affordable.

In many of the annotations, the authors have indicated every-other-year purchase as a reasonable alternative to consider. We have also indicated in some annotations that the needs of the users would dictate the purchase decision. In addition, the reader should think carefully about the other methods of resource sharing which are part of the prudent librarian's everyday operation. These might include:

1. Cooperating with a nearby library so that, by alternate-year purchase by the two libraries, the latest edition of a tool would be available to the patrons of both.
2. Assigning subject area coverage to specific neighboring libraries so that the entire list could be accommodated by several libraries working together.
3. Arranging access to special corporate library collections.
4. Persuading businesses within the area to donate funds for the purchase of specific items.
5. Suitable use of interlibrary loan or photocopying for items or parts of items that will not be heavily used.

In the first edition of this book, the author asked readers to suggest changes to the list, promising that an update was planned. The same request is made again, for the next edition, as well as the request for comments on the structured annotation brief (STAB) method used to prepare the annotations in this list.

Core List

Compiled by Virginia S. Vocelli

1.1. Accountants' Index. American Institute of Certified Public Accountants. New York: American Institute Publishing, 1921–. Quarterly, plus cumulative year-end volume. $200.00.

Authority and scope: Published by the professional accounting association, the American Institute of Certified Public Accountants, this index covers books, pamphlets, government documents, and periodical articles dealing with all aspects of accounting and related fields that have been published in English throughout the world. Authors, titles, and subjects are listed in a single alphabetized index, but entries are not annotated. Available online.

Evaluation: This is a convenient and comprehensive source for current literature in the field of accounting. Recommended especially for business and academic libraries.

1.2. Acronyms, Initialisms and Abbreviations Dictionary [year]. Julie T. Towell and Helen E. Sheppard, eds. 12th ed. Detroit, MI: Gale, 1987. $190.00.

Authority and scope: First published in 1960, this dictionary has grown from 12,000 entries to over 400,000. The acronyms are arranged in alphabetical order in a two-column arrangement, with the acronym on the left in boldface type and the definition and a brief explanation, if necessary, to the right. Available at an additional charge is a supplement service covering new acronyms and initialisms and a *Reverse Acronyms Dictionary* in which the complete terms are arranged alphabetically and the acronym is the definition.

Evaluation: The most comprehensive resource of abbreviations, containing thousands of business-related terms, this reference is recommended for all libraries. Smaller libraries may economize by buying every other edition.

1.3. Advertising Age. Chicago: Crain Communications. 1930–. Weekly. $55.00 yearly; $1.50 single copy.

Authority and scope: A respected trade journal, this weekly paper covers the current scene of advertising and marketing and extends to television, broadcasting, and newspapers as well. Regular columns carry information on personnel shifts, account changes, ratings, and new products. Several times a year, special surveys, such as the top national advertisers and top 100 leading media companies, are published. Available online.

Virginia S. Vocelli is director, West Hartford Public Library, West Hartford, CT.

Evaluation: Indexed in *Business Periodicals Index* (entry 1.22), *Reader's Guide,* and *Business Index* (entry 1.18), this is an excellent source for students and professionals following trends in the field or researching companies, and it is recommended for all libraries, except the very smallest.

1.4. Aljian's Purchasing Handbook. National Association of Purchasing Management. Paul V. Farrell, contributing ed. 4th ed. New York: McGraw-Hill, 1982. $67.95.

Authority and scope: In this handbook, formerly edited by George Aljian, retired purchasing executive Paul Farrell has brought together the contributions of 92 purchasing experts and has provided a comprehensive treatment of the policies, practices, and procedures used in purchasing and materials management. The information is presented in 32 sections and includes a glossary, bibliography and library suggestions, reference tables, and an index.

Evaluation: A good mixture of theoretical and practical information, this is the most comprehensive reference on this topic and belongs in every library.

1.5. Almanac of Business and Industrial Financial Ratios. Lee Troy. Englewood, NJ: Prentice-Hall. Annual. $44.95.

Authority and scope: This reference profiles financial and operating ratios for approximately 160 industries including manufacturing, wholesaling, retailing, banks, and financial industries and services. It profiles corporate performance in two analytical tables: Table 1 reports financial and operating information for corporations with and without net income. Table 2 provides the same information but only for those corporations that operated at a profit. There is a time lag, since the statistics are based on corporate activity reported in the latest published IRS tax returns.

Evaluation: Essential to the users of financial and operating information, this reference is recommended for academic and business libraries.

1.6. AMA Management Handbook. William K. Fallon, ed. 2nd ed. New York: ANACOM. 1983. $79.95.

Authority and scope: Fallon, author, consultant and business editor, and over 200 management experts, provide a comprehensive source of practices and techniques. The material is arranged in 14 subject areas including general management, finance, research and technology, manufacturing, purchasing, marketing, and personnel. It is indexed.

Evaluation: Covering a broad range of management topics, this is an excellent handbook and basic resource and is recommended for all libraries.

1.7. American Almanac of Jobs and Salaries. John W. Wright. 3rd ed. New York: Avon Books, 1987. $12.95.

Authority and scope: A comprehensive survey of hundreds of occupations, this reference provides complete job descriptions, salaries, and advancement opportunities in many career areas. Divided into such chapters as "Public Employment," "Science and Technology," "Key White-Collar Jobs," "Unions," "Health Care," and "The Workaday World," the volume concludes with a salary and wage history of a number of occupations. It is indexed.

Evaluation: Handy and easy to use, this popular almanac provides a current, complete, and in-depth picture of American jobs. It is recommended for all libraries.

1.8. American Bank Directory. Norcross, GA: McFadden Business Publications, 1836–. Semiannual. $175.00 complete edition; $16.00 single-state editions.

Authority and scope: Over 15,000 banks and bank holding companies in the United States are included in this directory. Information on bank name, address, Federal Reserve district, year established, branches, transit number, officers and directors, and principal correspondents is given for each entry. The same information is provided in the single-state editions.

Evaluation: A useful alternative to more expensive banking directories, this reference is recommended to all libraries, especially those whose clientele has no need of information on the foreign banking community.

1.9. American Statistics Index: A Comprehensive Guide and Index to the Statistical Publications of the U.S. Government. Washington, DC: Congressional Information Service, 1973–. Monthly, with annual cumulations. $2,015.00.

Authority and scope: Published by a reputable firm specializing in providing access to government publications, the ASI provides access to federal statistics. The abstract volume, arranged by agency, is composed of entries that contain complete bibliographic citations and thorough descriptions of all tables and narratives contained in the government documents. The index volume is composed of two indexes: (1) covering subjects and names; and (2) broken into the following categories: geographic breakdowns, economic breakdowns, and demographic breakdowns. Also included in the index volume are a title index, a guide to the Standard Industrial Classification code, the Standard Occupation Classification, and a list of Standard Metropolitan Statistical Areas (SMSAs). As a complement to ASI, since 1980 CIS has produced the *Statistical Reference Index; a Selective Guide to American Statistical Publications from Private Organizations and State Government Sources.*

Evaluation: Although comprehensive and thorough, price prohibits acquisition by many libraries. If, however, a library is centrally located, has statistical demands, or is in an academic setting, this excellent reference is essential.

1.10. Area Handbook Series. Washington, DC: U.S. Department of the Army, 1975–. Price varies.

Authority and scope: Published under the jurisdiction of the Department of the Army, this country-by-country study series is written by staff members of the Foreign Service Institute of American University. Each book in the series covers the historical, political, economic, and military background of an individual country and includes a lengthy bibliography, a glossary, maps, and statistical information. A three- to four-page profile is included at the beginning of the book, and photographs are featured as well. The studies are revised and updated on an irregular basis.

Evaluation: A basic, relatively inexpensive resource for information on various nations, this is of great use to the businessperson, student, and traveler. It is recommended that libraries circulate these volumes rather than keep them on the reference shelf.

1.11. Area Wage Surveys. U.S. Bureau of Labor Statistics. Washington, DC: Government Printing Office, 1950–. $103.00 for subscription; price varies for single issues.

Authority and scope: Since 1948, the U.S. Bureau of Labor Statistics has published surveys in which occupations common to a variety of manufacturing and other industries are studied on a community-by-community basis. The series has been expanded through the years to include more occupations and more areas. Presently, approximately 70 smaller metropolitan areas and broad industry divisions (manufacturing, transportation, communication and other public utilities, wholesale trade, retail trade, finance, insurance and real estate, and services) are surveyed. Weekly and hourly earnings data are published annually, while a complete earnings-and-benefits survey is published every three years. A U.S. summary is published annually.

Evaluation: Libraries will be most interested if the metropolitan area in which they are located is included; in this case, annual purchase of the report is recommended. Academic and larger business libraries will want the entire series.

1.12. ASPA Handbook of Personnel and Industrial Relations. Dale Yoder and Herbert J. Hememan, Jr. Washington, DC: U.S. Bureau of National Affairs, 1979. $65.00. Supplement, 1983. $22.50.

Authority and scope: Edited by two specialists in the area of personnel and management, this is the official handbook of the American Society for Personnel Administration. Seventy-two authors, all experts in the field, have contributed to 51 chapters (contained in the following eight sections): "Policy and Program Management," "Planning and Auditing," "Administration and Organization," "Staffing Policies and Strategies," "Training and Development," "Motivation and Commitment," "Employee and Labor Relations," and "The Professional in Personnel and Industrial Relations." Extensively footnoted, the handbook includes a literature survey, topical index, and name index. *Handbook Resources Management in the 1980s* was published as a supplement to the *ASPA Handbook.* The content of the eight chapters, presented in the same order as in the *Handbook,* reflects the changes and developments in the field of personnel management.

Evaluation: Designed for the professional in personnel administration, this handbook, along with the supplement, belongs in all academic, business, and larger public libraries.

1.13. Barron's. New York: Dow Jones, 1921–. Weekly. $86.00.

Authority and scope: Published for over 65 years, this national business and financial weekly carries timely articles on investment prospects for industries, individual companies, and business topics of interest to investors. The "Week's Statistics" section includes stock and bond quotations and current economic indicators and indexes. It is indexed in *Business Periodicals Index, Accountants' Index, Business Index,* and *The Wall Street Journal Index* (entries 1.22, 1.1, 1.18, and 1.172).

Evaluation: Indispensable for the professional or amateur investor, *Barron's* is recommended for all libraries.

1.14. Barron's Real Estate Handbook. Jack C. Harris and Jack P. Friedman. 2nd rev. ed. Woodbury, NY: Barron's, 1988. $25.50.

Authority and scope: Containing more than 1,300 terms used in real estate and related areas such as finance and architecture, the first half of this reference is arranged in alphabetical order, from "Abandonment" to "Zoning Ordinance." Most definitions are two to three sentences long, and all include an example of the term, and an illustration when applicable. The remainder of the book is made up of financial reference tables covering such topics as monthly mortgage payments, mortgage values, discount points, graduated mortgages, and depreciation percentages.

Evaluation: Concise and to the point, the examples used in the glossary assist in the understanding of complex terms. Although more of a dictionary than a handbook, this is an excellent book to serve as a basic resource in small libraries; larger libraries may want more detail.

1.15. Best's Insurance Reports: Life-Health, Property-Casualty, and International. Morrison, NJ: Alfred M. Best, 1906–. Annual and twice a year (International). $375.00 each volume.

Authority and scope: Alfred M. Best, a longtime publishing authority in the field of insurance, provides this reference source on all major or domestic insurance companies and groups in the U.S. and many insurance companies in the world. Information provided for each company includes history, management and operation, assets and liabilities, investment data, accident and health statistics, company growth, and current Best's rating, as well as five years of Best's ratings and profitability leverage and liquidity for each insurer. The international edition was added in 1984 and includes data on 700 non-U.S. insurance companies in Canada, Europe, Asia, Australia, South America, and Africa.

Evaluation: Together, these volumes form an extremely valuable source of information on the insurance industry and will be of use to the businessperson and consumer. Smaller libraries may economize by purchasing every other year, or limiting purchase to the domestic reports.

1.16. Black's Law Dictionary. Henry Campbell Black. 5th ed. St. Paul, MN: West Publishing, 1979. $19.95 paper.

Authority and scope: The fifth edition of this standard legal resource contains over 10,000 entries, including usage examples and precedents. Appendixes include the Constitution of the United States, listings of names and terms of justices of the Supreme Court, and an organizational chart of the United States government.

Evaluation: An authoritative and readable source, *Black's Law Dictionary* is considered to be the standard legal dictionary and should be in all libraries. Business clientele will have frequent need to refer to *Black's* in business law matters.

1.17. Broadcasting Cablecasting Yearbook. Washington, DC: Broadcasting Publications, 1935–. $105.00.

Authority and scope: Issued annually by Broadcasting Publications, this serves as a handbook and directory to the broadcasting industry in the U.S. and Canada. It is divided into sections covering broadcasting, television, radio, equipment and engineering, cable television, satellites, programming, advertising and marketing, and professional services and associations. Included is such information as TV and radio call letters, principal FCC regulations, TV market maps, special programming, and audience statistics. There is a general index.

Evaluation: The combination and amount of information in this yearbook justify its place in all reference collections, and annual purchase for larger libraries is indicated.

1.18. Business Index. Belmont, CA: Information Access Company. 1979–. Monthly. $2,450.00.

Authority and scope: Business Index provides comprehensive coverage of more than 810 journals, including the *Wall Street Journal*, *Barron's*, and the business and financial section of the *New York Times*. Library of Congress subject headings are supplemented with natural-language subject headings. Subscribers receive a monthly update which contains the year's cumulation on one microfilm reel; this is used in a company-provided microfilm viewer. A subscription also includes retrospective citations on microfiche.

Evaluation: Comprehensive, easy to use, and up-to-date, *Business Index* provides close competition to *Business Periodicals Index*. Libraries with a large business clientele should receive both, because of the more thorough indexing of BPI and the use of its bound volumes for retrospective searching.

1.19. Business Information: How to Find It, How to Use It. Michael R. Lavin. Phoenix, AZ: Oryx Press, 1987. $49.50.

Authority and scope: Lavin, a business librarian, lecturer, and consultant in business research, has written a handbook combining basic business concepts with in-depth descriptions of major business publications. Sixteen chapters are divided into four major sections: introduction to business information; information about companies; statistical information; and special topics such as marketing, business law, tax law, and job hunting. Each chapter begins with a list of topics to be covered and major sources to be discussed. Additional titles are suggested at the end of the chapter for further reading; and sample pages from selected sources are reproduced. It is indexed.

Evaluation: An excellent reference for the business researcher, this unique and well-written resource should be part of every academic and public library collection.

1.20. Business Information Sources. Lorna M. Daniells. Berkeley, CA: University of California Press, 1985. $40.00.

Authority and scope: Daniells, noted authority and bibliographer in the business field, and former head reference librarian at Harvard University's Graduate School of Business Administration, has compiled this basic guide to business sources and reference materials. Chapters 1 through 8 describe basic business reference sources such as indexes and statistical compilations. Chapters 9 through 20 concentrate on management functions and describe basic texts, handbooks and specialized sources. Books published in the last five years are emphasized, with brief but descriptive annotations included for each entry. A "basic bookshelf" of recommended titles for company libraries constitutes the final chapter. An index is provided.

Evaluation: An important contribution to the business bibliographic field, this completely revised and updated edition is an essential purchase for all libraries.

1.21. Business Organizations and Agencies Directory. Anthony T. Kruzas, Robert C. Thomas, and Kay Gill, eds. Detroit, MI: Gale, 1986. $290.00. Supplement, $85.00.

Authority and scope: Included in the 23 sections of this directory, by type of organization, are trade and business organizations, stock exchanges, Better Business Bureaus, Chambers of Commerce, diplomatic representations, trade and convention centers, educational institutions, data banks and computerized services, franchise companies, government agencies, publishers, and research centers. The master index, new to this edition of the *Directory*, is arranged by organization name and selected keywords.

Evaluation: Although much of the information contained in this volume can be found in other publications, many of them Gale-produced, the combination of materials makes this a very useful source of business information for business libraries and larger public libraries.

1.22. Business Periodicals Index. New York: H. W. Wilson, 1958–. Monthly except July, with periodic cumulations. Sold on service basis.

Authority and scope: H. W. Wilson, a leading publishing house, provides this subject index to over 300 periodicals in the business field. The periodicals indexed are English-language and come from trade and professional associations and government agencies. Citations include article title, volume and page, title of journal, and page length of article. Available online.

Evaluation: This is a valuable resource for businesspeople, students of business administration, or anyone interested in researching a particular area of business or economics. However, for institutions without a major interest in this area, the field is sufficiently covered by other, more general indexes.

1.23. Business Software Directory. Ruth K. Koolish, ed. Glenview, IL: Information Sources, Inc., 1986. 2 vols. $175.00.

Authority and scope: Over 7,300 listings for micro- and minicomputer software, as well as software listings for mainframe computers that interact with micro- and minicomputers, are contained in this directory. Volume 1 contains a user's guide, indexes (application-industry, hardware, software title and vendor), and a controlled vocabulary terms list (new to this edition). Volume 2 contains the software listings, which include title, descriptions, system and service information, availability, vendor address and contact. Available online, the directory was known by previous titles: *Small System Software and Services Software Sourcebook* and *Business Mini/Micro Software Directory*.

Evaluation: Designed to help users choose appropriate software for their business needs, this directory is easy to use and recommended for all libraries whose clientele needs a comprehensive guide to business software.

1.24. Business Statistics. U.S. Department of Commerce. Washington, DC: Government Printing Office. 1932–. Biennial. $18.00.

Authority and scope: Published by the Bureau of Economic Analysis of the Department of Commerce, this volume is a biennial supplement to the periodical *Survey of Current Business* (entry 1.160) and presents historical data for approximately 1,900 series that appear in the S-pages of that periodical. Data are shown on an annual basis for early years, quarterly for the last decade, and monthly for the most recent five years. Also included are sources and explanatory notes to tables.

Evaluation: This is a basic statistical report useful for any library, whether or not the *Survey of Current Business* is received. It is an economical purchase for the smaller library with business statistical needs beyond the *Statistical Abstract of the United States* (entry 1.157).

1.25. Business Week. New York: McGraw-Hill. 1929–. Weekly. $39.95.

Authority and scope: Covering all phases of business, including production, labor, finance, economics, labor relations, new marketing research, exports, transportation, and products, this weekly magazine contains short articles and usually one longer feature article in each issue. There are also regular columns publishing production statistics and leading indicators and book reviews. Special issues are published throughout the year on a regular basis and feature such topics as world economic outlook, a corporate balance sheet ranking the 900 largest U.S. nonfinancial and industrial companies, an executive compensation survey, and the investment outlook at year's end. Indexed in *Business Periodicals Index, Business Index* and other key indexes, *Business Week* is also available online.

Evaluation: Invaluable for keeping current with business trends and developments, this is recommended for all libraries.

1.26. Canadian Trade Index. Toronto, ON: Canadian Manufacturers' Association. 1968–. Annual. $75.00.

Authority and scope: Published by the Canadian Manufacturers' Association, the representative organization of Canadian manufacturers, this index provides basic information for approximately 13,000 Canadian manufacturers, including addresses, branches, export representatives, and trademarks and brands. It also includes a classified list of products, a geographical list of manufacturers, an alphabetical and classified list of agricultural producers, French translations of product headings, an alphabetical list of trademarks, trade and brand names, and a service section.

Evaluation: An international directory of basic information on manufacturers, this is a good reference source for any library, though alternate-year purchase would suffice for the smaller library.

1.27. Computer Dictionary. Charles J. Sippl. 4th ed. New York: Howard Sams & Co., 1985. $24.95.

Authority and scope: Charles Sippl, professor, business consultant and writer, has compiled a dictionary that has been updated frequently to reflect the changes in this complex and fast-changing field. The definitions range in length from one sentence to several and include acronyms, terms, and concepts unique to modern technology. The fourth edition lacks the useful appendixes that were part of previous editions.

Evaluation: Primarily for the advanced user, this is nevertheless a worthwhile reference for any library.

1.28. Consultants and Consulting Organizations Directory. Janice McLean, ed. 7th ed. Detroit, MI: Gale, 1986. Triennial with annual supplements. $344.00.

Authority and scope: This directory contains information on more than 10,000 firms, individuals, and organizations active in over 120 fields in the U.S. and Canada. Volume 1, organized into 14 general subject sections, contains the main listing for each organization: that includes complete name, address, telephone number, principal officers and management, and a description of specialties and activities. Volume 2 contains a geographical index listing consulting organizations by state and by city, a subject index of industries served, a personal name index, and a firm index. An alternative to this title is *Dun's Consultant's Directory.* Which is chosen is a matter of the library's personal preference.

Evaluation: One of the most extensive of its kind, this directory is recommended for all but the smallest public libraries.

1.29. Corporate Technology Directory. Wellesley Hills, MA: Corp Tech, 1986. $750.00.
Authority and scope: Access to over 12,000 private and public U.S. high-technology manufacturing firms whose products include computer hardware and software, fiber optics, robotics, biotechnology, artificial intelligence, and advanced materials is provided by this three-volume set. Volume 1 contains the indexes accessed by company name, key word, subject code, product and manufacturer, zip code, parent/subsidiary company name, and executive name. Volumes 2 and 3 contain the corporate profiles, which include telephone, address, description of company, staff, sales, executive names, product code (developed by Corp Tech for this directory) and a description and ownership characteristics.
Evaluation: While cost may prohibit many smaller libraries from purchasing this, it is a necessary acquisition for large public and academic libraries serving a "high-tech" clientele.

1.30. County and City Data Book. U.S. Bureau of the Census. Washington, DC: Government Printing Office, 1949–. Irregular. $24.00.
Authority and scope: Published as a supplement to the *Statistical Abstract of the United States* (entry 1.157), this volume presents a large and varied selection of items taken from the major decennial and quinquennial censuses and other statistical series. Subjects included are agriculture, business, city finances, education, housing, climate, health, manufacturing, population characteristics, and retail and wholesale trade and services. Geographical areas covered are cities, counties, divisions, states, and smaller urban areas. A special appendix on congressional districts is included.
Evaluation: A valuable reference source for any library, this book provides general and in-depth overviews of communities and their vital statistics.

1.31. County Business Patterns. U.S. Bureau of the Census. Washington, DC: Government Printing Office, 1946–. Annual. Price varies per single issue.
Authority and scope: Issued by the Bureau of the Census, this report series contains employment and payroll statistics by county and by industry, classified by two-, three-, and four-digit Standard Industrial Classifications (SIC). A separate report is issued for each state, Puerto Rico and outlying areas, the District of Columbia, and the U.S.
Evaluation: This is a handy reference tool for any library interested in annual employment and payroll statistics. Small libraries might consider limiting purchase to reports covering their own states, surrounding states, and the U.S. Although the reports are issued annually, the statistics lag approximately two years behind.

1.32. CRB Commodity Yearbook. New York: Commodity Research Bureau. 1939–. Annual. $49.95.
Authority and scope: Published since 1939, this source presents pertinent data about more than 100 commodities. Data included are price, production, shipment, etc.—in most cases for better than a five-year period and some by primary-production states. Also included are general feature articles on topics such as commodity price trends and futures markets. A supplement published three times a year is available through a separate subscription.
Evaluation: A reliable, inexpensive source of data on commodities, this reference belongs in all but the smallest public libraries.

1.33. Dartnell Advertising Manager's Handbook. Richard H. Stansfield. 3rd ed. Chicago: Dartnell, 1982. $49.95.

Authority and scope: Richard Stansfield and contributors, all authorities in the field of advertising, present a thorough treatment of modern advertising. All aspects of managing an advertising campaign are covered, including agency selection, campaign planning, prospect identification, copywriting, headlines, media, research, surveys, budget, and image building. Illustrations and case histories are used throughout the text. An index is included.

Evaluation: While it is oriented toward industrial advertising, this comprehensive treatise on the basic techniques utilized in a successful advertising campaign can serve as the core source in advertising for any reference collection.

1.34. Dartnell Marketing Manager's Handbook. Steuart Henderson Britt and Norman F. Guess, eds. 2nd rev. ed. Chicago: Dartnell, 1983. $49.95.

Authority and scope: Guess, senior vice-president of Dartnell, has completely revised Britt's original handbook, with the help of most of the original contributors and additional experts in the field. There are 76 chapters covering such topics as the marketing function, research, developing the marketing plan, putting it into action, promotion, and international marketing. There are suggestions for further reading at the end of most chapters, and the volume is indexed.

Evaluation: One of the most comprehensive handbooks in the field, this is recommended for all libraries as a basic resource.

1.35. Dartnell Office Administration Handbook. Robert S. Minor and Clark W. Fetridge. 6th ed. Chicago: Dartnell, 1984. $49.95.

Authority and scope: Published by one of the most respected business publishing companies, this handbook is composed of 36 chapters divided among seven parts: "Basics of Administrative Management," "Office Personnel Recruitment and Selection," "Administration of Office Personnel," "Office Manuals," "Office Practices and Procedures," "Office Environment," and "Administrative Skills Development." Illustrations and sample forms reflect recent trends in office technology. The appendixes include a list of electronic calculator terms, communication terms, and management terms and concepts.

Evaluation: A comprehensive handbook and basic resource on office administration practices and procedures, this reference is recommended for all libraries.

1.36. Dartnell Personnel Administration Handbook. Wilbert Scheer. 3rd ed. Chicago: Dartnell, 1985. $49.95.

Authority and scope: Wilbert Scheer, consultant, author and speaker, has provided a handbook covering all aspects of personnel administration: personnel management, recruitment, employment, indoctrination and orientation, training and development, health and safety, employee services, wage and salary administration, benefits, labor relations, administration, policy, and personnel statesmanship. It is indexed.

Evaluation: This handbook is recommended for all libraries as a basic resource in this field.

1.37. Demographic Yearbook. United Nations, Department of International and Economic and Social Affairs. New York: United Nations, 1949–. Annual. $90.00.

Authority and scope: Published by the United Nations and internationally recognized as authoritative on population statistics, this compilation presents detailed information on selected subjects, including natality, mortality, population distribution, trends and censuses, marriage and divorce, ethnic and economic characteristics, for approximately 220 geographical entities. Special topic tables that vary each year are also published in the yearbook.

Evaluation: Although usually two years behind in publication, this source provides a thorough reference to international population statistics. Smaller libraries can economize by buying every two or three years.

1.38. Dictionary of Banking and Financial Services. Jerry M. Rosenberg. 2nd ed. New York: Wiley, 1985. Hard-cover, $34.95; paper, $16.95.

Authority and scope: Rosenberg, professor and consultant, is the author of several dictionaries in the business and management field. First published as the *Dictionary of Banking and Finance*, this reference contains 15,000 terms used in the international banking and financial markets, securities, and insurance industry. The definitions are brief and include multiple meanings based on their use in related and varying fields. The second edition does not include the appendixes from the first edition.

Evaluation: An excellent ready-reference source, this dictionary is a good bargain and recommended for all libraries where more than one reference in this field is needed.

1.39. Dictionary of Business and Management. Jerry M. Rosenberg. 2nd ed. New York: Wiley-Interscience, 1985. Hard-cover, $36.95; paper, $14.95.

Authority and scope: Rosenberg, a professor and consultant in the field of management, has compiled a reference source for terms currently used in business and management. More than 10,000 entries are listed in alphabetical order, with an average entry length of two or three sentences. Terms, acronyms, and some slang are included. The appendix includes Celsius and Fahrenheit tables, a metric conversion table, sample and interest tables, a list of programs of graduate study in business and management, relevant business quotations, and a summary of major business and economic events in the United States, 1776–1983.

Evaluation: Useful for general access to business terms, this dictionary is readable, easy to use, and recommended for all libraries.

1.40. Dictionary of Computing. 2nd ed. New York: Oxford University Press, 1986. $24.95.

Authority and scope: Over 4,000 terms used in the field of computing and related fields such as electronics, math, and logic are defined in this reference. The entries, written by practitioners in the field and associated fields, are one to several sentences long; there is adequate use of illustrations and diagrams.

Evaluation: Easy to use and probably more useful to the novice computer user than the experienced professional, this dictionary is recommended for all libraries as a basic resource.

1.41. Dictionary of Insurance. Lewis E. Davids. 6th ed. Totowa, NJ: Littlefield, Adams and Co., 1984. Hard-cover, $24.95; paper, $7.95.

Authority and scope: Lewis Davids, a university professor and business author, has compiled this practical guide defining terms used in the insurance business. The definitions are brief and often limited to one sentence. Titles and locations of many of the nonbook sources of information on insurance are also included, as well as lists of state commissioners of insurance and organizations related to the insurance industry.

Evaluation: This dictionary provides quick access to the terms most often used in insurance. It is recommended as a convenient and relatively inexpensive purchase for all libraries.

1.42. Dictionary of Real Estate Appraisal. Chicago: American Institute of Real Estate Appraisers, 1984. $26.50.

Authority and scope: The institute has provided a dictionary of clear and timely definitions of terms that are important in the field of real estate appraisal. It also includes terminology from the related fields of accounting, agriculture, architecture, banking, construction, finance, insurance, law, urban planning, and computers. The definitions are concise, ranging in length from one to three sentences. There is a 32–page bibliography of books, periodicals, and U.S. government publications on real estate appraisal, and two pages of commonly used symbols.

Evaluation: While illustrations would have been useful, this dictionary is recommended for academic and business libraries, where it will be used by both students and professionals.

1.43. Direct Marketing Handbook. Edward L. Nash, ed. New York: McGraw-Hill, 1984. $59.95.

Authority and scope: Nash, president of his own direct-marketing firm and recognized authority in the field, together with 60 experts in this area, has compiled a comprehensive resource covering all aspects of direct marketing. Sixty chapters are divided into five areas: planning, media, creative, production, and applications. The appendix includes a glossary, guidelines for ethical business practices from the Direct Marketing Association, and sample size selection tables for direct mail testing. It is indexed.

Evaluation: Because of its comprehensiveness and currency, larger libraries may want to have a copy of this handbook in reference and the circulating collections. It is highly recommended as a basic resource in this field.

1.44. Directory of American Firms Operating in Foreign Countries. 10th ed. New York: Uniworld Business Publications, Inc., 1984. 3 vols. $150.00.

Authority and scope: Previously compiled by the late Juvenal L. Angel, this directory lists more than 3,200 American corporations which have over 21,000 subsidiaries and affiliates in 121 foreign countries. Volume 1 is an alphabetical index of the American companies listing U.S. address, officers, principal product or service, number of employees and foreign countries in which each operates. Volumes 2 and 3 have company listings by country (Afghanistan to Zimbabwe), each entry including the name and U.S. address of parent firm, principal product, or service.

Evaluation: For anyone interested in American business abroad, this is a useful directory recommended for all business, and large academic and public libraries.

1.45. Directory of American Savings and Loan Associations. Baltimore, MD: T. K. Sanderson Organizations, 1955–. Annual. $50.00.

Authority and scope: This comprehensive listing of all active savings and loan associations and cooperative banks in the U.S. is arranged alphabetically by state and city. Each entry includes street address, mailing address, branches, telephone number, key personnel, and assets.

Evaluation: This directory provides easy access for those interested in savings and loan associations. Business libraries with a banking clientele would find it most useful.

1.46. Directory of Business and Financial Services. Mary Grant and Riva Berleant-Schiller. 8th ed. New York: Special Libraries Association, 1924–. $35.00.

Authority and scope: Compiled by two research center administrators and professors, this recently revised directory describes over 1,000 business and financial services that are published periodically or with regular supplements. Arranged alphabetically by title, each entry contains publisher, description of contents, frequency, and price. New in this edition is a section describing over 100 databases and a list of investment consultants. There are three indexes: publisher, geographic, and subject.

Evaluation: Providing access to many of the business services available today, this is a handy reference recommended to all but the smallest public libraries.

1.47. Directory of Corporate Affiliations. Skokie, IL: National Register Publishing. Annual. $395.00.

Authority and scope: One of the many directories published by the National Register Publishing Co., this directory is a "who owns whom" listing of about 4,000 American parent companies. Section 1 is a cross-index of all divisions, subsidiaries, affiliates, etc., with parent company and page reference to section 2. Section 2 is an alphabetical listing of parent companies; each entry includes such information as address, telephone number, type of business, number of employees, sales, ticker symbol, stock exchange, and top executives. In addition, divisions and subsidiaries of that company are listed with address, telephone number, etc. There is also a geographical index and an index by Standard Industrial Classification number.

Evaluation: A valuable source of information for those interested in the corporate structure of the U.S. business community, this is a good published source in which to identify a smaller company. Easy to use as well, it is necessary for all but the smallest reference collection.

1.48. Directory of Directories. Cecilia A. Marlow, ed. 5th ed. Detroit, MI: Gale, 1988. $195.00.

Authority and scope: This standard reference source includes information on over 10,000 directories of all types. Arranged in 16 major subject classifications, each entry includes titles, publisher name and address, description, frequency, price, and availability in computer-readable format. There is a title index and a subject index of over 3,000 subject headings. In addition to printed directories, approximately 250 directory databases, microform collections, and other nontraditional publications are included. The *Directory of Directories* is kept current with a paperback supplement, *Directory Information Service*, available through a separate subscription. All directory publishers mentioned in *Directory of Directories* are accessible in a separate publishers volume.

Evaluation: Useful in all libraries but the smallest, this directory includes a great number of entries of value in business and technical areas.

1.49. Directory of Executive Recruiters. Fitzwilliam, NH: Consultants News, 1971–. Annual. $24.95.

Authority and scope: Designed to help people interested in changing jobs and organizations seeking professional assistance in filling key positions, this reference profiles over 2,000 executive recruiting firms in the United States, Canada and Mexico. Name, address, salary minimum, functions, and industry covered are specified. There is a separate list of retainer recruiting firms and contingency recruiters. Indexed by function, industry, and geographic location, there is also a helpful section on how to use an executive recruiter. A "corporate edition" with more information on the firms is planned for future publication.

Evaluation: While admittedly not complete, this reference is a good source to begin with, and affordable for most libraries.

1.50. Directory of Foreign Firms Operating in the U.S. 5th ed. New York: Uniworld Business Publications, 1986. $100.00.

Authority and scope: Approximately 1,300 foreign business firms in 36 countries which own or have substantially invested in 2,200 American firms are included in this directory. Arranged in three parts, the listing of foreign firm and American affiliate by country constitutes the largest part of the directory. Address, principal officer, and product or service are listed for both the foreign and American firm. Parts 2 and 3 are separate alphabetical listings of all foreign firms and American affiliates listed in Part 1, to which both subsequent parts are keyed.

Evaluation: A companion to the *Directory of American Firms Operating in Foreign Countries* (entry 1.44), this directory is considered a standard in the field. More frequent publication of subsequent editions (4th edition, 1978) would make it even more useful; large public and academic libraries will want it as part of their collection.

1.51. Directory of Foreign Manufacturers in the U.S. Jeffrey S. Arpan and David A. Ricks. 3rd ed. Atlanta, GA: Georgia State University Business Publications, 1985. $80.00.

Authority and scope: Arpan and Ricks, recognized authorities in direct foreign investment in the United States, have compiled this directory of firms located in the U.S. that are owned directly or indirectly by non-U.S. companies. The companies are listed alphabetically, with each entry including address, name of parent company, product, and four-digit SIC code. There is a geographic index, parent company index, parent-company-by-country index, and an index of products by SIC code.

Evaluation: Recommended for its comprehensiveness and ease of use, this directory should be in all business and medium-sized to large public libraries.

1.52. Directory of Management Consultants. 4th ed. Fitzwilliam, NH: Consultants News, 1986. $62.00.

Authority and scope: Over 860 management consulting firms are profiled in this reference. Each entry includes name, address, type of services offered, when founded, name of president, number of staff, branches, revenue range, and geographical areas served. The book is indexed by type of service, industries served, geographic location, and key personnel.

Evaluation: If need is limited to management consultants, this is the best and most convenient directory available. It is recommended where that need is present.

1.53. Directory of Obsolete Securities. New York: Financial Information, 1927–. Annual. $325.00.

Authority and scope: Compiled from the publishing company's Financial Daily Card Service and Financial Stock Guide Service, this is a list of companies whose identities have been lost as a result of name changes, mergers, acquisitions, dissolutions, reorganizations, bankruptcies, charter cancellations, and related changes. Each listing indicates the manner in which the company's identity has been changed, the name of the new company (if any), and the year in which the action took place. When possible an indication has been made as to whether the company's stock has any remaining value or any stockholder equity still exists. It is cumulative since 1927.

Evaluation: Recommended for all but the smallest public libraries, economy may be achieved by alternating years of purchase.

1.54. Directory of Online Databases. New York: Cuadra/Elsevier. Annual subscription includes 2 complete issues and 2 update supplements. $130.00.

Authority and scope: This comprehensive listing of online databases includes all databases available for use with remote computer terminals and microcomputers. Each entry includes name, type (numeric or textual), subject, producer, online service through which service is available, conditions of use, content, language, geographic coverage, updating frequency, and time span. In addition to the database descriptions, there are an alphabetical listing of vendor addresses and six indexes, which are divided by subject, producer, online service/gateway, telecommunications, and a master index.

Evaluation: Extremely valuable because it is continuously updated, this resource is recommended for all business libraries, academic and large public libraries.

1.55. Directory of Trust Institutions. Atlanta, GA: Communication Channels. Annual. $35.00.

Authority and scope: Issued by the publishers of *Trusts and Estates Magazine*, and offered as part of its subscription, this directory is a geographical listing of active trust institutions in the U.S. and Canada. Each entry provides names, addresses, trust assets, and key personnel. Additional information includes an index of state administrators of charitable and proprietary organizations, an index of nonbank services, a glossary of fiduciary terms, trust titles and abbreviations, and other brief, useful banking-related lists.

Evaluation: This is a practical guide which provides quick reference to over 3,800 trust institutions in the Northern Hemisphere. It is recommended for all libraries.

1.56. Directory of United States Importers. New York: Journal of Commerce. Biennial. $275.00.

Authority and scope: Published by a prominent company, this directory lists over 25,000 importers located in the U.S., Canada, and Puerto Rico. Arranged by state, and then alphabetically by company, each entry includes the address, officers, port of entry, date the company was founded, bank reference, and product description. The directory also contains an alphabetical index, a product section and listing of companies who handle that product, foreign trade zones in the U.S., international banks which provide import financing, and U.S. consulates/embassies of major trading nations.

Evaluation: The only complete guide to the U.S. import industry, this directory is recommended for business and large public libraries; smaller libraries will want to know which larger collection in their area may have it, in order to refer patrons.

1.57. Dow Jones Investor's Handbook. Phyllis Pierce, ed. Homewood, IL: Dow Jones-Irwin, 1966–. Annual. $10.95 paper.

Authority and scope: Data on the well-known Dow Jones averages for the most recent year are compiled in this handbook. Industrials, transportation, and public utility stocks are covered, with data including monthly closing averages, quarterly earnings, dividends, yields, and price–earning ratios for more than the last 10 years. The activities of the New York Stock Exchange, American Stock Exchange, and Barron's Group stock are reviewed, with the year's high and low prices, net change, volume, dividends, and most active stock identified. Retrospective statistics are available in Dow Jones Averages, 1885–1930.

Evaluation: Convenient and easy to use, this is recommended for all business and medium-sized to large public libraries.

1.58. The Dow Jones-Irwin Business and Investment Almanac. Sumner N. Levine, ed. Princeton, NJ: Dow Jones Books, 1977–. Annual. $24.95.

Authority and scope: Sumner Levine, finance professor and business author, has compiled a handy source of information on business, economics, and investments. Essays, charts, graphs, chronologies, and statistical tables cover such topics as regulatory agencies, finance, largest corporations, stock market, employment wages and productivity, the industrial real estate market, bank failures and corporate bankruptcies, government budgets, receipts and deficits, international business, and financial comparisons. It includes an index.

Evaluation: Recommended for all libraries, this volume is a handy ready-reference tool with an extremely useful and up-to-date combination of information.

1.59. Dun & Bradstreet's Principal International Businesses. New York: Dun & Bradstreet, 1974–. Annual. $495.00.

Authority and scope: Over 55,000 leading enterprises in over 133 countries are listed in this directory published by one of the most respected publishers in the business world. Arranged in three sections (geographical, SIC number, and alphabetical by company name), the most complete entry is provided in the first section and it includes company name, address, product, number of employees, sales expressed in local currency, executive officers, and SIC number. The other sections give name and location only.

Evaluation: As one of the most complete listings of international businesses, this directory certainly belongs in business and academic libraries. The price will probably prohibit small libraries from considering it.

1.60. Economic Census. U.S. Bureau of the Census. Washington, DC: Government Printing Office, 1929–. Quinquennial. Price and format vary.

Authority and scope: Published by the U.S. Bureau of the Census, the *Economic Census* includes individually published censuses of retail trade, wholesale trade, service industries, construction industries, manufacturers, mineral industries, and transportation, as well as the censuses of outlying areas (Puerto Rico, the Virgin Islands, and Guam), the Enterprise Statistics Program, the Survey of Minority–Owned Business Enterprises, and the Survey of

Women–Owned Businesses. Published at five–year intervals (covering the years ending in "2" and "7"), the economic censuses constitute the most comprehensive and periodic canvas of the nation's industrial and business activities. The data for the economic censuses are tabulated on the basis of the Standard Industrial Classification system. Geographic coverage varies, with the most detailed data published at the national level and fewer statistics appearing for states and smaller areas in order to avoid disclosing information on individual firms. The censuses are available on microfiche.

Evaluation: Recommended for all business and academic libraries, selection of the individual reports will depend on projected interest. Smaller libraries should consider obtaining reports for their own states for each census and perhaps the U.S. summary volume.

1.61. Economic Indicators. U.S. Council of Economic Advisers, Washington, DC: Government Printing Office, 1948–. Monthly. $32.00.

Authority and scope. Prepared with an emphasis on the concise presentation of factual data in tabular and chart form, data, covering latest months, quarters, and in some cases as long a period as ten years, are compiled from statistics collected by various government agencies on total output, income and spending; employment, unemployment and wages; production and business activity; prices; and currency, credit, security markets, and federal finance.

Evaluation: Of value to statisticians and economics and business analysts for up-to-date information on economic conditions, *Economic Indicators* is easy to read, and the table and chart format can be a useful combination. Data are available in other sources, however, and purchase is necessary only if the combination format is found valuable by patrons.

1.62. Economic Report of the President. Transmitted to the Congress in February of each year together with the Annual Report of the Council of Economic Advisors. U.S. Council of Economic Advisors. Washington, DC: Government Printing Office, 1947–. Annual. $8.50.

Authority and scope: This annual review of the nation's economic conditions presents projections of the current economic policy, a review of the existing economic conditions, and prospective changes in economic policies.

Evaluation: This prospectus will be of interest to students of political science, to economists, and to historians. Particular data or data combinations may be useful to the nonspecialist.

1.63. Economist. London: The Economist. 1843–. Weekly. $75.00.

Authority and scope: Published for over 125 years, this journal covers various aspects of the economic and political scene in the United Kingdom in brief and feature–length articles. While concentrating primarily on the U.K., the magazine also covers trends and developments of Europe, the international scene, and the United States. Available online, *Economist* is indexed in *Business Periodicals Index, Business Index, F&S* and other key indexes.

Evaluation: Considered an essential and highly respected source for news of the international economic scene, the *Economist* is recommended for all business, academic, and large public libraries.

1.64. Editor and Publisher Annual Market Guide. New York: Editor and Publisher, 1924–. Annual. $60.00.

Authority and scope: Published since 1924, this book surveys over 1,500 daily and weekly newspaper markets in the U.S. and Canada, as well as selected foreign markets. Arranged by state and city, the information includes population, location, trade areas, principal industries, retail businesses, colleges and universities, climate, and newspapers. A map is included for each state with shadowed areas marking Standard Metropolitan Statistical Areas and boxed areas representing Consolidated SMSAs.

Evaluation: A good reference source for people interested in the factors that make up a potential market or a place to live, the guide is easy to use, up-to-date, and warrants annual purchase by all but the smallest libraries, considering the general interest nature of the material.

1.65. Employment and Earnings. U.S. Bureau of Labor Statistics. Washington, DC: Government Printing Office, 1909–. Monthly subscription, $22.00; annual supplement, $8.00; historical volume, $17.00.

Authority and scope: Published by the Bureau of Labor Statistics, this compilation presents detailed statistics on the work force in the U.S. Included are data on both employed and unemployed persons, embracing characteristics such as age, sex, race, occupation, and industry attachment. Also covered is information on nonagricultural wages and salaries, including average weekly hours, average hourly earnings, and average weekly earnings for the nation, states, and metropolitan areas. The monthly report presents current statistics on a monthly or quarterly basis, with some data available for selected geographic areas. An annual supplement to *Employment and Earnings* presents revised detailed industry statistics arranged by SIC number and reported on a monthly sequence. Data from 1909 to 1984 are published in a comprehensive report, *Employment, Hours, and Earnings, U.S., 1909–84*, making available a complete statistical survey of the employment history of the U.S. Another report, *Employment, Hours and Earnings, States and Areas, 1939–82*, makes available this same data in geographic breakdown.

Evaluation: Recommended for all business and academic libraries; in addition, smaller public libraries should consider alternate–year purchase of the annual volume or may make do with the historical volume.

1.66. Encyclopedia of Associations. Katherine Gruber, ed. 21st ed. Detroit, MI: Gale, 1987. Annual. Vol. 1, $220.00; Vol. 2, $200; Vol. 3, $210.00; Vol. 4, $185.00.

Authority and scope: This comprehensive reference source is a classified directory of over 20,000 organized groups of people who have voluntarily associated themselves for stated purposes. Details provided for each group include name, address, acronyms, chief officer, membership, purpose and activities, staff size, special committees, budget, and meetings and publications. Entries in Volume 1, arranged in 17 categories, are national organizations of the United States. There is a name and key–word index. Volume 2 includes the geographical and executive indexes, allowing organizations to be located by city and state and association executives to be identified. Volume 3 is the supplement to use between new editions; it includes new associations and projects. Volume 4 lists international organizations whose headquarters are located outside the United States.

Evaluation: This is an indispensable reference tool for all libraries. Annual purchase of volume 1 is recommended. Less frequent purchase of volumes 2, 3, and 4 should also be considered.

1.67. Encyclopedia of Banking and Finance. Glenn G. Munn and Ferdinand L. Garcia. 8th ed. Boston: Bankers Publishing, 1984. $94.00.

Authority and scope: First edited by Glenn G. Munn and edited later by equally recognized authorities (the latest being F. L. Garcia) this comprehensive work contains brief definitions of terms such as cheque, money order, etc.— and a number of encyclopedia articles on money, credit, banking practices, pertinent business laws and federal regulations, investment, insurance, brokerage, and other topics that require in-depth coverage.

Evaluation: The encyclopedia has no competitor. It furnishes authoritative and readable information on the entire spectrum of banking and related subjects and is an indispensable reference work for all libraries.

1.68. Encyclopedia of Business Information Sources. James Woy, ed. 6th ed. Detroit, MI: Gale, 1986. $210.00.

Authority and scope: Considered a standard in business bibliography, this reference is a comprehensive guide to 23,000 sources of information on over 1,000 specific topics designed to meet the research needs of executives and researchers. Categories are in alphabetical order and range from "abbreviations" and "abrasives" to "zoning" and "zoological gardens." Complete citations are provided in each source. Arrangement is by type of source, such as handbooks and manuals, directories, price sources, trade associations, and commercially available online databases.

Evaluation: An excellent place to start when researching unfamiliar topics, this is an essential purchase for all reference collections. The specificity of subjects, as well as the different types of sources covered, make it particularly useful.

1.69. Encyclopedia of Economics. Douglas Greenwald, ed. New York: McGraw-Hill, 1982. $77.50.

Authority and scope: Greenwald, a well-known consulting economist and author, together with 178 experts in the area, has compiled this comprehensive reference source covering the entire field of economics. The length of articles, arranged alphabetically, ranges from one page to several, and each article includes definition, explanation, relationship to other concepts, and charts and graphs where appropriate. There are references at the end of most entries, and the work is liberally cross-referenced and indexed.

Evaluation: Recommended as a good source for the person who wants in-depth definitions of over 300 important economic terms, this is readable, easy to use, and thorough. It is also expensive for a single-volume book.

1.70. Encyclopedia of Information Systems and Services. Amy Lucas, ed. 7th ed. Detroit, MI: Gale, 1987. United States volume, $210.00; international volume, $185.00; 3-volume set, $360.00.

Authority and scope: Published by the well-established Gale Research Company, this is an international guide to computer-based information systems, services, organizations and products. It covers computer-readable databases, database producers, online vendors and time-sharing companies, consultants, networks, government agencies, libraries, fee-based services, and more. The information (international or domestic) is published in two volumes according to the geographic location of system or service. Listed alphabetically by parent organization, each entry contains complete address, name of director, description of system or service, scope, input sources, holdings, storage media, publications, computer-based products and services, clientele, projected publications and services, microform products and services, and contact personnel. The index volume, which is included even if only one geographic volume is purchased, contains eight separate indexes to the information in the main volumes: master index, databases, publications, software and function (service, personnel, geographic, and subject). An update supplement is issued between editions.

Evaluation: Although expensive, this is a basic resource providing access and a general overview to a fast-growing field. It is essential for any library serving a substantial number of patrons with an interest in this field.

1.71. Encyclopedia of International Commerce. William J. Miller. Centreville, MD: Cornell Maritime Press, 1985. $37.50.

Authority and scope: Active in export/import management for many years, Miller has compiled a comprehensive reference in international trade. Arranged alphabetically, the entries range in length from one or two sentences to several paragraphs. The definitions are accompanied by sample illustrations, sample forms, tables, and cross–references. A detailed table of contents serves as an index to the additional information in the appendixes; also included are information on the Shipping Act of 1984, statistical compilations, related laws and regulations, and commonly used abbreviations.

Evaluation: Concise and easy to understand, this reference is recommended for any library with a clientele interested in foreign trade.

1.72. Encyclopedia of Management. Carl Heyel, ed. 3rd ed. New York: Van Nostrand, 1983. $62.95.

Authority and scope: With the help of 203 expert contributors, Heyel, a business consultant, author and professor, has compiled a reference source for a broad range of business management topics. In dictionary arrangement ("accounting" to "zero defects"), the length of entries ranges from one paragraph to several pages. Most articles cite additional references, and there is liberal use of "see" and "see also" cross-references. A "Guide to Core Subject Readings" pulls related topics together and suggests an order of reading, so that the book might also be used as an extended learning tool. It is indexed.

Evaluation: An excellent, comprehensive resource, this could serve as a basic reference for management information for all libraries.

1.73. Europa Year Book: A World Survey. Detroit, MI: Gale, 1926–. Annual. 2 vols. $265.00.

Authority and scope: Published for over 50 years, this has become a standard source of information on the countries of the world. Volume 1 contains international organizations and the first part of the alphabetical survey of countries of the world (Afghanistan to Jordan). Volume 2 covers Kampuchea to Zimbabwe. The information provided includes essential data, such as recent history, government, economic affairs, education, tourism, and a statistical survey.

Evaluation: This is a truly authoritative handbook known for its up-to-date, accurate, and comprehensive coverage of the political, economic and commercial institutions of the world. It is recommended for all but the smallest libraries. Smaller libraries may wish to note its accessibility elsewhere in the immediate area.

1.74. Exporters' Directory/U.S. Buying Guide. New York: Journal of Commerce. Biennial. 2 vols. $250.00.

Authority and scope: Produced by a respected publishing company, this directory/buying guide lists over 32,000 exporting firms in the U.S. and Puerto Rico. Volume 1 contains listings of companies, brand names, an alphabetical product index, and cross–index of exported products (Schedule B), and other miscellaneous information of interest to exporters. Volume 2 lists exporters in each state in alphabetical sequence. Each entry contains complete address, telephone number, principal company officers, and product description.

Evaluation: With the exception of the smaller library, this reference is essential for any library whose clientele has marketing or managing interests in international commerce.

1.75. Exporters' Encyclopedia. New York: Dun & Bradstreet. Annual with twice-monthly updates. $395.00.

Authority and scope: This guide from one of the top publishers of business resources covers every phase of exporting to over 200 world markets. Divided into six sections, the export market profile section constitutes most of the volume. Arranged alphabetically by country, the following information is provided: country profile, communications data, key contracts, trade regulations, documentation regulations, marketing data, transportation, and business travel. The other sections contain such data as export information of a general nature, pertinent organizations and government agencies, communications, port descriptions, and instructions on handling an export order and communications. Published separately is the *Export Documentation Handbook*, which contains details on documentation required for exporters.

Evaluation: While expensive, this is an excellent reference in the exporting field. Useful, too, from a travel standpoint, it is recommended for business and large academic and public libraries.

1.76. Facts on File Dictionary of Personnel Management and Labor Relations. Jay Shafritz. 2nd ed. Revised and expanded. New York: Facts on File, 1985. $35.00.

Authority and scope: Shafritz, a professor and author in the field of personnel management, has compiled a reference which contains terms, phrases, processes, names, laws, and court cases "with which personnel managers should be familiar." The definitions range in length from one sentence to several and contain illustrations when appropriate. There are many cross-references and suggested texts for further reading. The appendix contains official names of national unions with popular names and acronyms, popular names with official names and acronyms, and the National Labor Relations Board style manual.

Evaluation: The definitions in this dictionary are concise and easy to use, making this reference recommended for any business collection serving either the private or public sector.

1.77. Fairchild's Financial Manual of Retail Stores. New York: Fairchild Publications. Annual. $60.00.

Authority and scope: Statistical information on retail stores in the U.S. is provided, including sales and earnings, net income, assets, and liabilities. Listed for each entry are officers, directors, business activities, subsidiaries, transfer agents, and number of stores. The index includes reference to the owning corporation if applicable.

Evaluation: Recommended for all libraries, this provides easy access to this segment of business for all business professionals, students, and job hunters. Smaller libraries can economize by purchasing in alternate years.

1.78. Federal Reserve Bulletin. U.S. Board of Governors of the Federal Reserve System. Washington, DC: Publications Services, U.S. Board of Governors of the Federal Reserve System. Monthly. $20.00.

Authority and scope: From the U.S. Board of Governors of the Federal Reserve System, this monthly periodical presents current articles on economics, money and banking, policy, and other official statements issued by the Board. The "Financial and Business Statistics" section makes up the second half of each issue and is composed of current U.S. banking and monetary statistics. The statistics are presented monthly or quarterly for the current year and annually for the previous three years. Available online.

Evaluation: An excellent source for a survey of U.S. banking and monetary statistics, this periodical is particularly useful for academic and special libraries.

1.79. Forbes, Annual Directory Issue. New York: Forbes, 1917–. Annual. $4.50.

Authority and scope: Forbes, a leading publisher in the field of business, provides a listing of the 500 largest companies in the U.S. Published each May, the issue ranks the companies separately by sales, profits, assets, and market values and then lists them in alphabetical order. Each entry in the latter section summarizes all rankings and financial data for that company. Available online.

Evaluation: This is a quick, convenient source for any library and also comes as a part of the subscription to the magazine. The list may not be as well known as the *Fortune* magazine's "500" (entry 1.81), (the companies listed are usually the same on both lists), but the information provided is more varied. Subscribers to the magazine also benefit from other studies published on a regular basis, such as the mutual fund survey, the 200 best small companies, and the richest people in America.

1.80. Foreign Economic Trends and Their Implications for the United States. U.S. Bureau of International Commerce. Washington, DC: Government Printing Office, 1968–. Irregular. $75.00 per year.

Authority and scope: Published by the Bureau of International Commerce, Department of Commerce, as compiled by the various U.S. embassies abroad, this series of over 100 brief country-by-country reports surveys current economic situations and trends and implications for the United States. Data provided are gross national product, foreign trade, wage and price indexes, unemployment rates, and construction.

Evaluation: This is a basic series useful for a concise overview of overseas economic conditions and their implications for the U.S. economy. It is recommended for all business libraries that can afford it, especially those with clientele involved in overseas business.

1.81. Fortune Directory of the 500 Largest U.S. Industrial Corporations. Chicago: Fortune Magazine, 1967–. Annual. $3.95.

Authority and scope: Prepared by one of the most well known and prestigious business magazines, the "Fortune 500" lists the largest U.S. industrial corporations. Appearing in April or May of each year, the rankings include sales, assets, net income, stockholders' equity, employees, net income as percent of stockholders' equity, earnings per share, and total return to investors. They also include rankings of the 500 based on separate measures such as sales, assets, etc., as well as who did the best and worst in 11 categories including sales, assets, changes in profits, and total return to investors. The magazine also publishes other lists: the survey of the next 500 largest corporations is published in June, and that of the "International 500" (the largest industrial corporations outside the U.S.), in August.

Evaluation: As a special feature of one of the best-known business magazines, this source is a handy and reliable ranking that should be in all libraries. (See also entry 1.79, *Forbes, Annual Directory Issue*).

1.82. Franchise Annual: Handbook and Directory. Edward L. Dixon, Jr., ed. Lewiston, NY: Info Press, 1969–. Annual. $24.95.

Authority and scope: A directory of over 3,000 listings for American, Canadian, and overseas franchises, this volume also includes consultants, distributors, and licensors. Arranged by type of franchise, most entries include name, address, and telephone number of contact person, nature of franchise, number of units, date of establishment, and investment cost. There are also several chapters that explore and explain the intricacies of the franchise industry.

Evaluation: The general-interest potential and reasonable price would make this a recommended item for all public and business-oriented libraries.

1.83. Franchise Opportunities Handbook. U.S. Bureau of Domestic Commerce, Washington, DC: Government Printing Office. 1967–. Annual. $15.00.

Authority and scope: The U.S. Bureau of Domestic Commerce has provided a handbook of equal opportunity franchisors with the following information: descriptive information, number of existing franchises, training provided, requirements, and a brief history. There is useful information on selecting and evaluating a franchise, a list of government assistance programs, and a bibliography. The franchises are listed by category, and an alphabetical index and an index by category are included.

Evaluation: This is a relatively inexpensive and up-to-date reference source for a growing field of business. It is recommended for all libraries because of its general-interest value.

1.84. Fundamentals of Legal Research. J. Myron Jacobstein and Roy M. Merskey. 3rd ed. Mineola, NY: Foundation Press, Inc., 1985. $22.95.

Authority and scope: Considered a standard in legal research, this book provides answers to basic questions about legal research tools and how to use them. Appendixes include legal abbreviations, state guides, loose-leaf services, and more.

Evaluation: A valuable resource in the area of legal research, this reference should be held by even the smallest public and academic libraries. It can provide sound guidance to the business law researcher.

1.85. Gale Directory of Publications, An Annual Guide to Newspapers, Magazines, Journals and Related Publications. Detroit, MI: Gale. Annual. $135.00.

Authority and scope: The new publisher has left unchanged the format and content of this reference, formerly the *Ayer/IMS Directory of Publications.* In existence for over 100 years, this directory contains information on more than 23,000 newspapers, magazines, and trade publications in the U.S., Canada, and Puerto Rico. Geographically arranged by state or province, and then by city, each entry contains cost, circulation, frequency, advertising rates, names of editor and/or publisher, and mailing address of each publication listed. A map for each state is included. An alphabetical index and several classified indexes are included: agricultural publications, magazines of general interest, college publications, trade and technical publications, and weekly, semi-weekly, and tri-weekly newspapers.

Evaluation: One of the best known and respected directories of its kind, this reference is recommended for all libraries.

1.86. Government Regulation of Business: An Information Sourcebook. Robert Goehlert and Nels Gunderson. Phoenix, AZ: Oryx Press, 1987. $55.00.

Authority and scope: Compiled by bibliographic specialists in political science and business to provide access to the literature on the government regulation of business and industry, this bibliography is for researchers, government personnel and businesspeople. It is divided into six major sections covering core library collection, economics of regulation, politics of regulation, regulatory activities, major regulatory agencies, and reference works. Focusing on regulation at the national level, entries are limited to English-language works published between the years 1945 and 1985. Annotations are included for the core library list and reference works. There are three indexes: subject, author, and title.

Evaluation: A comprehensive source for a somewhat specialized area, this is recommended for larger libraries whose patrons have solid business research interests.

1.87. Guide to American Directories: A Guide to Major Directories of the United States Covering All Trade, Professional and Industrial Categories. Bernard Klein and Glenn S. Schacher, eds. 11th ed. Coral Springs, FL: B. Klein Publications, 1956–. Irregular. $55.00.

Authority and scope: Klein, a well-known editorial consultant, with the assistance of Schacher, has compiled an extensive listing of over 6,500 directories arranged in several hundred categories. A descriptive annotation is provided, with publication data for each title.

Evaluation: While not as complete as Gale's *Directory of Directories* (entry 1.48), this reference is heavy on business listings and could be selected as a cheaper alternative to the other source.

1.88. Guide to Special Issues and Indexes of Periodicals. 3rd ed. New York: Special Libraries Association, 1985. $35.00.

Authority and scope: Compiled by members of the Special Libraries Association and published by the same organization, this reference tool provides detail on over 1,362 periodicals in the U.S. and Canada that publish on a regular basis special issues, buyers guides, convention issues, statistical outlooks or reviews and other features. The periodicals are listed in alphabetical order. Each entry, in addition to providing complete subscription information, includes the title of the special issue or index, description, release date, history of special issue, computerized databases where the periodical is indexed or abstracted, and price. Added features include a classified list of periodicals, a subject index to the special issues, and a separate list of Canadian periodicals.

Evaluation: A valuable tool for identifying regularly appearing issues and indexes that attempt to gather together statistical or other types of useful data, this is recommended for all libraries.

1.89. Handbook for Professional Managers. Lester R. Bittel and Jackson Ramsey. New York: McGraw-Hill, 1985. $59.95.

Authority and scope: Bittel and Ramsey, both business authors, consultants and professors, have edited the contributions of 229 experts in the field to provide a thorough treatment of management techniques, terms, practices and philosophy. Each entry, one to six pages in length, supplies a definition of underlying principles, a description of concrete applications and procedures, and evaluations of the usefulness of the concept or technique. Illustrations are included when applicable, and most entries are accompanied by a list of references. It is generously cross-referenced and indexed. Originally published under the title *Encyclopedia of Professional Management.*

Evaluation: This up-to-date and comprehensive treatment of management concepts useful to managers and students should be included in all library collections.

1.90. Handbook of Accounting and Auditing. John C. Burton, Russell E. Palmer, and Robert S. Kay. Boston: Warren, Gorham, and Lamont, 1981. Update, 1987. $96.00, basic volume; $49.00, update.

Authority and scope: The authors have compiled this handbook with the help of over 50 contributors, all accounting professors or accountant professionals. It is composed of 49 chapters in seven parts: general issues of accounting measurement and disclosure, overview of accounting concepts and procedures, specific areas of current financial accounting reporting and auditing, accounting for specialized industries, major accounting institutions, legal aspects of accounting and auditing, and an overview of research in both fields. Each chapter includes suggested readings, and these lists are combined into a bibliography at the end. It is indexed. The update, edited by D. Gerald Searfoss and Alfred M. Yates, is organized according to the 49 chapters of the handbook. Introductory pages include a list of the chapters that have been extensively updated. A comprehensive index refers to both volumes. The Update is essential to keep current with new information and trends.

Evaluation: A basic resource in an important field, the approach, content and comprehensiveness of this handbook recommend it and the update as an essential purchase for all libraries but the smallest.

1.91. Handbook of Basic Business Economic Statistics. Washington, DC: Bureau of Economic Statistics. Monthly; annual cumulation. $132.00.

Authority and scope: The Bureau of Economic Statistics, a private research organization, publishes this basic source book of more than 1,800 current statistical series on the national economic situation, including comparable data back to 1913, if available. Data on labor, prices, production, general business indicators, social security, and national product and income, all condensed from federal government sources, are included.

Evaluation: Comprehensive, reliable, and approachable, this handbook is useful when statistics are needed but the patron is unsure of availability and format wanted. Expensive, though plain in appearance, this is a basic reference tool for business, academic, and larger public libraries. For a smaller subscription fee, it is available on a less frequent basis.

1.192. Handbook of Construction Management and Organization. Joseph P. Frein, ed. 2nd ed. New York: Van Nostrand-Reinhold, 1980. $56.95.

Authority and scope: Frein, along with experts in their fields, has compiled a comprehensive handbook on every phase of organizing and operating a construction business. The information is divided into 32 chapters, beginning with the basics of contracting and following through to contract completion and settlement. There is also coverage on financing, equipment maintenance and repair, basic management techniques, bid strategy, taxes, and estimating. An index is included.

Evaluation: This is an invaluable reference work directed to the general contractor, specialty contractor, and subcontractor, as well as to the student and professor. It is recommended for the business and medium-sized public library as a basic resource in the field.

1.93. Handbook of Corporate Finance. Edward I. Altman, ed. New York: Wiley, 1986. $60.00.

Authority and scope: The classic, *Financial Handbook*, 4th ed, 1981, was split into two volumes: this, and its companion, *Handbook of Financial Markets and Institutions* (entry 1.94). Contributors from the academic and business world have compiled this compendium on corporate finance and investment theory and practice. Among the topics covered in 19 sections, are planning and control techniques, forecasting, statement analysis, small–business finance, pension and profit sharing, leasing, mergers, and bankruptcy and reorganization. It is indexed.

Evaluation: This newest version of the classic treatment of corporate finance continues to deserve a place in all business and academic libraries.

1.94. Handbook of Financial Markets and Institutions. Edward I. Altman, ed. New York: Wiley, 1987. $75.00.

Authority and scope: Altman, university professor, with the assistance of other experts in this field, has compiled this guide to financial markets and institutions. In some 30 sections, the following are covered: money and capital markets, U.S. debt obligations, deregulation, insurance, reinsurance, and risk management. The new edition includes sections on the microcomputer and investments, bond rating process, investment banking, high yield bonds, and small business financing. Like its companion volume (entry 1.93), it is indexed.

Evaluation: Considered the authoritative handbook to which business and finance professionals turn, this reference is recommended for all business and academic libraries.

1.95. Handbook of Human Resources Administration. Joseph J. Famularo, ed. 2nd ed. New York: McGraw-Hill. 1986. $79.95.

Authority and scope: Famularo, formerly senior vice-president of human resources for McGraw-Hill and the author of several business texts, has assembled the contributions of over 80 experts in the field of human resources and personnel administration. The resulting handbook deals with all aspects of human resources in the workplace. Eighteen sections, subdivided into 80 chapters, cover such topics as recruitment, training and development, selection, benefits, performance appraisal, labor relations, and communication. Recently revised, this edition reflects the changes in the workplace, such as computer technology and employee relocation. It was originally published under the title *Handbook of Modern Personnel Administration.*

Evaluation: Comprehensive and exhaustive in its coverage of human–resources administration, this reference is recommended for all libraries.

1.96. Handbook of International Business. Ingo Walter and Tracy Murray, eds. New York: Wiley, 1982. $79.95.

Authority and scope: Walter and Murray, professors, authors, and consultants to government in the field of international business, have compiled forty-two chapters on six major subject areas: environment of international business, international trade, finance, legal aspects, marketing, and management. Each chapter has a list of sources and suggested reading list. It is indexed.

Evaluation: This concise, comprehensive reference in standard handbook format is recommended as a basic for all students and other individuals interested in international business.

1.97. Handbook of International Financial Management. Allen Sweeney and Robert Rachlins, eds. New York: McGraw-Hill, 1984. $54.95.

Authority and scope: Twenty–one practicing professionals have contributed nineteen chapters covering the fundamentals of foreign exchange, management of international finance, political and economic risk, international banking and other capital markets, accounting, auditing, tax questions, leasing, licensing, and budgeting. Some chapters have useful lists of references for further reading, and the handbook is indexed.

Evaluation: A comprehensive resource, this belongs in every library whose patrons are interested in international finance, whether as students or business executives.

1.98. Handbook of Labor Statistics. U.S. Bureau of Labor Statistics. Washington, DC: Government Printing Office, 1924/26–. $16.00.

Authority and scope: This handbook presents in one volume all major statistical series produced by the U.S. Bureau of Labor Statistics. Its contents consist of statistical tables relating to employment, unemployment, productivity, compensation, prices, unions, industrial injuries, and foreign labor. Each table begins with the earliest reliable data, although some intervening years have been omitted because of space limitations.

Evaluation: This indispensable publication of current U.S. labor statistics is useful for any library.

1.99. Handbook of Modern Accounting. Sidney Davidson and Roman Will. 3rd ed. New York: McGraw-Hill, 1983. $80.00.

Authority and scope: Accounting professor Davidson, provides an encyclopedic treatment of the subject with a series of articles written by 50 specialists. Topics range from basic concepts to the more specialized areas of cost analysis and dividends. The information is contained in 42 chapters, most with bibliographies, and the volume is indexed. The appendix is composed of compound interest, annuity, and bond tables.

Evaluation: This is one of the most useful professional handbooks in the field of accounting and provides a solid core of information for any library.

1.100. Handbook of Modern Marketing. Victor P. Buell, ed. 2nd ed. New York: McGraw-Hill, 1986. $84.95.

Authority and scope: Victor Buell, an associate professor of marketing and an active member of professional associations, has extensively revised this comprehensive reference work in the field of marketing. Each of the 107 chapters is written by a different authority and covers aspects such as modern marketing concepts, classification of markets, planning the product line, distribution, pricing, marketing research, planning the marketing program, selling and sales management, communications, customer service, and international marketing. The new edition contains information on the new developments in the field of marketing such as computer-assisted telephone interviews, environmental scanning, telemarketing, and social marketing.

Evaluation: Although particularly applicable to a business library, this handbook can be recommended for general library collections as well.

1.101. Handbook of Sales Promotion. Stanley M. Ulanoff, ed. New York: McGraw-Hill, 1985. $49.95.

Authority and scope: Ulanoff, a consultant and professor in the field of marketing, has assembled the contributions of 30 specialists in sales promotion into a comprehensive resource. Eight parts are divided into chapters covering all aspects of sales promotion: management, sales promotion in manufacturing and retailing, special personnel in sales promotion, creation and distribution of items and services, and legal issues. The appendix includes a checklist of trade shows, organizations, and associations involved in sales promotion, and periodicals related to the topic. There are both a glossary and an index.

Evaluation: This up-to-date handbook is a basic resource in the field. It is accordingly recommended for all libraries.

1.102. Handbook of United States Economics and Financial Indicators. Frederick M. O'Hara and Robert Sicignano. Westport, CT: Greenwood Press, 1985. $35.00.

Authority and scope: More than 200 major measures of economic activity that are used in the United States, such as the GNP and the CPI, are defined in this reference. Each entry includes the name of term or activity, description, derivation of indicator or how it is produced, frequency of publication, and a list of publications that publish the indicator. Arranged alphabetically, most entries contain brief bibliographies of sources of further information and are liberally cross-referenced. Appendixes include lists of nonquantitative indicators (Super Bowl predictor), an abbreviations list, and a guide to sources and compilers of the indicators.

Evaluation: Useful as a dictionary of key economic indicators and a directory of sources of those indicators, this reference will be a valuable addition to any library where this information was available previously only in piecemeal form.

1.103. Historical Statistics of the United States, Colonial Times to 1970. U.S. Bureau of the Census. Bicentennial Edition. Washington, DC: Government Printing Office, 1976. 2 vols. $35.00.

Authority and scope: Prepared by the Bureau of the Census with the cooperation of the Social Science Research Council, this two-volume set serves as a historical supplement to the annual *Statistical Abstract of the United States* (entry 1.157). Like the *Abstract,* it is a prime source for U.S. social, economic, political, and industrial statistics, with cross references made between data in the two reference sets. One major difference is that here statistics are presented on a national basis only, with no breakdowns by region, state, or local areas.

Evaluation: This is essential for every reference collection. Issued just twice since the first edition in 1945, it remains an affordable and easy-to-use statistical source for any library.

1.104. How to Find Information About Companies. 5th ed. Washington, DC: Washington Researchers, 1987. $125.00.

Authority and scope: Written to "show researchers sources of information about public and private companies, both foreign and domestic," and as a "corporate intelligence source book," this reference details sources in federal, state, and local government as well as in the private sector. It covers finding the appropriate office at state and federal levels when seeking information on such subjects as air pollution, banking, economic development, insurance, etc. Also listed are U.S. district and state courts and Freedom of Information Act offices in each federal agency. For the private sector, resources such as trade unions, investigative services, credit-reporting and bond-rating services, and databases are noted. The section on electronic databases is substantially updated in the latest edition and includes an evaluative chart of the 100 most helpful databases.

Evaluation: This relatively simple, straightforward and convenient guide to resources on companies is recommended for all business and academic libraries.

1.105. Insurance Almanac: Who, What, When and Where in Insurance; An Annual of Insurance Facts. Englewood, NJ: Underwriter Printing and Publishing, 1912–. Annual. $75.00.

Authority and scope: This directory from the Underwriter Printing and Publishing Company, a leader in insurance publications, provides names of officers, type of insurance written, and, for a few larger companies, the corporate history and company statistics, all separated into the six major lines of insurance. It also lists names of agents and brokers, actuaries and consultants, public adjusters, organizations, state officials, and management and insurance groups.

Evaluation: This basic insurance directory is a useful quick reference source for any library. Smaller libraries may economize by purchasing in alternate years.

1.106. International Dictionary of Business. Hano Johannsen and G. Terry Page, eds. 3rd ed. Englewood, NJ: Prentice-Hall, 1986. $7.95 paper.

Authority and scope: Hano Johannsen and Terry Page, both noted business researchers in Great Britain, have compiled a dictionary of over 5,000 entries covering the language of management in international usage. Definitions are thorough, ranging in length from one sentence to a paragraph. When necessary, examples, italicized cross-references and colloquialisms are included. Published in Great Britain as *International Dictionary of Management.*

Evaluation: This comprehensive, practical, and easy-to-use reference tool is recommended for all libraries, though some users may find the British and European slant confusing.

1.107. International Trade Statistics Yearbook. United Nations, Department of International and Economic and Social Affairs. New York: United Nations, 1950–. Annual. $80.00.

Authority and scope: Published by the Statistical Office of the United Nations, this yearbook provides export and import statistics for 154 countries, in light of overall trends in current values as well as volume and price. The data in Volume 1 are arranged by country, with commodity figures given in Standard International Trade Classification code. Also included in Volume 1 are basic summary tables on various aspects of world trade. Volume 2 contains data arranged by commodity and by country. The statistics in both volumes cover at least four years of activity.

Evaluation: Comprehensive in coverage and detail, this reference is recommended for larger collections or special libraries whose companies have extensive international business.

1.108. Introduction to United States Public Documents. Joe Morehead. 3rd ed. Littleton, CO: Libraries Unlimited, 1983. $19.50.

Authority and scope: A basic reference and bibliographic source for federal government publications, Morehead's book includes information on public documents, the Government Printing Office, the Superintendent of Documents Office, the depository library system, technical report literature, selected information sources for federal government publications, legislative branch materials, legal sources of information, and publications of the president's office and selected executive branch and independent agencies.

Evaluation: Widely used as a text in documents courses, this is recommended for use in all types of business-oriented libraries.

1.109. Investors Encyclopedia. Chet Currier. New York: Franklin Watts, 1985. $24.95.

Authority and scope: Currier, a financial reporter for the Associated Press since 1974, has compiled this guide to over 75 investment alternatives, from annuities to zero-coupon bonds. Each entry includes a description; how and where to get information for investing; cost of buying, owning, and selling; reports on capital gains, income potential, risks and drawbacks; liquidity; and tax advantages and disadvantages. The appendixes show how to read and understand financial data and include 1984 year-end prices for various securities. The book is indexed.

Evaluation: This is an excellent ready-reference source that is reliable, easy to use, and especially helpful for the novice investor. It would be a valuable source in any library.

1.110. Kelly's Manufacturers and Merchants Directory. East Grinstead, West Sussex, England, 1880–. Annual. $165.00.

Authority and scope: With a long publishing history behind it, this directory contains an alphabetical and classified listing of the names, addresses, products, and services of over 90,000 British companies. The classified listing makes up half of the directory, with brief entries containing company name and addresses. There is also a brand and trade name listing. New to recent editions is a classified list of manufacturers, merchants, and wholesalers offering services to the offshore oil industry.

Evaluation: An old favorite for access to British companies, this directory is recommended for business libraries and public libraries whose clientele has an interest in foreign enterprise.

1.111. Kohler's Dictionary for Accountants. W.W. Cooper and Yuii Ijiri, eds. 6th ed. Englewood Cliffs, NJ: Prentice- Hall, 1983. $58.95.

Authority and scope: Cooper and Ijiri have extensively revised and expanded this standard in the field, formerly known as *Dictionary for Accountants,* by Eric L. Kohler. Over 4,538 terms and concepts in accounting and related areas are included with definitions ranging in length from one to two pages. Charts and diagrams are used effectively.

Evaluation: Authoritative and readable, this reference will be useful in all libraries.

1.112. The Language of Real Estate. John W. Reilly. 2nd ed. New York: Real Estate Education, 1982. $24.95.

Authority and scope: John Reilly, an attorney and licensed real estate instructor, has compiled this handy reference of over 2,200 definitions of current terminology in real estate. Presented in dictionary format, the entries range in length from one paragraph to one page. Examples are given when necessary to understand the term. It is liberally cross-referenced and includes an appendix of abbreviations, a sample closing problem, and the realtors' code of ethics.

Evaluation: Comprehensive, readable, and affordable, this handbook is recommended for all libraries.

1.113. Legal Thesaurus. William C. Burton. New York: Macmillan, 1980. $19.95.

Authority and scope: Prepared by attorneys and research librarians, this source lists some 5,000 terms that range from purely legal to those in constant use in many business-oriented professions. It is organized alphabetically, with the main entry listing definition, part of speech, synonyms, associated legal concepts, foreign phrases and translations (keyed to concepts), multiple meanings, and alternate parts of speech.

Evaluation: Burton's book would be especially useful for business libraries that search full-text databases.

1.114. Lesly's Public Relations Handbook. Philip Lesly. 3rd ed. Englewood Cliffs, NJ: Prentice-Hall, 1983. $42.50.

Authority and scope: Using the contributions of over 40 experts, Lesly, a noted consultant and author in the field of public relations, has produced this extensive introduction to public relations. Fifty-five chapters are subdivided into eight sections: what public relations is, issues of management, what it includes, how an organization utilizes public relations, the techniques of communication, the practice of public relations, and emerging principles and trends. A bibliography, codes of practice, a glossary, lists of international/foreign public relations associations and public relations in specialized areas, and an index are included.

Evaluation: Brought up to date to reflect the changes in the field, this handbook has long been considered the most comprehensive resource in public relations. It is recommended for all libraries.

1.115. Letitia Baldridge's Complete Guide to Executive Manners. New York: Rawson Associates, 1985. $23.95.

Authority and scope: Editor of the *Amy Vanderbilt Complete Book of Etiquette* and former chief of staff for First Lady Jacqueline Kennedy, Baldridge maintains that "good manners are cost effective." Divided into two parts, "Human Relations at Work" and "Business Protocol," the guide sets down the rules of etiquette in the business world. Traditional points, such as making introductions and proper forms of address, are covered, but there are also guidelines for international situations, male-female relations at work, business entertaining, and gift giving. Illustrations are generous and the book is indexed.

Evaluation: Comprehensive and practical, this handbook is recommended for all libraries.

1.116. Life Insurance Fact Book and Life Insurance Fact Book Update. Washington, DC: American Council of Life Insurance, 1946–. Annual. Single copies free.

Authority and scope: First published in 1946, this booklet summarizes, with texts, tables, and charts, the year's developments in the life insurance business in the United States. The data are taken from annual statements provided by life insurance companies and include statistics in summary form on annuities, payments, pension, and retirement programs. In most cases, the statistics are presented for the present year, as well as for the previous 20 to 30 years. Beginning in 1985, *Life Insurance Fact Book* has been issued in alternate years in a condensed edition as the *Life Insurance Fact Book Update.* The *Update* contains all available new data to supplement those which appeared in the previous *Fact Book.*

Evaluation: Most useful as a single source of information about the life insurance business. No library would go wrong in obtaining a copy of this handy fact book and update every year.

1.117. Life Rates and Data. Cincinnati, OH: National Underwriter, 1971–. Annual. $19.00.

Authority and scope: More than 300 insurers have contributed information to this compilation of premium rates, cash values, dividends, costs, and policy conditions for the life plans of the insurers listed. It is a companion volume to *Life Reports: Financial and Operating Results of Life Insurers* (entry 1.118).

Evaluation. Recommended as an inexpensive source for financial data on life insurers, this publication is extremely useful for both the professional and the layperson and should be in every library.

1.118. Life Reports: Financial and Operating Results of Life Insurers. Cincinnati, OH: National Underwriter, 1971–. Annual. $40.95.

Authority and scope: This companion volume to *Life Rates and Data* (entry 1.117) presents basic financial information on over 1,000 life insurers, plus detailed corporate and operating statistics on more than half of those companies.

Evaluation: Libraries that cannot afford *Best's* (entry 1.15), but need basic financial information about life insurance companies, will be particularly interested in this reference tool, which is recommended for all libraries.

1.119. McGraw-Hill Dictionary of Modern Economics. Douglas Greenwald, et al. 3rd ed. New York: McGraw-Hill, 1983. $49.95.

Authority and scope: Greenwald, a well-known economics editor and consultant to government and business, has compiled with other economic experts a dictionary of over 1,420 frequently used modern economic terms. Also included are descriptions of approximately 235 private, public, and nonprofit agencies, and organizations concerned with economics and marketing. The definitions are practical and to the point, ranging in length from a few words to several sentences. A bibliographic citation is provided where further explanation may be needed.

Evaluation: Highly recommended as an easy-to-use, authoritative reference for any library, the usefulness of this dictionary goes beyond the field of economics to many related fields.

1.120. McGraw-Hill Handbook of Business Letters. Roy W. Poe. New York: McGraw-Hill, 1983. $39.95.

Authority and scope: Roy Poe, business educational consultant and publishing executive specializing in business books, has compiled this handbook covering more than 160 different letter-writing situations and showing how to handle them effectively. All the major categories of business letters are covered, such as transmittals and confirmations, credit and collection letters, and job applications and resignations. The situation calling for each type of letter is described, followed by a model letter and analysis.

Evaluation: While not as comprehensive as the older *Handbook of Business Letters* (L.E. Frailey, 1965), this is a helpful contribution to the business communications field that would find use in any library.

1.121. MacRae's State Industrial Directories. New York: State Manufacturing Directories, 1959–. Annual. Price varies from $44.00 to $135.00.

Authority and scope: This series includes individual directories for all states. Manufacturers and processors are listed in each directory in four different ways: by product/service, company name, geographically by county and city, and SIC number. The geographical listing includes the most complete information for each company: names and corporate affiliations, street and mailing addresses, telephone numbers, names and titles of key personnel, products manufactured, year of establishment, sales, plant and property size, SIC codes, number of employees, locations of branch plants and research facilities, and export-import status.

Evaluation: These directories are easy to use and up-to-date. All libraries should hold the directory for their own state and, perhaps, those for surrounding states.

1.122. Mail Order Business Directory: A Complete Guide to the Mail Order Market. 14th ed. Coral Springs, FL: B. Klein Publications, 1986. $65.00.

Authority and scope: Klein Publications has prepared this directory of over 9,000 of the most active mail-order and catalog houses. Arranged geographically, state by state, each company is described (address, specialty, etc.), with a list of buyers included. There is also a very select list of mail-order firms outside the U.S. and Canada. It is not indexed.

Evaluation: While somewhat limited in scope, this directory is recommended for medium-sized and larger libraries as a basic resource in this popular field.

1.123. Marconi's International Register. New York: Telegraphic Cable and Radio Registrations, 1898–. Annual. $85.00.

Authority and scope: This international cable address directory has a long history of publication. The company name section includes name, address, nature of business, telex numbers, and cable address. Another section presents trade headings, arranged in alphabetical order, each with a list of companies dealing in that trade. Also provided are an international trade index, listing companies by industry and then by country; a list of trade and brand names; a legal section; and a cable address index.

Evaluation: Marconi's is useful as a directory for international companies and as a supplement to other international directories. The access to foreign trade names could be helpful to special and larger public libraries, but smaller libraries can do without its acquisition.

1.124. Million Dollar Directory. New York: Dun & Bradstreet, 1964–. Annual. 5 volumes. $990.00.

Authority and scope: Published by a leading provider of business information, this well-known directory has been expanded to five volumes. Industrial firms are listed, as well as utilities, banks and trust companies, transportation companies, mutual and stock insurance companies, wholesalers and retailers, and domestic subsidiaries of foreign corporations. In Volumes 1–3, the businesses are listed in alphabetical order, with the following information: address; headquarters; annual sales and number of employees; stock exchange number and company ticker symbol; SIC number; name; titles, and functions of officers, directors and other principals; and the principal product. Volumes 4 and 5 are cross-reference tools, providing access by geographical area and industry.

Evaluation: Although expensive, these directories are essential for all business libraries and academic libraries, and for the public library with a large business clientele.

1.125. Monthly Bulletin of Statistics. New York: United Nations, 1947–. Monthly. $105.00.

Authority and scope: Published by the Department of International Economic and Social Affairs of the United Nations, this comprehensive bulletin provides statistical data for over 200 countries and territories of the world in 74 subject areas such as industrial production, trade, transportation, national accounts, wage and price indexes, population, manpower, forestry, mining, manufacturing, construction, electricity and gas, and finance. Where possible, figures are given for at least five different years and for the most recent 18 months. This bulletin is the monthly update to the annual *Statistical Yearbook* of the United Nations (entry 1.158).

Evaluation: Comprehensive and relatively up-to-date, this reference is recommended for business and academic libraries where there is appreciable interest in materials about foreign countries.

1.126. Monthly Labor Review. U.S. Bureau of Labor Statistics. Washington, DC: Government Printing Office, 1962–. Monthly. $23.00.

Authority and scope: The *Monthly Labor Review* provides authoritative coverage of employment, prices, wages, productivity, job safety, and economic growth. The first part of the journal is composed of articles on the labor scene; the second part contains current labor statistics on the labor force, labor compensation, and collective bargaining and prices. It is indexed in *Business Periodicals Index* (entry 1.22) and *Business Index* (entry 1.18).

Evaluation: This resource's authoritative nature and the extent of its statistical treatment make it a must for all libraries.

1.127. Moody's Handbook of Common Stocks. New York: Moody's Investors Service. Quarterly. $145.00.

Authority and scope: Basic business and financial information on over 900 stocks with high investor interest is provided in this handbook. With one page allotted to each company, the information given includes capitalization, quarterly interim earnings and dividends, company background, recent developments, prospects, and a table of 10–year comparative statistics and ratios. There is a companion volume: *Moody's Handbook of OTC Stocks*, with over 500 over-the-counter stocks of high investor interest.

Evaluation: An excellent resource for capsuled current data on companies, this resource is recommended for small libraries as a basic source. Larger libraries will also find it useful as a quick reference tool.

1.128. Moody's Manuals. New York: Moody's Investors Service, 1955–. Annual, with semiweekly supplements. Individually priced; $2,434.00 for entire service.

Authority and scope: Issued by one of the best-known financial publishing companies, *Moody's Manuals* provide information on every U.S., Canadian, and foreign company listed on the U.S. exchanges. The information is presented in seven separate manuals: *Industrial, Bank and Finance, OTC, Public Utility, Transportation, Municipal and Government* and *International*. Included are detailed company histories, including subsidiaries, properties, management individuals, up to seven years of income accounts and balance sheets, and seven-year comparisons of statistical records and financial and operating ratios.

Evaluation: One of the most comprehensive sources for information of this kind, this service is recommended for all business, academic, and public libraries medium-sized and larger. The price is restrictive, however, and smaller libraries will want to be selective or take advantage of library purchase plans available from the publisher.

1.129. National Construction Estimator. Lisa Andrews, ed. Carlsbad, CA: Craftsman Book Co. Annual. $19.00.

Authority and scope: Compiled with information from building professionals all over the United States, this reference is an encyclopedia of building costs. Divided into residential and commercial-and-industrial construction, it lists estimated material prices, excavation, and general contracting costs for the current year. An area modification table is provided to help account for local wages, productivity, and material cost differences.

Evaluation: Useful for any library whose clients need to know the cost of construction, in which case annual purchase is essential.

1.130. National Roster of Realtors Directory. Cedar Rapids, IA: Stamats Publishing, 1919–. 2 vols. Annual. $75.00.

Authority and scope: In its 68th edition, this directory provides a listing by state of all realtors (names, addresses, and those who are members of the National Association of Realtors), within states, by realtor boards in the United States and Canada. Also provided is information on the institutes, councils, and societies of the National Association of Realtors, including officers, directors, and executive staffs.

Evaluation: While most of this information can be obtained from the telephone book, this directory is a convenient resource to use instead. Libraries may consider purchasing in alternate years or obtaining an older edition from a local realtor.

1.131. National Trade and Professional Associations of the United States and Canada. Washington, DC: Columbia Books, 1966–. Annual. $45.00.

Authority and scope: This directory lists more than 6,000 trade and professional associations and labor unions with national memberships. The organizations are first listed alphabetically, and include name, chief executive officer, size of staff, membership, year founded, annual budget, meetings, and publications. Three indexes provide access to the associations listed: subject, geographic, and budget (divided into eight categories ranging from under $10,000 to over $5 million).

Evaluation: Overshadowed by the *Encyclopedia of Associations* (entry 1.66), this directory is nevertheless useful. It has also been known to list organizations not included by other publications. Purchase by business and larger libraries is recommended.

1.132. Overseas Business Reports. International Trade Administration. Washington, DC: Government Printing Office, 1961–. Irregular. $26.00.

Authority and scope: Prepared by the U.S. Department of Commerce, working with material provided by U.S. Foreign Service Officers in embassies from all over the world, each report covers detailed information on trade and investment conditions and on marketing opportunities in the country reviewed. Areas included are trade patterns, industrial trends, distribution and sales, natural resources, population, transportation, credit, trade regulations, market prospects, and finance and economy.

Evaluation: These readable analyses are recommended for any business library with patrons interested in overseas markets. They can also serve smaller libraries as sources of information about foreign countries.

1.133. Oxbridge Directory of Newsletters. Matthew Manning, ed. New York: Oxbridge Communications. Annual. $125.00.

Authority and scope: Over 13,500 U.S. and Canadian newsletters are described in this directory. Grouped under 168 subject categories, then alphabetically by title, each entry includes publisher, address, editor, description, book reviews accepted, history, frequency, price, circulation, size, printing method, availability in nonprint form, and primary readership. It is indexed.

Evaluation: Comprehensive and easy to use, this directory is recommended for all libraries as the best source in this fast-growing field.

1.134. Polk's World Bank Directory. Nashville, TN: Polk and Co., 1895–. The North American edition is issued twice per year at $168.75; the International edition is issued annually for $135.00.

Authority and scope: Polk's geographic listing of world banks gives names of officers and directors, correspondents, assets, and liabilities. A map accompanies each state and country section. Additional information in the North American edition includes a list of state banking officials, holidays, an explanation of the Federal Reserve System, transit numbers and holding companies. The world volume includes a list of U.S. banks offering international banking services.

Evaluation: A basic banking directory is necessary for all libraries, and this is recommended as one of the best and most complete that is available. Smaller libraries may want to limit their purchase to the North American edition, depending on their clientele.

1.135. Predicasts Basebook. Cleveland, OH: Predicasts. Annual. $525.00.

Authority and scope: This loose-leaf reference provides historical data on U.S. business and economic activities. Arranged by a modified, seven-digit SIC number, the industry statistics include production, consumption, plant and equipment expenditures, payroll, and exports/imports. The figures cover approximately 15 years' of activity. The source of the statistic and annual growth are also provided. Available online.

Evaluation: Comprehensive and easy to use, this is considered a basic sourcebook of industry statistics. While the cost of this reference is prohibitive for the small library, medium-sized business and academic libraries should have it.

1.136. Predicasts Forecasts. Cleveland, OH: Predicasts. Quarterly with annual cumulations. $725.00.

Authority and scope: Nearly 50,000 short and long-range projections for products and industries, along with leading economic indicators for U.S. business are available in this reference. Arranged by modified seven-digit SIC code, each forecast gives the subject, quantities for a base year, short- and long-term projections, unit of measure, source of data and projected annual rate. Available online. *Worldcasts,* a companion volume, publishes similar statistics for foreign countries.

Evaluation: The best and first place to look for short- and long-range forecasts for U.S. business, this service is recommended for business and academic libraries; small libraries will want to know where it is in their areas and refer patrons to it.

1.137. Predicasts F&S Index, United States. Cleveland, OH: Predicasts, Inc. Monthly with annual cumulations. $800.00.

Authority and scope: Company, product, and industry information from over 750 trade journals, major business newspapers, and business magazines, as well as reports and publications from government and industry organizations, are indexed in this service. Part 1 is organized by a modified SIC code and reports new products, demand, sales, etc. Part 2 is arranged by company name with cross-references to subsidiaries. Entries include a one-line abstract and shortened bibliographic citation. Major articles are noted with a large dot. Available online. There are two companion services also available: *F&S Index, Europe* and *F&S Index, International.*

Evaluation: Although an excellent source when searching for information on a public or private company, the price is prohibitive for small libraries. Business, academic, and large public libraries should hold the *F&S Index* and may want to consider the companion services, would their clientele warrant that level of purchase.

1.138. Prentice-Hall Dictionary of Business, Finance and Law. Michael Downey Rice. Englewood Cliffs, NJ: Prentice-Hall, 1983. $39.95.

Authority and scope: Rice, an experienced financial lawyer, has compiled a dictionary of terms, acronyms, statutes, and regulations commonly used in business. Covering a broad range of subjects—corporate law, taxation, securities transactions and regulations, bankruptcy, labor administrative law, and contracts—its definitions are clearly written and range in length from one sentence to several. This work is set up like a legal dictionary, with references to statutes and regulations relating to the term or agency when applicable.

Evaluation: Definitely intended for the nonlawyer, this reference is easy to use and understand and therefore recommended for all libraries but the smallest.

1.139. Production Handbook. John A. White, ed. 4th ed. New York: Wiley, 1986. $75.00.

Authority and scope: John White, professor of materials handling, has compiled the contributions of experts in the field and produced a comprehensive text on every stage of planning, operation and control in modern industrial management. Its 22 sections cover all phases of production, and a helpful outline is provided at the beginning of each section. Diagrams, charts, and formulas are included where appropriate, and there is a list of references at the end, as well as an index. New and timely information such as the changing role of employees, forecasting, and robotics is included in this revised edition.

Evaluation: Now thoroughly revised, this is recommended as the basic resource in its field, particularly for business libraries and medium-sized and larger public libraries.

1.140. Questions and Answers on Real Estate. Robert W. Semenow. 9th ed. Englewood Cliffs, NJ: Prentice-Hall, 1979. $16.95.

Authority and scope: Considered the foremost real-estate license law experts in the United States, Robert Semenow has authored a text that has become the chief resource for individuals taking the real estate license examination. It covers all the major aspects of real estate, such as agreements, valuation, condominiums, syndicates, and appraisal, and it includes a question-and-answer section.

Evaluation: Because of its importance to the real estate community, this is an essential purchase for every library. Though more frequent updating would be desirable, it can still serve as a basic resource in the field.

1.141. Rand McNally Commercial Atlas and Marketing Guide. New York: Rand McNally, 1876–. Annual. $250.00.

Authority and scope: Published by a company known to the general populace for its maps, the *Commercial Atlas* contains a map for each state, but it is especially valuable for its excellent statistical and demographic data. It provides statistical indicators of market potential for U.S. cities, counties, and regions. In addition it includes such useful lists as American colleges, the largest corporations in America, railroad and air distances, and postal information. The place-name index provides for each entry, population, elevation, zipcode, post office (if different) and symbols to indicate commercial activity. (e.g. banking town, principal business center, railroad). The *Road Atlas* appears as a supplement to the *Commercial Atlas* and is received with it.

Evaluation: This is a standard reference that belongs in all libraries.

1.142. Real Estate Law. Robert Kratovil and Raymond J. Werner. 9th ed. Englewood Cliffs, NJ: Prentice-Hall, 1983. $34.50.

Authority and scope: Written by authors of several books in this field, this reference covers the basic principles of real estate law and includes such topics as titles, deeds and acknowledgements, contracts, sales, escrows, mortgages, real estate finance, insurance, and, in this latest revision, condominiums, mobile homes, and zoning changes. The coverage is thorough and follows an easy-to-use numbered paragraph format.

Evaluation: Recommended for all libraries, this will be useful to the general public, students, and professionals interested in real estate transactions.

1.143. Robert's Rules of Order. Gen. Henry M. Robert. Newly revised. Glenview, IL: Scott, Foresman & Co., 1981. $16.95.

Authority and scope: An authoritative manual of parliamentary law and the basic guide to fair and orderly procedure in meetings, the revised *Robert's* will not disturb the established practice in organizations that have used the preceding editions.

Evaluation: This most widely-used and comprehensive source for parliamentary practices is recommended for use in all types of business-oriented libraries.

1.144. Sales and Marketing Management. New York: Bill Communications, 1918–. Biweekly. $38.00.

Authority and scope: Published for many years as *Sales Management,* this periodical offers information on all phases of the marketing process. In short- to medium-sized articles, it covers strategies, tactics, research and evaluation, and success stories. Of particular note are the four annual statistical issues, the most well known being *Survey of Buying Power,* Part 1 appears as the second July issue, and Part 2, as the second October issue. Part 1 reports statistical data on buying power, population, households, income, and retail sales for cities, counties, and metropolitan areas. Part 2 reports metropolitan market projections, annual surveys of television and newspaper markets, merchandise line sales, and zip code characteristics. Also published annually are *Survey of Selling Costs,* a statistical report issued each February on a broad range of selling expenses, and *Survey of Industrial and Commercial Buying Power,* the second April issue, which provides shipments and receipts totals for approximately 2,800 counties with manufacturing and nonmanufacturing industries. Indexed in *Business Periodicals Index* (entry 1.22) and *Business Index* (entry 1.18).

Evaluation: Presenting information on all phases of the marketing process, this periodical is unsurpassed in its field. It belongs in all but the smallest public library, because of its general interest to the business community.

1.145. Savings Institution Sourcebook. Chicago: U.S. Savings and Loan League, 1954–. First 9 copies are free.

Authority and scope: Published by a major trade association in the United States, this booklet, formerly called the *Savings and Loan Sourcebook,* is a consolidation of factual information on savings, mortgage lending, housing, the savings and loan business, and related federal government agencies. Data are given for the latest year and, in some cases, for 10 to 20 years. A short text explains the basics of the savings and loan business, and a table of major federal laws affecting the business and a glossary of terms are included. There is an index.

Evaluation: This is a handy, useful booklet whose easy availability makes it a recommended item for all libraries.

1.146. Small Business Sourcebook. Robert J. Elster. 2nd ed. Detroit, MI: Gale, 1986. 2 vols. $185.00.

Authority and scope: An annotated guide to a multitude of sources on starting a small business, this *Sourcebook* includes information on 150 specific small businesses, as well as on general information sources. The first part contains detailed listings of sources of information for the small business person: from accounting/tax preparation to word-processing services. The profiles list up to 16 categories: associations, educational programs, trade periodicals, and consultants in the field. The second part contains a wide range of general information sources: federal and state government agencies, trade and professional organizations, small business development, consultants, and venture capital firms. There is an index which lists all sources of information included in Parts 1 and 2.

Evaluation: An excellent starting point for the entrepreneur, this comprehensive resource belongs in all public libraries.

1.147. The [year] Sourcebook of Demographic and Buying Power for Every Zip Code in the U.S.A. Fairfax, VA: CACI, Inc. Annual. $295.00.

Authority and scope: An international professional and high-technology services organization that is also an official U.S. Census summary-tape processing center, CACI, Inc. has produced a reference that provides key demographic and socioeconomic characteristics for every residential zip code in the U.S. Section 1 contains complete profiles, with statistics on population, housing, income, employment and buying power. Section 2 contains business statistics such as the top five zip codes ranked by the previous year's employment. CACI, Inc. also publishes the same information in a *Sourcebook for Every County in the U.S.*

Evaluation: This easy-to-use reference simplifies marketing and research tasks by providing important data in one volume. Of interest to students and businesspeople, this is recommended for all business and academic libraries.

1.148. Standard and Poor's Register of Corporations, Directors and Executives. New York: Standard and Poor's, 1928–. Annual. $425.00.

Authority and scope: Standard and Poor's, a leader in the field of business publications, has compiled this comprehensive directory to over 45,000 U.S. corporations. Volume 1 contains an alphabetical listing of the companies; each entry includes addresses, names of officials, products, company accounting firm, primary bank and law firm, and number of employees, as well as total sales figures when available. Volume 2 is a straight alphabetical listing of over 70,000 individuals serving as officers, directors, partners or board members. Volume 3 is divided into color-coded sections: Standard Industrial Classification (SIC) numbers and explanations, a list of companies by four-digit SIC number, a geographical index, corporate family indexes (subsidiaries, divisions, affiliates), an obituary section, new individual listings, and new company additions.

Evaluation: One of the best known of all directories, this is recommended for all libraries. If the library is limited to only one business directory, this should be it.

1.149. Standard and Poor's Security Dealers of North America. New York: Standard and Poor's. Bi-Annual. 2 vols. $320.00.

Authority and scope: A noted publishing company in the field of business, Standard and Poor's provides this listing of brokers/dealers and investment banking firms in the U.S. and Canada. Completely revised twice a year, it lists security administrators and active security dealers geographically. A separate listing of discontinued security dealers is also included. Listings include names of partners, officers, branch managers, and department heads. In addition, complete addresses and telephone number for each office, exchange memberships, specialization, clearing facilities, and wire services are given.

Evaluation: This is a necessary, although expensive, reference source for all business libraries and large public library systems. A current subscription is necessary and probably places the source out of the reach of smaller libraries.

1.150. Standard Directory of Advertisers. Skokie, IL: National Register Publishing Co. Annual, with biweekly supplements and 5 cumulative supplements. 2 vols., Classified and Geographical. $235.00 each.

Authority and scope: This directory lists over 17,000 companies allocating annual appropriations for national or regional advertising campaigns in 50 product classifications. Each entry includes name, address, telephone number, type of business, key management and sales executives, approximate sales and number of employees, advertising agency, account executive, time and amount of appropriations, and advertising media. Also included are an alphabetical index, a trade name index, and a list of Standard Industrial Classification group numbers and their relation to the product classification used in the directory.

Evaluation: Recommended for all but the smallest libraries, this is a handy source of basic information on nationally known companies. While some of the same information can be found elsewhere, the arrangement of the information and the trade name index expand the usefulness of this directory.

1.151. Standard Directory of Advertising Agencies. Skokie, IL.: National Register Publishing Co. Published 3 times a year; $292.00 for subscription; $129.00 for single issue.

Authority and scope: Over 4,800 companies appear in this directory of advertising agencies in the U.S. and Canada. Besides being published three times a year to keep up-to-date in a rapidly changing business, it is supplemented by a news sheet issued nine times a year. Agencies are arranged alphabetically, and each entry contains the following information: address and phone number, chief officers, specialization, annual billing, number of employees, and names of clients. At the front of the directory are a geographical index of domestic agencies, an index of foreign advertising agencies, including U.S. companies with foreign branches, and a special market index. This tool is also known as the "Agency Red Book."

Evaluation: An essential resource for researchers and individuals in the advertising business and related fields, this directory is recommended to libraries serving those patrons. Other libraries may elect to purchase only one volume per year.

1.152. Standard Handbook for Secretaries. Louise Hutchinson. 8th ed. New York: McGraw-Hill, 1969. $14.95.

Authority and scope: This standard desk reference for secretaries covers a wide variety of topics, including reports, minutes of meetings, letter writing, filing, grammar, legal papers, patents, copyrights, trademarks, and weights and measures.

Evaluation: Though dated, there is nothing to replace Hutchinson's, and it is recommended as an essential handbook for all libraries.

1.153. Standard Industrial Classification Manual. U.S. Bureau of the Budget. Washington, DC: Government Printing Office, 1987. $24.00.

Authority and scope: Issued by the federal Office of Management and Budget, the SIC manual is the guide to one of the most comprehensive and widely used classification systems in the United States. It divides U.S. industries by type of activity and assigns an industry code number that is determined by the product or service rendered. The entire field of economic activity (agriculture, forestry, construction manufacturing, wholesale and retail trade, finance, real estate, etc.) is covered. The book has been extensively revised from the 1972 edition to reflect the changes in technology and American business in general. Tables in the appendix show the relationship of previous revisions to those of the 1987 edition.

Evaluation: Because of the extensive use of this classification system in government and private industry, this is an essential purchase for all but the smallest libraries. Since it will take a while for publishers and databases to change their files over to the revised code, libraries will want to keep both editions for a time.

1.154. Standard Periodicals Directory. Margie Domenech and Matthew Manning, eds. 11th ed. New York: Oxbridge Communications, 1988. Annual. $295.00.

Authority and scope: Irregularly published at first, but now annual, this directory contains information on over 65,000 periodicals published in the United States and Canada. It is arranged by subject, and each entry includes title, publishing company, address, telephone, key staff names, description of contents, book review acceptance, year established, frequency and circulation, advertising and subscription rates, printing method, size, and color, if used. There is also an index by title.

Evaluation: Recommended for all libraries, this directory lists more periodicals than *Ulrich's* (entry 1.166) and is easier to use. Since it does not contain foreign titles, libraries may want to purchase both on an alternate-year basis.

1.155. Standard Rate and Data Service. Chicago: Standard Rate and Data Service, 1919–. Frequency and price vary with issue.

Authority and scope: Separate directories are available from this service, providing advertising rates and circulation information for newspapers, business publications, consumer magazines and agri-media, community periodicals, direct mail, co-op source directories, Canadian advertising media and spot-television and radio markets. Other information provided, such as demographic characteristics, metro area rankings, spendable income, retail sales, and media market maps (when appropriate), is also useful.

Evaluation: Recommended to any library whose patrons are buyers of advertising time and space. Libraries may wish to subscribe or purchase single copies selectively, because of the high cost.

1.156. Statesman's Year-book. John Paxton, ed. New York: St. Martin's Press, 1864–. Annual. $49.95.

Authority and scope: With a long history of reliable publication, this manual provides a wide variety of information about the United Nations, other international organizations, and the nations of the world, in addition to statistical tables on some commodities. For each country, information includes history, area and population, constitution and government, defense, international relations, economy, energy and natural resources, industry and trade, communications, justice, religion, education and welfare, and diplomatic representatives.

Evaluation: Reliable and relatively inexpensive, this is recommended for all libraries.

1.157. Statistical Abstract of the United States. U.S. Bureau of the Census. Washington, DC: Government Printing Office, 1879–. Annual. $29.00 and $22.00 (paper copy).

Authority and scope: Published regularly by the U.S. Bureau of the Census since 1879, this is the "standard summary of statistics on the social, political, and economic organization of the United States." National data are featured, although data for regions, states, metropolitan areas, and cities are sometimes provided as well. Included are tables of statistics for population, vital statistics, health and nutrition, education, law enforcement, geography and environment, social insurance, national defense, labor, income, prices, banking and finance, elections, science, transportation, agriculture, fisheries, mining, construction, manufacturers, domestic trade, foreign commerce, and government finances and employment at the federal, state, and local levels. Most tables cover several years; some go back to the 1800s.

Evaluation: An indispensable and inexpensive source, this is a must for all libraries.

1.158. Statistical Yearbook. United Nations. Department of International and Economic and Social Affairs. New York: United Nations, 1948–. Annual. $45.00.

Authority and scope: Published by the Statistical Office of the United Nations, this reference tool is a digest of statistics for over 270 U.N. countries and territories. Arranged by broad subject areas and then presented by individual countries, the statistical tables include data on manufacturing, energy resource, agricultural production, finance, construction, transportation, import/export trade, balance of payments, education and culture, general socioeconomic statistics, and wages and prices.

Evaluation: Though generally about four years behind in publication, this is a valuable reference source for larger libraries; smaller libraries may rely on more general titles for this kind of information or elect to purchase in alternate years.

1.159. Statistics Sources. Jacquelyn Wasserman O'Brien and Steven R. Wasserman, eds. 11th ed. Detroit, MI: Gale, 1987. $280.00.

Authority and scope: Providing access to over 60,000 statistical sources issued by both the private sector and the government, this guide is arranged in some 20,000 very detailed subject categories, and each entry includes titles, name of publisher, and address. While emphasis is on U.S. statistical sources, coverage of international sources has expanded with each edition. New to the 11th edition is the "Selected Bibliography of Key Statistical Sources," a list of major general statistical sources, arranged by categories, such as "Encyclopedias" and "Almanacs."

Evaluation: Recommended for all libraries as a basic resource on which to base referrals, this is the purchase to be made if only one such reference tool can be afforded. It represents an alternative to *American Statistics Index* (entry 1.9).

1.160. Survey of Current Business. U.S. Department of Commerce. Washington, DC: Government Printing Office, 1921–. Monthly. $30.00.

Authority and scope: Published by the Bureau of Economic Analysis of the Department of Commerce, this periodical presents significant economic indicators for business use. Each issue contains articles on the current business situation and current business statistics for the latest month, quarter, or year. The latter section covers the following topics: general business indicators (personal income, business sales, manufacturers' inventories, etc.), commodity prices, domestic trade, labor force, employment and earnings, finance, and production and export statistics for major industry categories. The *Survey* is indexed in *Business Periodicals Index* (entry 1.22) and *Business Index* (entry 1.18) and the current business statistics are cumulated in the biennial publication *Business Statistics* (entry 1.24). Available online.

Evaluation: Considered by many to be the most important single source for current business statistics, this is recommended for all libraries.

1.161. Television and Cable Factbook. Washington, DC: Television Digest, 1982–. Annual. 2 vols. $225.00.

Authority and scope: Published by a specialist in the industry, the *Factbook* provides access to all aspects of the business of television. The "Stations" volume contains operating information for U.S. and Canadian television stations, and, to a lesser degree, those in foreign countries. Arranged geographically, the information includes: personnel, ownership and history of station, technical facilities, a map of the market, and advertising rates. There is also a directory of public educational TV stations, and lower power television stations. The "Cable and Services" volume includes information on cable systems, networks, and related industries, such as production firms, advertising agencies, and equipment manufacturers.

Evaluation: This directory is the most comprehensive guide to the television and cable industry and is highly recommended. Smaller libraries may purchase it in alternate years to save money, or may note its availability in other libraries in their areas.

1.162. Thomas' Register of American Manufacturers. New York: Thomas Publishing, 1905–. Annual. 21 vols. $225.00.

Authority and scope: This comprehensive directory to American manufacturing firms is offered in three parts. Part 1 lists products and services in detailed subject categories with helpful cross-references. All known manufacturers or sources are listed alphabetically by product and service and then by state and city within the state, with addresses and telephone numbers included. Part 2 lists, in alphabetical order, all companies included in the *Register* with complete addresses and phone numbers, asset ratings, subsidiaries, and affiliates. There is also a brand-name listing with owner company's name and address. Part 3 is composed of reprints of company catalogs. Subscribers may elect to receive one of two supplements: *Thomas' Registers' Guide to Data/ Information Processing Products* or *Thomas' Registers' Guide to Factory Automation.* Both paper volumes provide listings of products, services, suppliers, and sources in these specialized fields.

Evaluation: Somewhat like a telephone directory, this is recommended for all libraries as a very comprehensive access to American manufacturing. Smaller libraries may alternate years or purchase or obtain the next to the latest set from a larger library or friendly local business.

1.163. Thorndike Encyclopedia of Banking and Financial Tables. Boston: Warren, Gorham, and Lamont, 1980–. Basic volume, $84.00; yearbook, $53.00.

Authority and scope: Published by a respected publishing firm, this reference is a comprehensive collection of tables of banking, investment, mortgage and financial computations compiled by David Thorndike, Wall Street Consultant. There are tables for interest rates or yields on mortgage and real estate, simple and compound interest on savings and bonds, and rates on various types of loans. The yearbook, intended to complement and not replace preceding yearbooks, contains more tables, updated to reflect the changing monetary scene, and a revised section on state usury and bad-check laws, foreign exchange rates, taxation, and a glossary of terms.

Evaluation: Comprehensive and kept up-to-date with the yearbook, this reference is recommended for all libraries except the smallest public libraries.

1.164. Trade Names Dictionary. Donna Wood, ed. 5th ed. Detroit, MI: Gale. $285.00.

Authority and scope: With emphasis on consumer-oriented products, this dictionary contains over 200,000 entries for products, manufacturers, and distributors. Each trade name appears in alphabetical order in boldface and is followed by a brief description, the manufacturer's name and a symbol indicating the source of information. In the "Company Index" of the *Dictionary*, all companies appear with a complete address and list of products. The list of information sources includes complete name, publisher's address, and current price. The "Company Index" is available at an added cost.

Evaluation: Recommended for all libraries, this easy- to-use reference is the most comprehensive such list in a single source.

1.165. Trade Shows and Professional Exhibits Directory. Robert J. Elster, ed. 2nd ed. Detroit, MI: Gale, 1987. Biennial. Main volume, $150.00; Supplement, $80.00.

Authority and scope: Over 3,500 exhibitions, trade shows, conventions, and similar events, held in the U.S. and Canada and some foreign countries, are described in this directory from a well-known and respected publisher. Arranged by 33 general subject categories, each entry contains name, sponsor, and description of event (manager, attendance, number of exhibits, cost, frequency of event, dates, and location of future meetings). The indexes are by show/exhibition name, key word, geography, chronology, organization, and subject.

Evaluation: Although some of the information is outdated quickly, this is the best reference source reporting such information, and purchase by larger public libraries is recommended.

1.166. Ulrich's International Periodicals Directory. New York: Bowker, 1932–. Annual. $159.95.

Authority and scope: Bowker, one of the largest and most respected companies in publishing, produces this classified listing of over 68,800 periodicals from around the world. Arranged in 534 subject areas, each entry provides titles, frequency, publisher name and address, cost, and indexing or abstracting information. Also included are a list of publications that have ceased publishing, an index to publications of international organizations, a title index, and lists of periodicals available online and vendors of online periodicals. *Ulrich's* is also available online.

Evaluation: This comprehensive and up-to-date resource is considered a basic part of every reference collection. Its classified arrangement provides easy access to a large amount of information.

1.167. U.S. Government Manual. U.S. General Services Administration. Office of the Federal Register. Washington, DC: Government Printing Office, 1935–. Annual. $19.00.

Authority and scope: Published by the federal General Services Administration, this manual provides comprehensive information on the agencies of the federal government, as well as on the quasi-official agencies, commissions, committees, boards, and international organizations in which the United States participates. Each entry includes a list of principal officials, organization chart, agency purpose, history, legislative and executive authority, address, description of programs and activities, and sources of information. The appendixes offer additional useful information: abolished or transferred agencies, commonly used abbreviations, acronyms, the text of several information acts, names of regional councils and boards, and a list of Code of Federal Regulation titles. It is indexed by name, subject, and agency.

Evaluation: Recommended for all libraries, this handbook provides indispensable access to the agencies of the federal government.

1.168. U.S. Government Purchasing and Sales Directory. 10th ed. Washington, DC: Government Printing Office, 1984. $10.00.

Authority and scope: Compiled by the Small Business Administration (SBA), this is an alphabetical listing of the products and services bought by military departments and civilian agencies. Divided into two sections, "Military" and "Civilian," the directory provides a list of products, keyed to a separate listing of agencies with addresses and military and civilian departments with major research and development activities. The directory also includes ways in which the SBA can help a business get government contracts and data on surplus property for sale.

Evaluation: Informative and comprehensive, this relatively inexpensive directory is recommended for all libraries, particularly small and medium-sized public libraries serving the small-business owner or entrepreneur.

1.169. [Year] U.S. Industrial Outlook: Prospects for over 350 Manufacturing and Service Industries. U.S. Department of Commerce. International Trade Administration. Washington, DC: Government Printing Office, 1960–. Annual. $24.00.

Authority and scope: Published by the Department of Commerce this report presents projections and statistics for 350 major U.S. industries. Generally following the Standard Industrial Classification System (SIC), it provides coverage of industries not covered by the SIC, such as franchising and travel services. The text covers the current situation, outlook for the coming year, and long-term prospects. The statistics include historical trends and forecasts for coming years.

Evaluation: Recommended for all libraries, this is a reliable resource for information on recent trends and outlook for industries.

1.170. Value Line Investment Survey. New York: Arnold Bernhard, 1937–. Weekly. $395.00.

Authority and scope: This weekly review and analysis of over 1,700 stocks includes, for each stock, a stock chart, tabular statistics and opinions on longer-term quality, performance and income, and yield expectations. The statistics and charts are reviewed and updated on a rotating basis, industry by industry, so that the information on every company is revised quarterly. Also included in the subscription is a weekly "Summary and Index," a weekly "Selection and Opinion" newsletter, which includes an analysis of the stock market, prospects for business, and recommendations for investment strategy, and a "Quarterly Economic Review" issue. The *Survey* is available online.

Evaluation: Considered to be one of the most respected, and certainly most popular, investment surveys, this reference tool is recommended for all libraries.

1.171. The Wall Street Journal. New York: Dow Jones, 1889–. Daily except Saturday and Sunday. $119.00.

Authority and scope: Generally recognized as the basic newspaper for the businessperson, the *Wall Street Journal* is also a useful source of information for the general reader. A summary of general news accompanies detailed factual reports on companies, industries, and business personalities. The latest stock market statistical information is included, as is a classified section advertising positions available.

Evaluation: Because of its coverage of all news important to business, this basic reference tool should be held by all libraries.

1.172. The Wall Street Journal Index. Princeton, NJ: Dow Jones Books, 1958–. Monthly with annual cumulations. Monthly, $333.00; monthly with annual cumulation, $550.00; annual cumulation, $305.00.

Authority and scope: This index is compiled from the final eastern edition of *The Wall Street Journal* (entry 1.171) and is arranged in two parts: "Corporate News" and "General News." The entries are listed alphabetically, with a chronological listing within each topic. An abstract of each article is followed by the date, page, and column where the article appears. It is issued monthly and then published in an annual cumulation. The annual volume includes an index to *Barron's*, a convenient listing of articles and special reports in the *Journal*, and the closing Dow Jones Averages for that year.

Evaluation: A necessity for libraries that maintain back files of the *Journal*; smaller libraries that do not subscribe or do not keep the *Journal* for any length of time can probably do without this index.

1.173. Ward's Business Directory. Belmont, CA: Information Access Company. Annual. $990.00 for 3 volumes, $350.00 each.

Authority and scope: Expanded recently into three separate directories, *Ward's Business Directory* is the most comprehensive computerized list of companies ranked by industry. Volume 1 includes more than 37,000 private and 8,000 public companies. Companies are ranked by sales within SIC industry codes, and the information given includes up to 30 financial indices from annual reports of the public companies. Volume 2 includes demographic information, basic information on the company (CEO, sales, number of employees), and ranking by sales for 35,000 private companies. Volume 3 carries data on 15,000 of the largest companies from the major industrial countries of the world, plus emerging countries. Basic data included are: address, divisions and subsidiaries, and comparison of sales and employees between U.S. and non-U.S. industries.

Evaluation: This is one of the few directories to rank public and private companies together by SIC number. It is recommended for all special, academic, and medium to larger public libraries.

1.174. Who's Who in Finance and Industry. 25th ed. Chicago: Marquis Who's Who, 1936–. $170.50.

Authority and scope: Now in its 25th edition, this directory provides career sketches of leaders in the field of business and finance. Information provided includes: name, position, vital statistics, parents, educational background, marital status, career and related activities, professional and other memberships, writings, and home and office address. The "Standards of Admissions" statement indicates that executives are selected because of special prominence in their particular branch of business or because of positions held in financial and industrial concerns of certain sizes, defined by assets or sales, or other specialized rating criteria.

Evaluation: Marquis's long tradition of quality in preparing biographical directories is borne out here. All libraries with a business collection of any size should hold this directory.

1.175. Wiesenberger Investment Companies Service. New York: Wiesenberger Financial Services, Division of Warren, Gorham and Lamont, 1941–. Annual with supplements. $345.00.

Authority and scope: Wiesenberger Financial Services, a respected publisher in the financial field, has provided a guide to mutual funds and investment companies. The information is taken from annual reports to stockholders and other statistical sources and gives "background, management policy and financial record for all leading companies in the U.S. and Canada." It is divided into four parts: general information about investment companies, the use of investment companies, and closed-end investment companies, and mutual-fund management companies. Also provided are a list of investment company managers/advisers and an index. Three quarterly newsletters plus an annual "Panorama," which is meant to be a convenient but not complete reference to all mutual funds registered for sale in the U.S., are included in the subscription.

Evaluation: Considered to be the best single source for basic information on mutual funds and investment companies, this service is recommended for all business libraries and for smaller and medium-sized public libraries that can justify the price. Smaller libraries should consider sharing the purchase or simply identifying availability at other libraries in the areas.

1.176. World Almanac and Book of Facts. New York: Newspaper Enterprise Association, 1868–. Annual. $5.95.

Authority and scope: First published in 1868 and annually since 1886, this compilation of information and statistics covers almost every subject of interest to Americans. It contains statistics on social, industrial, political, financial, religious, and educational topics, lists of associations and societies, biographies of famous personalities, and important current events of the previous year. Sources for many of the statistics are given, and a good general index appears at the front of the volume.

Evaluation: No library should be without this indispensable ready-reference tool.

1.177. World Wide Chamber of Commerce Directory. Boulder, CO: Johnson Publishing, 1967–. Annual. $22.00.

Authority and scope: This directory provides a compact listing, arranged alphabetically, state by state, town by town, of all Chambers of Commerce in the United States. Information includes the manager or president of the chamber, address, telephone number, and the population served. There are lists of American Chambers of Commerce abroad, Chambers of Commerce in Canada and Mexico, and foreign chambers in the principal cities of the world.

Evaluation: The usefulness of data, convenience, and low price make this a recommended purchase for all but the smallest libraries.

PART II

The Literature of Business Reference and Business Libraries: 1976–1987

Introduction

by Rashelle S. Karp

The compilation of abstracts of pertinent literature, 1976–1987, which makes up Part II of this book, is organized alphabetically by first author. Index access by author, journal, book title, publisher, and subject is provided in the dictionary-type index at the back of the book.

Several comments should be made about the compilation of literature of 1976-1987.

1. The total amount of literature is small (244 items over the 11–year period, including all items in series). Within the total output there is a heavy preponderance of journal articles (210), with a slight upward trend in volume of publication over the past five years, as indicated in Table 1. (It should be noted that 1987 is not complete.) The total number of items upon which the following statistics are based is higher than the total numbered items in the annotations because the statistics include all annual publications of articles in series which are only annotated once in the numbered listing.

Table 1. Volume of Publication

	1976	1977	1978	1979	1980	1981	1982	1983	1984	1985	1986	1987	Totals
Journal	18	18	22	15	17	16	21	22	12	25	20	4	210
Other	5	3	2	0	4	4	0	2	7	5	1	1	34
Totals	23	21	24	15	21	20	21	24	19	30	21	5	244

2. The interest in business reference and business libraries, as measured by the publishing record, seems higher in the United States than elsewhere. Of the 244 items, only 45 (18.4 percent) are attributable to other than U.S. sources. (In the 1983 edition of this book, the percentage was 19.2.)

Rashelle S. Karp is assistant professor at the College of Library Science, Clarion University of Pennsylvania, Clarion.

3. Table 2 presents the breakdown of major subject interests in the literature.

As can be seen, business reference sources overwhelmingly make up the greatest subject of interest. Of the 244 items, 128 treat business reference sources (51 of these general reference sources, 20 automation/databases). Another 14 are concerned with reference/information service itself, and an additional 14 are devoted to education in business reference. A smaller portion of the literature is devoted to peripheral reference interests: availability of business information (6), fees (5), indexing (1), information brokers (1), information needs of patrons (8), publishing (4). In all, 181 (74.1 percent) have a reference focus. The other significant subject interest is in business/company libraries, both specific and general. Forty-eight items (19.6 percent) are included in this category. These two large groupings account for 229 (93.8 percent) of the items published in the 11–year period.

Table 2. Major Subject Interests in the Business Literature 1976–1987

Subject	Number of Articles
Availability of Business Information	6
Business/Company Libraries	48
Specific	30
General	18
Business Reference Sources	128
Automation/Databases	20
Banking	2
Children's Materials	1
Companies/Industries	4
Economics	4
Financial Services	7
Foreign Trade	10
Franchises	1
General	51
Maps	1
Marketing	4
Money Management	1
Serials	12
Small Business/Entrepreneurs	3
Statistics/Statistical Studies	7
Education in Business Reference	14
Fees	5
Indexing	1
Information Brokers	1
Information Needs of Patrons	8
Maintenance and Organization of Materials	8
Public Relations	7
Publishing	4
Reference/Information Services	14

4. It would seem that persons writing in business literature do so, for the most part, alone. Of the 221 items with identified authors, 185 are a result of single authorship, 29 the work of 2 authors, and 7 were written by three or more authors.

5. Over the 11-year period, only three authors contributed more than three papers each to the literature: Balachandran (8), DiMattia (12), and Popovich (4). Fifteen others contributed more than one paper: Behles, Brown, Eddison, Heckman, Kavass, Kerbel, Legett, Matarazzo, Norton and Gautschi, Reid, Ternberg, Vernon, and Webb (all with 2); and Campbell (3). In all, 213 authors are represented.

6. Of the 74 journals that published items on the list, only 24 published more than one. *Special Libraries* published the most (28), followed by *Library Journal* (25), *Reference Services Review* (15), *ASLIB Proceedings* (14), *Canadian Library Journal* and *Unabashed Librarian* (each with 8), and *Publisher's Weekly* and *RQ* (each with 6). The remaining 16 journals published more than one, but less than 6 of the articles listed. They are: *Library Association Record* (5), *Serials Review* (5), *Online* (5), *College and Research Libraries* (3), *American Libraries* (3), *Show-Me Libraries* (3), *Behavioral and Social Science Librarian* (3), *Illinois Libraries* (3), *Database* (3), *Drexel Library Quarterly* (2), *Law Library Journal* (2) *Online Review* (2), *Australian Academic and Research Libraries* (2), *Business Computing* (2), *College and Research Libraries News* (2), and *Collection Building* (2).

Bibliography

Compiled by Rashelle S. Karp

2.1. Abraham, Deborah, and Pelcher, Annette. "Information for Tennessee Economic and Community Development." *Tennessee Librarian* 30 (Spring 1978): 24–26.

The special library of the Tennessee Department of Economic and Community Development serves as a resource to department staff, state and local officials, and the public. In addition to the primary functions of acquiring, organizing, and disseminating information, the library staff has developed informational brochures and statistical studies and has conducted research projects. The library houses materials on all aspects of the Tennessee economy, from the local scene to topics of national interest. One of its special collections is the Office of Minority Business Collection, which includes information on the economic status of women in the work force.

2.2. Allott, A. M. "Confusion and Fragmentation in Service to Business." *Library Association Record* 79 (December 1977): 687.

The 1970s have focused attention on the information needs of the business world. Yet England still has no centralized national business library, a situation that has resulted in confusion and fragmentation for those seeking information. The same state exists in many companies where it may take an internal crisis for different departments to share information. Paradoxically, the same information is often readily shared with outside agencies and even with rival companies. On the national level, an improvement in the availability of statistical serials has been achieved through the cooperative efforts of librarians and statisticians. Their hope is that this example will serve as a model for a national business library in the near future, perhaps with an interim facility being designated soon.

2.3. Altman, Elizabeth C. "A History of Baker Library at the Harvard University Graduate School of Business Administration." *Harvard Library Bulletin* 29 (April 1984): 169–96.

The intrigues and professional development of Baker Library are narrated from its beginnings in 1908 through 1978.

2.4. Andrade, Priscilla. "Banking on Micrographics." *Journal of Micrographics* 15 (April 1982): 60–62.

Transferring a bank's hard copy of legal documents, correspondence, and cash reports onto microform with a computer random access retrieval system has benefitted the bank in many ways. The benefits include staff reduction, higher morale, reduction of storage costs and overtime salaries, and improvement of file integrity.

2.5. "At Chase Manhattan Bank: Library Service for a Fee." *Library Journal* 103 (August 1978): 1456.

Research and library services available to the business public on a one-shot fee basis or by yearly retainer are identified.

2.6. Awe, Susan. "The Wisconsin Small Business Development Center Information Service-A Model." *Special Libraries* 77 (Summer 1986): 152–56.

In accordance with 1978 federal legislation, the U.S. Small Business Administration supports over 40 state Small Business Development Centers whose purpose is to provide information services for small businesses within the state. The Wisconsin SBDC recommends that the following procedures be used in order to adequately serve the community: (1) determine the needs; (2) identify, collect, classify, and disseminate the needed information; (3) develop a referral system to other information centers within the state; (4) use automated databases; (5) use a variety of commercial and government sources; (6) aggressively market the service; and (7) evaluate at periodic intervals.

2.7. Baade, Harley D. "The Corporate Environment and the Librarian." In *Special Librarianship: A New Reader*, edited by Eugene B. Jackson, pp. 298–304. Metuchen, NJ: Scarecrow, 1980.

Every corporation reflects a distinct attitude toward information which affects the total library environment. Areas that may vary are the company's treatment of information professionals, placement of the library within the organization, and the degree of development of policies and procedures. Generally, corporations offer information professionals unique opportunities for individualism and career growth in a competitive, dynamic atmosphere.

2.8. Bailey, Martha J. "Functions of Selected Company Libraries/Information Services." *Special Libraries* 72 (January 1981): 18–30.

A survey of 108 industries established functions characteristic of company libraries or information services. Analysis is presented by function (acquisitions, cataloging and indexing, circulation, distribution of information, publication, and references), and by nine industry categories: advertising, aircraft and missiles, chemicals, foods, law firms, newspapers, office machines, petroleum, and pharmaceuticals.

2.9. Bakewell, Kenneth Graham Bartlett. "The London Classification of Business Studies." *International Classification* 6 (1979): 29–35.

The London Classification of Business Studies (LCBS) was initiated in London, England, in 1970 as an alternative to the Harvard Classification. Illustrative examples of the classification system and of the differences between the first and second editions are presented. An increasing number of libraries throughout the world are adopting LCBS.

2.10. Balachandran, Madhava. *Basic Economic Statistics*. Exchange Bibliography No. 971. Monticello, IL: Council of Planning Libraries, 1976.

This descriptive bibliographic essay covers 112 economic statistics references in three broad categories: (1) historical, (2) current economic indicators, and (3) economic forecasts and projections.

2.11. ———. "Foreign Trade Statistics." *Reference Services Review* 4 (October 1976): 870–90.

Statistical data on international trade are available from numerous reference sources. Some provide purely statistical data on import and export trade, while others are analytical in nature and provide insights to current trends. Over 30 of the more important titles in this area are discussed briefly in terms of scope and emphasis. The majority of the titles are published by the U.S. Bureau of the Census.

2.12. ———. "International Economic Statistics: A Selected List of Documents." *Reference Services Review* 5 (October/December 1977): 53–57.

Seventy-three statistically oriented publications selected from materials available from the U.S. federal government, foreign governments, and regional and international organizations are covered in this bibliographic essay.

2.13. ———. "Marketing Information Sources." *Reference Services Review* 4 (July 1976): 87–91.

A variety of demographic and socioeconomic information is available to professionals in marketing and product management, sales merchandising, advertising, and market research, covering both quantitative and qualitative market indicators. The majority of the sources come from the federal government, but private sources such as trade associations, trade journals, and commercial publishers also contribute. Over 50 titles in this field are discussed briefly in terms of emphasis and scope.

2.14. ———. "Research Guide to Economics." *Reference Services Review* 5 (July 1977): 33–37.

This guide to business reference sources is divided into the following categories: guidebooks and manuals; journal selection tools; comprehensive sources of historical statistics; publications on current economic indicators; and survey-type publications. Sources of information are noted for economic data, forecasts and projections, receipts and expenditures of governmental organizations, and government finance.

2.15. ———. "State of the Art Survey of Reference Materials in Business." *Reference Services Review* 4 (October 1976): 7–16.

An annotated survey of significant sources of information on business published in 1975 and 1976 discusses the content and scope of databases, indexes, dictionaries and directories, and microforms. Some 58 evaluative reviews of titles in the fields of economics, marketing, accounting, real estate, women and minorities, and energy are included. Federal government publications are given special emphasis.

2.16. ———. "State of the Art Survey of Reference Sources in Business and Economics." *Reference Services Review* 6 (January 1978): 21–40.

This article presents an annotated survey of outstanding reference sources in business and economics which became available in 1976 and 1977. The content and scope of online databases, indexes, and micropublications are discussed, and evaluative reviews of over 100 titles are included in the categories of accounting, advertising, business information and management, business and technical writing, currency and banking, economics, finance and investment, labor and industrial relations, marketing, minorities and women, and real estate. Special mention is made of recent trends in the publication of current research in economics and business.

2.17. ———. *A Subject Approach to Business Reference Sources.* Occasional Paper No. 128. Champaign, IL: University of Illinois Graduate School of Library Science, June 1977.

The author evaluated information contained in almost 200 business reference sources discussed in this article. The first section examines both primary and secondary sources of information on specific companies, regardless of industry category. Sources that provide a broader perspective on the entire area are categorized in the second section under the headings of "Multi-Industry Studies," "Single-Industry Studies," and "Consumer Market Analysis."

2.18. Balke, Faye M., and Irby, Jane. "The Selling of the Public Library." *Drexel Library Quarterly* 12 (January/April 1976): 149–58.

A closer partnership between public libraries and the information industry in supplying of information is urged. Librarians, the authors suggest, must be willing to take already developed systems of storage and retrieval and apply them imaginatively rather than passively depending on commercial sources. An example of this is a project in San Mateo, California, where the public library is building its own online database within an already existing information retrieval system.

2.19. Bauer, Charles K. "Managing Management." *Special Libraries* 71 (April 1980): 204–16.

At the Lockheed Georgia Company, a continuous interaction between the information center and the administration earns the center recognition as a dynamic, integral partner in the management team. The information specialist must possess attitudes and behaviors that will clearly demonstrate the value and usefulness of information. Knowledge about the company, its products, and its information resources, as well as skills in salesmanship, supervision, and establishment of rapport with clients are essential. Support for the information center must come from all levels of management, starting from the top administrator.

2.20. Behles, Richard J. "Business America." *Serials Review* 6 (April/June 1980): 7–8.

Although it has undergone several name changes, *Business America* remains a primary serial title for current information on international trade and commerce. It includes two or three short articles, per issue as well as regular departments, such as "Domestic Business Report," "Economic Highlights," "Business Outlook Abroad," and "Worldwide Business Opportunities." It is indexed in *Index to U.S. Government Periodicals* and *Business Periodicals Index.*

2.21. ———. "Business Periodicals." *Serials Review* 6 (April/June 1980): 9–16.

An annotated list of 24 business periodicals is divided into general periodicals, and those covering management, finance, marketing, industrial psychology, international business, and retail business. Discussions of each periodical are descriptive and give evaluative guidelines for making acquisition decisions.

2.22. Bernhard, Lenore H. "The Business Firm Library." In her *How to Organize and Operate a Small Library*, 39+. Fort Atkinson, WI: Highsmith, 1976.

The chapter on setting up a small business library includes a profile of the staff, collection, cataloging system, and purchasing policies of a library in a large utility company.

2.23. Bernstein, Judith R. "Corporate Annual Reports in Academic Business Libraries." *College and Research Libraries* 47 (May 1986): 263–73.

A survey of 500 academic business libraries in the United States resulted in the findings that (1) over half collect hard-copy corporate annual reports, which are usually housed in the reference room, special alcoves, or filing cabinets throughout the library; (2) the major uses of corporate annual reports are for career, financial, company history, or marketing-research information; and (3) few libraries collect foreign corporate annual reports.

2.24. Black, Bernard A. "Fortune." *Serials Review* 4 (January/March 1978): 7–12.

The origins and development of *Fortune* magazine are discussed. *Fortune* has major index coverage in *Industrial Arts Index, Business Periodicals Index, Readers Guide to Periodical Literature, Social Science Citation Index*, and *Public Affairs Information Service-Bulletin*.

2.25. Blick, A. R., and Ward, S. M. "Microform Policy to Reduce the Physical Growth of Industrial Libraries." *ASLIB Proceedings* 36 (April 1984): 165–76.

The Beecham Pharmaceuticals Research Division libraries make extensive use of microfiche for journal holdings in order to avoid storage problems. The development and implementation of this policy are described here, as are user reactions.

2.26. Brown, Barbara E. "Update to *Canadian Business and Economics: A Guide to Sources of Information*." *Canadian Library Journal* 33 (December 1976): 493–99.

This supplement to the 1976 book includes more titles annotated in both English and French. Subject headings similar to those utilized in the book appear here.

2.27. ———. "Update to *Canadian Business and Economics: A Guide to Sources of Information*." *Canadian Library Journal* 35 (February 1978): 5–15.

A listing of 105 titles which supplements the 1976 book is presented in both English and French. The annotations are divided into 40 categories and indicate titles specific to each province.

2.28. Brown, Barbara E., ed. *Canadian Business and Economics: A Guide to Sources of Information.* Ottawa, ON: Canadian Library Association, 1976.

This reference tool presents a comprehensive list of publications for Canadian business. Brief annotations are included for many, and French as well as English front and back matter are incorporated. The entries are arranged first by province and then within each province, under more than 60 subject and form headings (bibliographies, atlases, business finance, ethnic groups, etc.). Entries are indexed by author, title, former title, publisher, and series.

2.29. *Business Books and Serials in Print.* New York: Bowker, 1977.

Over 37,500 titles in the area of business—over 6,000 of which are serials—from some 1,580 publishers are included in the latest volume. Information includes author, title, and subject. Coverage emphasizes administrative and commercial (rather than industrial) aspects and extends to the areas of economics, agriculture, industry, finance, investment, insurance, taxation, prices, employment, wages, production, income spending and forecasting, and managerial functions.

2.30. "Business, Financial and Management Books: A Selection of Fall Titles." *Publisher's Weekly* 230 (October 24, 1986): 32–34+.

Titles are listed by publisher and descriptively annotated.

2.31. Cabell, David W. E. *Cabell's Directory of Publishing Opportunities in Business and Economics.* Beaumont, TX: Cabell Publishing, 1985.

Over 250 business publications are listed with descriptions of the types of manuscripts each publishes, its manuscript guidelines, editorial policy and objectives, editorial review processes, acceptance rates, time required for reviews, availability of reviewers' comments, circulation, type of readership, frequency of publication, sponsorship, percentage of invited articles, fees (if any) to publish manuscripts, and subscription rates. A subject index by field of business is included.

2.32. Cady, Susan A., and Richards, Berry G. "The One Thousand Dollar Alternative." *American Libraries* 13 (March 1982): 175–76.

Speed and confidentiality are critical to the subscription services for business offered by Lehigh University in Pennsylvania. An annual subscription pays for corporate borrowing privileges, copies of the library's serial lists, staff-prepared bibliographies and guides to literature, monthly lists of new acquisitions, and bibliographic instruction in the library. Computer literature searching, telefacsimile transmission, SDI, and some reference services are charged against the subscriber's original deposit. Funds left over at the end of the year revert to the library's book-collection budget; excess costs are billed to the client.

2.33. Campbell, Malcolm J. *Business Information Services.* 2nd ed. London: Clive Bingley, 1981.

The structure and organization of British business information sources are described, and special problem areas are highlighted.

2.34. ———. *Manual of Business Library Practice.* 2nd ed. London: Clive Bingley, 1985.

In this updated edition of a 1975 publication, the author provides a basic text for the British would-be business librarian.

2.35. ———. "Running Dogs in the Reference?" *New Library World* 77 (December 1976): 232–33.

Business, as a major taxpayer, is entitled to access to information through "free" public libraries. It is noted that 48 percent of public business library patrons come for personal, and not company, business. Online information retrieval services that eliminate the need for some expensive periodicals are suggested as one way of lowering costs.

2.36. Ceppos, Karen Feingold. "Corporate Climate and Its Effect on Information Management." *Special Libraries* 73 (October 1982): 238–44.

A survey of three companies indicates that corporate climate or the composite behavior and values of corporate employees influence the provision and use of library services. For example, some libraries are evaluated in terms of staff opinions, while others are evaluated in terms of money saved. Direct access to management is cited as very helpful in obtaining financial support.

2.37. Cheney, Debora, and Malecki, Sharon. "Industrial Directories: A Closer Look." *RQ* 26 (Winter 1986): 221–30.

The best sources for information about private companies are industrial directories. Major publishers of industrial directories are listed, along with the specific sources that they publish.

2.38. Cheo, Francis. "Singapore Library and Information Needs of and Services for End Users in Economics, Business and Finance." In *The Library in the Information Revolution*, pp. 433–39. Singapore: Maruzen, 1983.

The author identifies the users of business information in Singapore, and describes their demands, how librarians attempt to satisfy the information demands, and librarian success ratios. Specific information sources such as the National University of Singapore, DIALOG, and the National Library and Documentation Centre—Southeast Asia, are discussed.

2.39. Christensen, Rod. "Sources of Information on International Marketing: A Checklist." *Reference Services Review* 9 (July 1981): 53–59.

Over 60 annotated general sources, guides to reference sources, international regional sources, directories, and international statistics sources are listed.

2.40. Chung, Catherine. *Directory of Periodicals Online; Indexed, Abstracted, and Full-Text.* Volume 1 News, Law and Business. 2nd ed. Washington, DC: Federal Document Retrieval, 1986.

Instead of describing databases, this source lists journals (in alphabetical order by title) which are included in databases. Entries provide information about which database carries the journal; years of online coverage; first time between hardcopy publication of the periodical and online accessibility; whether online coverage is full-text, abstract or citation; and the database vendor. All periodicals covered by English-language, public-access databases are included.

2.41. Clausen, Nancy M. "Your R&D Library Can Help You More Than You Think as You Take Advantage of Your Records and Information Center." *Industrial Research/Development* 20 (September 1978): 164–67.

The information specialist in a research and development library can provide professional services to support the research activities of the company. For example, (1) current publications evaluated as relevant to patrons' interests could be disseminated to appropriate staff, or (2) the specialist's expertise in searching online databases might increase access to corporate and research literature and to data not readily available.

2.42. Cojeen, Robert H. "International Business Publications in the Seventies." *Choice* 15 (March 1978): 21–27.

Increased interest in multinational business dealings will result in greater demand for information on international business. This bibliographic essay covers around 80 sources, including government publications, popular works, and corporate literature, that are useful in understanding international business in fields like accounting and area studies. Items recommended for basic collections are indicated.

2.43. Coon, Carol. "San Francisco Public Library Small Business Resources." *Unabashed Librarian* 56 (1985): 21.

This reprint of a brochure lists and annotates the small-business resources of the San Francisco Public Library in the subject areas of exporting and importing.

2.44. Cooney, Jane; Gervino, Joan; and Hendsey, Susanne. "United States and Canadian Business and Banking Information Sources." *Law Library Journal* 70 (November 1977): 561–69.

The authors present an annotated bibliography with an emphasis on banking sources. Their list comprises more than 60 American and more than 40 Canadian sources. The categories include bibliographies, dictionaries, indexes, biographies, directories, bank directories, corporate information, statistics, and periodicals. Items the authors believe should be part of a core collection are also indicated.

2.45. Cox, Eli P., III; Hamelman, Paul W.; and Wilcox, James B. "Relational Characteristics of the Business Literature." *Journal of Business* 49 (April 1976): 252–65.

Scholarly business literature can communicate new information to the professional community. Systematic analysis of content, authorship, and relational characteristics of research journals yields insights into the development of the field as a research-oriented discipline. Citation indexes are an especially important tool in this regard. Nonmetric multidisciplinary scaling is a more refined technique for investigation of the relationships among journals and evaluation of their research characteristics.

2.46. Culley, James D., et al. "Business Students and the University Library: An Overlooked Element in the Business Curriculum." *Journal of Academic Librarianship* 2 (January 1977): 293–96.

Whether university schools of business are training students adequately in the use of business information sources is questioned on the basis of research on student knowledge and use of major business-related information sources, student use of business periodicals, and student attitudes toward use of the university library.

2.47. Culnan, Mary J. "What Corporate Librarians Will Need to Know in the Future." *Special Libraries* 77 (Fall 1986): 213–16.

Technology and changes in the foreign and domestic business world will force library schools to (1) broaden education beyond traditional skills, (2) include technology as a critical component of the curriculum, (3) teach analytic and quantitative skills, and (4) foster an understanding of the corporate library's unique role within the corporation.

2.48. Cupoli, Patricia. "Reference Tools for Data Processing, Office Automation and Data Communications: An Introductory Guide." *Special Libraries* 72 (July 1981): 233–42.

Information from current reference tools in the areas of data processing, office automation, and communications is available either through loose-leaf services and catalogs or through online retrieval systems and printed indexes. A discussion of the content of these various reference sources is presented. A list of almost 70 of these tools also includes vendor information.

2.49. Curtis, John, and Abram, Steven. "Special and Corporate Libraries Planning for Survival and Success." *Canadian Library Journal* 40 (August 1983): 225–28.

Unless inputs to the corporate library are measured in terms of how users are made more productive, the corporate library will fall victim to organizational reviews. Suggestions for looking at the library in the business context of the entire organization are outlined.

2.50. Cveljo, Katherine. "Business Librarianship: Information Services and Research." *Special Libraries* 70 (August 1979): 320–27.

Library services in business should respond to the clientele's changing and growing information needs. Successful librarians should be aware of the current information requirements and have a thorough knowledge of the organization, its staff, and its subject areas. Adequate education and training are essential. The author discusses a model business information course, utilizing a variety of instructional methods and combining theoretical and practical aspects.

2.51. Dahlin, Robert, and Maryles, Daisy. "Books on Money Matters: A Current Checklist." *Publishers Weekly* 215 (April 16, 1979): 53–55+.

The inflationary economy has led to an increase in the number of financial self-help books. This checklist includes over 125 current or forthcoming titles on money management for the consumer from 55 publishers. Categories include general money management, consumer advice, personal/family finances, women, stock market, real estate, taxes, estate planning, retirement, antiques and collectibles, and first-person accounts.

2.52. Darnay, Brigitte T., ed. *Subject Directory of Special Libraries and Information Centers.* Volume I - Business Law Libraries. 9th ed. Detroit, MI: Gale, 1985.

Volume 1 of this companion to Gale's *Directory of Special Libraries and Information Centers* (1982) provides directory information on over 1,000 business libraries. Four other volumes provide information on libraries in 26 other subject areas.

2.53. Davis, Joann. "Books on Money Matters: Current Checklist." *Publishers Weekly* 221 (March 5, 1982): 31–42.

Government deficits, unemployment, and recession continue to stimulate the publication of financial self-help books. This checklist annotates over 250 titles for consumers on taxes, real estate, the stock market and investments, Reaganomics, retirement, credit and borrowing, inflation, personal finances, general consumer advice, salaries, estate planning, economic analysis and history, the psychology of money, women and money, and fundraising.

2.54. Delany, Oliver. "Selling to the Government." *Oklahoma Librarian* 28 (January 1978): 15–16.

Information on how businesses can sell their goods and services to the federal government can be obtained from several sources. The *Supply Catalog* and *Sources of Supply and Service*, both published by the federal General Services Administration (GSA), the *U.S. Government Purchasing and Sales Directory* published by the Small Business Administration (SBA), and the *Commerce Business Daily* of the Department of Commerce provide a variety of information on the kinds of goods and services used by government agencies. The purpose and use of specifications and ordering procedures are spelled out in SBA's *Guide to Federal Specifications and Standards*, GSA's *Index to Federal Specifications and Standards*, and the *Index to Specifications and Standards*, published by the Department of Defense. Information on how to obtain each publication is included.

2.55. Dermyer, Angela. "Try on a Company Library." *Industry Week* 194 (1 August 1977): 56–57.

A company library is the necessary antidote when informational chaos is perceived by management. A librarian not only can bring order to that chaos, but can also provide professional services that can further the company's goals. Key issues to be considered before establishing a library include: where the library will stand within the organizational hierarchy; provision of an adequate budget, space, and clerical staff; and determination of the library's anticipated scope and subject coverage. The qualified librarian should have management skills as well as a background in all aspects of library work. Ideally, the librarian should also be viewed both as a part of the management support structure and as a full-fledged member of the professional staff.

2.56. Dessouky, Ibtesam A. "Libraries in Kuwaiti Financial Institutions: Their Functions and Potentials." *Special Libraries* 76 (Summer 1985): 198–203.

A survey of Kuwaiti financial institutions found that information services in Kuwaiti banks with libraries include traditional reference services, foreign-exchange information, evaluation of foreign and local situations, statistics, summaries of investments and loans, and selective dissemination of information (SDI). Banks without libraries obtained information through informal collections scattered throughout the bank departments and through personal collections. All cited the need for a library. The recommendation is made that Kuwaiti financial institutions develop a union catalog and engage in resource sharing.

2.57. DiMattia, Susan. "Business Books of [year]." *Library Journal*, [volume] (March 1, [year]).

In each March 1 issue of *Library Journal*, DiMattia provides an annotated listing of approximately 60–80 "best" or "most significant" business books from the past year. The list is organized into categories such as corporations, entrepreneurs/intrapreneurs, ethics, finance and investments, industry studies, the international marketplace, management, marketing/sales, success and career planning, women in business, economics, business/government relations, industries/companies, computers and related technology, strategic planning, human resources management, personal finance planning, the futures market, concerns of retired persons, and dual-career marriages. An essay precedes each year's listing of titles, in which the author highlights business publishing trends of the past year.

2.58. ———. "Business Reference Services." *RQ* 22 (Winter 1982): 135–39.
Business reference service differs from general reference service because seekers of business information (1) need their information more quickly; (2) often demand confidentiality; (3) need absolutely up-to-date and accurate answers; (4) request information which is difficult to find and often available only in expensive or obscure sources; (5) make tremendous use of online databases; (6) do not want to learn how to use the library themselves; and (7) are willing to pay for services rendered. Librarians must encourage and attract these patrons and the additional funds that they bring to the institution.

2.59. DiPiesse, Larry, and Hunhold, Maggie I. "Business Basics: A Bibliography for Better Business." *Show-Me Libraries* 34 (January 1983): 10–18.
This annotated bibliography identifies a core of business information sources that will most likely be used on a daily basis in a public library and whose total cost does not exceed $9,000.

2.60. Dodd, James B. "Information Brokers." *Special Libraries* 67 (May/June 1976): 243–50.
The author discusses the appearance in the 1970s of information brokers who obtain information, for a fee, for users who often come from industrial and business libraries. The author indicates that the information provided comes from the brokers' own collections as well as the collections of large libraries . Thirty-two information brokers were contacted. The variety of services those brokers offer includes document delivery, literature searches whose output is user friendly, translation, library management, writing and editing, and indexing. Issues addressed by the author include conflict of interest, fees, ethics, and relationships with libraries used.

2.61. Drummond, Janet. "Business Information Centers: New Resources Are Not Used." *Canadian Library Journal* 41 (October 1984): 259–61.
A survey of Canadian information centers specializing in business, economics, or finance asked questions about staffing, services, and public relations procedures. It was found that, although a majority of the centers were staffed by at least one librarian, nontraditional information services such as SDI, indexing, and market reports were seldom offered. Additionally, corporate libraries tended to rely on word-of-mouth public relations, rather than formal promotional methods.

2.62. Eddison, Elizabeth Bole. "Who Should Be in Charge?" *Special Libraries* 74 (April 1983): 107–09.

Would-be corporate librarians must be trained to assume the corporate position of vice-president of information. To achieve this training, library schools must include courses on records management, information analysis, data-processing management, systems analysis, business administration, marketing, and corporate finance.

2.63. Eddison, Elizabeth Bole, and Lyman, Lois B. comps. *Words that Mean Business: 3,000 Terms for Access to Business Information.* New York: Neal-Schuman, 1981.

Intended for use in indexing and organization of business library materials, this thesaurus lists over 3,000 main terms and related concepts, selected and systematically compiled in the course of indexing and cataloging more than 50,000 business resources. Four authority lists are included: agencies and organizations, major companies, currencies of the world, and standard subject heading subdivisions.

2.64. Engstrom, Theresa. "Whither Business Books?" *Publisher's Weekly* 23 (October 24, 1986): 25–30.

Sales of business books have seen tremendous growth in the 1980s because of paperback issues of previously hardcover publications, more aggressive promotions, the use of direct mail solicitation for sales, and better analysis of the market.

2.65. Escriu, Maria A. "A Canada-Latin America Private Business Collection." In *Seminar on the Acquisition of Latin American Library Materials.* 26th, 1981. Tulane University. Latin America Economic Issues. Los Angeles: University of California Latin American Center, 1984, pp. 266–74.

The Canadian Association-Latin America and Caribbean (CALA) was established in 1969 to provide business information from Latin America to Canada and to serve as a liaison between the two for marketing goods and services. CALA's information center provides specialized documents on Latin America, including many which are unobtainable anywhere else in Canada. Other agencies from which information may be obtained are also described.

2.66. Fay, Catherine. "The Corporate Information Center." In *Online Searching: The Basics, Settings and Management,* edited by Joann H. Lee, pp. 105–13. CO: Libraries Unlimited, 1984.

The development, purpose, organization, holdings, staffing, online services, record keeping, and promotion of a corporate information center are outlined.

2.67. Feingold, Karen, and Ward, Jane. "A Survey of Library User Demands in an Industrial Corporate Library." In *Quantitative Measurement and Dynamic Library Service,* edited by Ching-Chih Chen, pp. 103–12. Phoenix, AZ: Oryx Press, 1978.

Projections of future library services in the branch locations of Digital Equipment Corporation were based on the analysis of a 60-hour user study. The frequency distribution of current services and the type of user group were cross-tabulated with job location. Patrons most likely to make use of library services were those located near the library. The findings of this study helped substantiate a successful request for the purchase of a bookmobile and the expansion of library services to outlying locations.

2.68. Figueroa, Oscar, and Winkler, Charles. *A Business Information Guidebook.* New York: AMACOM, 1980.
Sources of information in business and economics are presented in three sections. Part I considers the broad aspects of information retrieval, including geographic considerations, and discusses the Standard Industrial Classification (SIC) and the Establishment Standard Industrial Classification (ESIC) coding systems, as well as the federal government Documents Depository System. Part II is an annotated list of sources of information in 82 subject categories particularly applicable to planning and managing a business. The final section contains sources on personal investing under the categories of securities, mutual funds, security dealers, the New York and American Stock Exchanges, investment companies, and securities research.

2.69. Finley, John D. "Documenting Missouri: Department of Revenue Publications." *Show-Me Libraries* 37 (September 1986): 29-31.
The major information publications from the Missouri Department of Revenue are described and evaluated.

2.70. Fisher, William H. "Weeding the Academic Business/Economics Collection." *Behavioral and Social Sciences Librarian* 42 (Winter 1984–85): 29–37.
A study of the business and economics section in a California university library indicates that, to be accurate, weeding must be based upon a combination of methodologies. In this case, materials were weeded if they were over 20 years old and had not been used within the past five years. Using age alone resulted in an 8 percent reduction of the collection; using last circulation date resulted in a 30 percent reduction. A combination of the two yielded a more reasonable collection reduction of 4.6 percent.

2.71. Fjällbrant, Nancy, ed. *International Association of Technological University Libraries. Meeting (11th 1985). Oxford England. The Future of Information Resources for Science and Technology and the Role of Libraries.* Stockholm, Sweden, International Association of Technological University Libraries, 1985.
The various papers discuss subjects including fee-based library services to industry, the industrial use of libraries in Europe, Australia, Israel, and Holland, and nonbibliographic databases.

2.72. Flower, Clara K. *Guide to Sources: Business Administration* and *Guide to Sources: Economics.* Orono, ME: University of Maine, 1980.
The major sources of information in business administration and economics available at the Raymond H. Fogler Library at the University of Maine at Orono are listed in these two introductory resource guides. Over 90 titles are included in the following categories: "Abstracts and Indexes," "Bibliographic Guides," "Biographies," "Dictionaries," "Directories," "Encyclopedias," "Government Publications," "Handbooks," and "Statistical Sources." The *Guide to Sources: Business Administration* also identifies the library's holdings of looseleaf business services.

2.73. Forest, Robert B. "Let's Go to the Library." *Infosystems* 24 (December 1977): 78.

The products of batch computer systems can be organized into a programming support library. The person in charge of the library, besides performing supportive clerical tasks, can also serve as the link between the programmers and the stored information. Some of the benefits of an organized library include improved employee efficiency, more consistent communications among staff members, and better control over the computer programs.

2.74. Foster, Allan. *Which Database? An Evaluative Guide to Online Bibliographic Databases in Business and the Social Sciences.* London: Headland Press, 1981.

The author gives guidance to the information professional on the initial selection of appropriate databases, in the form of evaluations of ABI/Inform, Accountants Index, Economic Abstracts International, Fintel, Labordoc, Management Contents, Predicasts, SCIMP, and Textline.

2.75. Freeman, Mike. "Business Basics: A Bibliography for Better Business." *Unabashed Librarian* 46 (1983): 21– 26.

This annotated bibliography of major sources of business information for a public library reference collection identifies only those materials that are most likely to be used by patrons on a daily basis.

2.76. Fries, James, and Brown, Jonathan. "Business Information on CD-ROM: The Datatext Service at Dartmouth College, New Hampshire." *Program* 21 (January 1987): 1– 12.

Datatext is a value-added database of bibliographic, biographical, textual, and numeric data on over 10,000 United States public companies. It is derived from six commercial online databases and loaded onto CD-ROM disks. The data is repackaged so that end users can manipulate the retrieved data in various ways. Compared to traditional databases, Datatext and the technology of CD-ROM are recommended as more useful.

2.77. Futas, Elizabeth, and Vidor, David L. "How Business Professionals Use Libraries." *Library Journal* 111 (November 1, 1986): 35–39.

A survey of part-time and full-time MBA students reveals that (1) part-time students used more books than full-time students; (2) both groups made greater use of popular business journals than scholarly ones; and (3) online searching was heavily used. It is suggested that loan periods for periodicals be examined in order to allow access for part-time students.

2.78. Ganly, John. "Consider the Source: Developing Business Collections." *Collection Building* 5 (Summer 1983): 24–28.

The author lists and describes major guides to business information from federal, state and local governments, international and multinational agencies, trade and professional associations, universities, Chambers of Commerce, research institutions, and private industry.

2.79. Georgi, Charlotte. "A Baker's Dozen Plus: Management Magazines for the Serials Librarian." *Serials Librarian* 9 (Fall 1984): 57–64.

This annotated listing of 13 major management periodicals also mentions 30 other sources which are highly recommended.

2.80. Goeldner, C. R., and Dirks, Laura M. "Business Facts: Where to Find Them." *MSU (Michigan State University) Business Topics* 24 (Summer 1976): 23–36.

An annotated list of information sources of material on analyzing and controlling business operations is presented, including references both to prime data sources and to bibliographical publications. The information is organized in two broad categories: (1) "Sources of Primary Data and Statistical Information," including the subheadings of "Government Publications," "Trade Publication Statistical Issues," and "Business Guides and Services," and (2) "General Reference Sources," with the subcategories of "Indexes," "Periodicals," "Bibliographies and Special Guides," "Trade Associations," and "Other Basic Sources." Over 80 publications are included.

2.81. Goodman, Jan. "From Lemonade Stands to Wall Street: Children's Books' Messages About the Economy." *Interracial Books for Children Bulletin* 16 (nos. 2–3, 1985): 4–9.

Examination of 15 commonly available nonfiction children's books on business indicates that an unrealistic picture of our economy is presented. Distortions in the books include their contentions that (1) everyone in the U.S. has money; (2) the difference between the poor and rich is not how much money they have; but rather how they spend their money; (3) there is no unemployment in the U.S.; (4) workers are only valuable as long as they provide a profit for management; and (5) capitalism is the best system. Sexism and racism are also problems in business materials for children, as white men are pictured in positions of power while women are illustrated as secretaries.

2.82. Greenwood, Molly. "Can Corporate Libraries Survive?" *Canadian Library Journal* 39 (December 1982): 353.

In order to be able to justify their existence, as well as provide effective services, would-be corporate librarians must receive practical rather than theoretical education in online searching and database design and operation.

2.83. Haines, Michael. "Company Correspondence: An Important Information Resource." *ASLIB Proceedings* 31 (August 1979): 401–11.

First discussed are the problems of making business correspondence accessible as an information resource, including multiple generation, indexing, subject and security classification, and multiple storage locations. The Charter Consolidates, Ltd. system for correspondence files is then treated, with special attention given to the indexing access points of company, country, commodity, and hierarchical subject classification. Finally, the finer points of computerization are presented.

2.84. Hanson, Janet R. "Teaching Information Sources in Business Studies: An Application of the Theories of J. Bruner and R. M. Gagne." *Journal of Librarianship* 17 (July 1985): 185–99.

The key to effective bibliographic instruction in the area of business is to teach for transferability of skills. To this end, Bruner's theory of instruction is outlined and then applied to construct an overall framework for the ordering of course content material by the librarian. Gagne's theory of instruction is outlined and applied to the development of teaching strategies.

2.85. Hatzfeld, Lois A. "Business." In *Periodical Indexes in the Social Sciences and Humanities: A Subject Guide*, pp. 22–26. Metuchen, NJ: Scarecrow, 1978.

A listing of key indexing sources that provide access to periodical literature in business is presented. The annotations define the scope and explain the arrangement and indexing of each source. The publications listed are *Accountants' Index, Accounting Articles, Anbar Management Services, Business Periodicals Index, Consumers Index to Product Evaluations and Information Sources, F&S Index International, F&S Index of Corporation and Industries,* and *Personnel Management Abstracts.*

2.86. Heckman, Lucy. "Finance and Investment Periodicals." *Serials Review* 8 (Summer 1982): 9–14.

An annotated listing of 19 periodicals judged most important by investment advisors for their securities and investment information is presented.

2.87. ———. "Statistical Sources in Business and Economics." *Reference Services Review* 11 (Summer 1983): 72–76.

The annotated listing includes indexes to general statistical sources, indexes to business statistical sources, business and economics statistics, directories, periodicals and almanacs, as well as statistical services.

2.88. Hornbeck, Julia. "An Academic Library's Experience with Fee-Based Services." *Drexel Library Quarterly* 19 (Fall 1983): 23–36.

The fee-based commercial information services provided by the Georgia Tech Library include document delivery from its collections, manual and online searching, bibliographic verification, and agent services to obtain original translations of non-English materials. These services are provided by regular staff, who use an hourly fee structure which is detailed in the article.

2.89. "Hotline to Offer Online [Business] Information." *Online Review* 10 (December 1986): 10.

The online business information service, *Hotline,* from British Telecom, covers all aspects of the business world, including market and company information and news. Additionally, it provides access to the Dow Jones Retrieval services. The product was developed in order to compensate for bias in U.S. business information services.

2.90. Howe, Robert. "A Bibliographic Guide to Latin American and Caribbean Government Publications on Foreign Investment, 1965–1981." *Government Publications Review* 10 (1983): 459–77.

The annotated guide lists serials which deal with investment laws and regulations, investment publications of international intergovernmental organizations, and investment-related publications of regulatory agencies, central banks, planning departments, and statistical services.

2.91. Hulser, Richard P. "Weeding in a Corporate Library as Part of a Collection Maintenance Program." *Science and Technology Libraries* 6 (Spring 1986): 1-9.

Weeding is necessary in corporate libraries because storage space is fixed, corporate missions often change, and materials tend to fall apart from repeated use or old age. It is suggested that monographs, unless classics, be weeded if they have not been used within the past five years. Short-run periodicals and periodicals which can be obtained in microform are also candidates for weeding. Internal technical reports must be kept (microform is suggested as a suitable medium), and networking is emphasized as a way to weed without permanently losing the discarded materials.

2.92. *Illinois Libraries* 62 (March 1980). Entire issue.

Articles relating to libraries in business and industry are included in this issue devoted to special libraries. The role of the business library and information center and its relation to the national information network are considered in "Library and Information Services for Business and the Professions," by David E. King (pp. 228–31). The services and collections of specific Illinois business libraries are discussed in "Clark Dietz Engineers, Inc.: A Library Profile," by Felicia Rodriguez Bagby (pp. 231–33); "Profile of a Library Serving a Corporate Headquarters," by Betty S. Hagberg (pp. 239–42); "Portland Cement Association Research and Development/Construction Technology Laboratories Library," by Marilyn Macku LaSalle (pp. 242–45); "Technical Information Center: Caterpillar Tractor Company," by Carol E. Mulvaney (pp. 256–58); and "An Advertising and Public Relations Agency Library," by Ellen Steininger (pp. 272–74).

2.93. "Information for Business: Problems of Availability and Access." *ASLIB Proceedings* 30 (September 1978): 316–41.

Papers presented at a 1977 ASLIB conference dealt with the problems of gaining access to business information. The papers collected here include: "Business Information: A Review of User Difficulties," by Judith Collins, a discussion of a survey that identified problems inherent in the information being sought as well as on the part of the information seeker; "Government Statistical Information," by Brian Mower, which considers the organization and role of the Government Statistical Service of the United Kingdom; "Some Problems in the Provision of Market Research Information," by Harry Henry, a commentary not only on problems, but also on the identification of primary market research information sources; and "Public Libraries," by Malcolm J. Campbell, which gives suggestions for strengthening the provision of business information, primarily for British public libraries.

2.94. "Instant Data from the *New York Times*." *Canadian Business* 50 (October 1977): 13+.

The *Information Bank* of the *New York Times*, which makes available to business subscribers items from 81 different publications, includes information from 12 U.S. daily newspapers; 12 daily, weekly, and monthly business publications; 12 foreign affairs publications; 5 scientific publications; and 40 news weeklies, monthlies, and quarterlies. Nearly 1.5 million items are available, with 20,000 items added monthly.

2.95. Jackson, Celia. "Information Systems at the Business Archives Council." *Indexer* 14 (October 1985): 257–58.

The services and organization of Great Britain's Business Archives Council are described.

2.96. Järvelin, Kalervo. "Cardinality Estimation in Numeric On-Line Databases." *Information Processing Management* 22 (6) (1986): 523–48.

Charges for online searching are usually based on connect time. It is suggested that charges for numeric databases be item-based or processing-based, in order to more accurately reflect the product being sold. A method for determining the charges is described.

2.97. Jensen, Rebecca J.; Asbury, Herbert O.; and King, Radford G. "Costs and Benefits to Industry of Online Literature Searches." *Special Libraries* 71 (July 1980): 291–99.

A telephone survey of clients of the NASA Industrial Application Center, University of Southern California, and the NASA Small Business Administration Technology Assistance Program examined the dollar costs and benefits of an online literature search. Over 50 percent of those interviewed reported dollar benefits, especially in acquiring technical information more efficiently. The survey indicates that when more dollars are invested in the service, more dollar benefits are realized. Interactive searches were found to be the most expensive type of search, but also the most cost-effective. Overall, the ratio of dollar benefit to investment averaged 2.9 to 1.

2.98. Jones, Herbert. "Why the Bookmen Turn to Business." *Director* 29 (December 1976): 33–34.

In England, prior to 1930, books and magazines about business were almost all American in origin. Only the Finsbury Public Library in London had a business collection. World War II, with its emphasis on production management and the creation, by Henry Luce's *Fortune*, of an international audience for business management, changed the situation; in 1949, *Director* became the forum for discussion of British business. The *Director's* "Bookshelf" book-review feature, remains important. Significant publishing firms that have emerged include Allen and Unwin, Hutchinson, Harrap, Longman, Macdonald and Evans, Macmillan, McGraw-Hill, Routledge and Kegan Paul, Penguin, and Pan. The Economist's Bookshop in London remains a place to consider when seeking books on business subjects.

2.99. Junge, Alfred R. "Business Information Sources on Asia." *Special Libraries* 70 (February 1979): 82–90.

Although the diverse economic practices in Asia make business trade and investment more difficult than in other parts of the world, Asia has significant potential as an economic market. Information on potential markets is available in standard business tools, such as the publications of the United Nations and the U.S. Department of Commerce. However, these sources need to be supplemented. Banks, trade organizations, and corporations provide a wide variety of useful periodicals, often available on a complimentary basis. A discussion of these documents is accompanied by an annotated list of almost 30 free publications.

2.100. Katz, Toni. *Guide to Sources: Company/Industry Information.* Orono, ME: University of Maine, 1981.

Listed are over 65 reference sources that provide information on companies and industries, available at the Raymond H. Fogler Library, University of Maine at Orono. The coverage includes general, regional, state, and Canadian corporate directories, as well as directories of industries in 18 specific areas. The final section is composed of sources for financial information and guides, investment services, and statistical sources for industry analysis.

2.101. Kavass, Igor I. "International Business Transactions: A Guide to Research Sources." *Law Library Journal* 76 (Summer 1983): 497–564.

The author presents an annotated bibliographic guide to treatises, compendia, collections of laws, periodicals, individual journal articles, documents, and other information sources of value for current research in the area of international business law.

2.102. ———. "The Problems of Legal Research in International Business Transactions." *International Journal of Legal Information* 10 (December 1982): 344–58.

Researching the legal aspects of international business is difficult because international business embraces many unrelated topics of law. Additionally, sources of information are scattered over a wide range of publications, and access to necessary information sources is often unavailable. The author illustrates these difficulties by citing examples and concludes by suggesting solutions.

2.103. Keating, Michael. "Taking Stock of Two Services: Moody's *Investors Fact Sheets* and Standard and Poor's *Stock Reports.*" *Reference Services Review* 7 (April/June 1980): 37–46.

Two major stock reporting services, Moody's *Investors Fact Sheets* and Standard and Poor's *Stock Reports* are compared. The author notes differences and similarities in format, price, photocopying policies, history, circulation, coverage, revision policies, and industry review. A point-by-point comparison is made of the services' treatment of selected companies. Some of the major differences noted are price, the "Industry Review" feature in *Investors Fact Sheets*, and the greater user familiarity with Standard and Poor's *Stock Reports*.

2.104. Keith, David. "The Databases of F. P. Sharp and How They Are Accessed with a Program Called MAGIC." *Database* 6 (August 1983): 52–61.

Time series data from over 80 financial, economic, aviation and energy databases can be accessed and manipulated into report formats through the use of the programming language APL and Sharp's access program, called MAGIC.

2.105. Kendrick, Aubrey W. "A Primer on Corporate Reports." *Reference Services Review* 13 (Winter 1985): 53–56.

The different types of corporate reports are identified and described, including 10-Ks, proxy statements, prospectuses, 10-Q's, and other less-used reports. How to acquire the reports is detailed, and a listing of companies and addresses for obtaining microform editions is provided.

2.106. Kennington, Don. "Information for Business and Commerce." *Library Association Record* 87 (July 1985): 257–59.

The results of the British Library's investigation into information cooperatives for business information is the recommendation that such a cooperative be (1) membership-based, with each member subscribing to the cooperative, (2) have its own staff, but make liberal use of volunteers, (3) be financially self-supporting, and (4) be independently and internally monitored to ensure adequate evaluation of progress and success.

2.107. Kerbel, Sandra S. "A Librarian's Primer on Financial Ratios." *RQ* 21 (Spring 1982): 268–73.

Current ratios, quick ratios, debt-equity ratios, inventory turnover ratios, and profit margins are explained so that corporate librarians can apply them. An annotated bibliography of resources which provide general information on the definitions and uses of ratios is also included.

2.108. Kerbel, Sandra S., and Myers, Mildred S. "Business and Society: A Bibliographic Essay." *Choice* 20 (October 1982): 223–25.

The accountability of business within the political, social, and physical environment of society is examined.

2.109. King, David E. "Library and Information Services for Business and the Professions." *Illinois Libraries* 62 (March 1980): 228–31.

Special libraries differ from other types of libraries in that (1) they are focused on information for utilitarian purposes only, (2) they serve employees of the institution in which they are located, (3) their collections are devoted to single subject areas, (4) they are not supported by public funding, and (5) they are usually unknown to the general public. The needs for resource sharing and provision of information from the federal government are underscored.

2.110. King, Richard L., ed. *Business Serials of the U.S. Government.* Chicago: American Library Association, 1978.

This annotated list of 105 U.S. serial publications includes information on pagination, the kinds of illustrations typically included, where the serial is indexed, sources for the data reported, and a description of each serial's purpose, coverage, and utility. The volume's 10 chapters cover the following subjects, reflected in their titles: "National Economic Conditions," "Domestic Commerce," "International Commerce," "Industry," "Agriculture," "Labor," "Small Business," "Consumerism," "Patents and Trademarks," and "Environment."

2.111. Kingman, Nancy M., and Vantine, Carol. "Commentary on the Special Librarian/Fee-Based Interface." *Special Libraries* 68 (September 1977): 320–22.

Fee-based information services such as INFORM can efficiently provide corporate librarians with accurate and pertinent business information. However, a high-quality service requires professional commitment to participate in the system and to support its goals. An improved interface between the librarian and the information broker will provide higher-quality information to the business community and will ultimately improve the professional caliber of librarianship.

2.112. Koch, Jean E., and Pask, Judith M. "Working Papers in Academic Business Libraries." *College and Research Libraries* 41 (November 1980): 517–23.

Working papers provide a means for circulating current research results in the fields of business and economics. The acquisition, collection, maintenance, and use of these documents vary among libraries. A survey of 119 academic business libraries indicated that a minority (33 percent) actively collect working papers, usually selecting them on the basis of the publishing institution's reputation and on specific requests from library patrons. Most of the libraries surveyed do not catalog or bind working papers. A parallel user study of the business libraries of Purdue University and the University of Illinois indicated that faculty are the main users of working papers and consider them an essential research tool.

2.113. Kok, John, and Strable, Edward G. "Moving Up—Librarians Who Have Become Officers of Their Organizations." *Special Libraries* 71 (January 1980): 5–12.

Special librarians (23) in business-finance and advertising who became officers in their organizations cited hard work and a service-oriented library staff as crucial to their promotions. And, although many of the appointments were not accompanied by increased salaries, increased prestige was very beneficial, psychologically and practically.

2.114. Kulibert, Marie. "Business Corner: A Booklist." *Unabashed Librarian* 54 (1985): 9–10.

The annotated listing of general business reference sources in the areas of insurance, investment, and taxation includes major newsletters, newspapers and magazines It is designed to be used as a handout for presentations.

2.115. Lavin, Michael R. *Business Information: How to Find It, How to Use It.* Phoenix, AZ: Oryx Press, 1987.

This detailed research guide explains to researchers at all levels how to use the most important business sources. The author discusses basic business concepts and terminology. Chapters cover the sources and forms of business information, basic finding tools, business directories, searching registered trademarks, corporate finances, investment information, statistical reasoning, census information, economic and industry statistics, marketing information, business law sources, tax law publications, and business resources in nonbusiness environments.

2.116. Lee, Missy. "The Entrepreneur and His Search for Information." *Mississippi Libraries* 47 (Spring 1983): 14–16.

A short annotated list of serial and monograph business information sources useful for entrepreneurs includes titles on marketing, internal financial management, franchise purchases, as well as general how-to sources.

2.117. Leggett, Mark. "Bank Letters, Bulletins, and Reviews." *Special Libraries* 68 (December 1977): 425–29.

Several commercial banks and all 12 Federal Reserve System district banks publish letters, bulletins, and reviews that deal with facets of the national and international economy. The publications vary in cost, frequency, format, content, and scope. As a whole, they provide coverage of past, current, and future economic events. A bibliography of 26 commercial bank publications, the 12 federal reserve system titles, and 10 indexing tools is included.

2.118. ———. "Employment Announcements in Business, Science and Technology Periodicals—A Checklist." *Southeastern Librarian* 29 (Fall 1979): 158–60.

Periodicals in business, science, and technology have generally been overlooked as potential sources for advertisements of employment and career opportunities. A list of 205 periodicals (including over 50 relating to business) that carry job announcements is presented. A key that indicates the average number of listings per journal is also provided.

2.119. McCleary, Hunter. "A Practical Guide to Establishing a Business Intelligence Clearinghouse." *Database* 9 (June 1986): 40–44.

Corporate librarians must organize the vast amounts of information that they collect through the use of file-indexing and -retrieving software packages, as well as database management systems.

2.120. McConnell, Karen S. "Automation." *Texas Library Journal* 60 (Summer 1984): 52–53.

A successful library was established at the Gulf States Utility Company with the immediate use of library vendors, online searching, OCLC, and approval plans.

2.121. McDermott, David. "Hallmark of Publishing for Professionals." *Publishers Weekly* 210 (October 11, 1976): 35–36.

The business of publishing books for business is seen as one in which direct mail advertising and sales are still overwhelmingly strong, and in which authors quickly become professional consultants, spending much of their time on speaking engagements or writing for journals.

2.122. McDonald, David R., and Maxfield, Margaret W. "The Reference Library: Resource for the Small Business." *Journal of Small Business Management* 17 (January 1979): 51–56.

Information essential to the small-business manager is readily accessible through an understanding of basic reference tools and with the help of a reference librarian and interlibrary loan. Some examples of tools commonly used by the small-business manager include: *The Business Owner's Advertising Handbook, U.S. Industrial Outlook..., Census of Population,* and *County Business Patterns.*

2.123. McGowan, Timothy. "Business Reference Tools for a Small or Medium-Sized Library." *Unabashed Librarian* 50 (1984): 15–18.

An annotated listing of business periodicals whose costs smaller libraries can afford. Listings are ranked in order of usefulness, and special issues of each periodical are identified.

2.124. McKee, David H. "Business Reference Review." *Reference Services Review* 4 (July 1976): 93–95.

The author reviews the following business reference sources: *Trade Names Dictionary, Dictionary of Development Terminology, Executive and Management Development for Business and Government: A Guide to Information Sources, The Institutional Investor, Business People In the News, Consultants and Consulting Organizations Directory: A Reference Guide to Concerns and Individuals Engaged in Consulting for Business and Industry,* and *New Consultants: A Periodic Supplement to Consultants and Consulting Organizations Directory.*

2.125. "Marketing Literature: How to Find it with a Computer." *Journal of Marketing* 42 (April 1978): 12–13+.

Researchers at the University of Oregon examined the efficiency of computer-assisted literature searches for the marketing scholar by determining which databases most thoroughly index the "core" journals in the field. The major journals were judged to be: *Academy of Marketing Science Journal, Journal of Advertising Research, Journal of Consumer Research, Journal of Marketing, Journal of Marketing Research, Proceedings of American Marketing Association,* and *Proceedings, Association of Consumer Research.* Marketing literature from these journals is more likely to be found in the *Management Contents* and *Social Scisearch* databases.

2.126. Marsh, Sharon G. "Strategic Planning Information Online." *Database* 7 (June 1984): 20–25.

The strategic planning cycle in business includes four major steps: (1) environmental analysis (surveying the external environment in which the business operates), (2) structural analysis (determining where the business fits within its external environment), (3) trend analysis (determining the trends in the business environment), and (4) business analysis (examination of the business itself). The article identifies databases which can be used to complete the planning process and describes how they can be most effectively used.

2.127. Marshall, Peter. "Guiding Business—Via Prestel." *Library Association Record* 83 (February 1981): 78–79.

Prestel, a British computerized Viewdata system, provides the business community with the best sources of information on a topic, identifies which sources are available at reference libraries, provides a directory of libraries, gives guidance on what publicly available records contain information not available from published sources, and recommends contact points for some categories of unpublished information. "Business London," one component of Prestel, consists of data appropriate to the London area. Although the potential of this system has not been fully realized, it is pointed out that, while Prestel can provide immediate access to some information, the public library will continue to be valuable because of the comprehensiveness of its resources.

2.128. Matarazzo, James M. "A Field Study Defines Corporate Library Excellence." *American Libraries* 17 (September 1986): 588+

A survey of 13 special libraries defines corporate library excellence in terms of levels of service to users, levels of management commitment to the library, and the amount of staff nurturing provided by library managers.

2.129. ———. "Lessons from the Past: Special Library in Times of Retrenchment." *Canadian Library Journal* 40 (August 1983): 221–23.

A study of corporate library closures reveals that the decision to close the corporate library is often made by senior management, who do not use the library and therefore do not perceive it as useful. It is recommended that corporate librarians evaluate library services before the organization does, and that they work to involve senior management in the library's services.

2.130. Mechanic, Sylvia. "Investment Bibliography." *Unabashed Librarian* 41 (1981): 19–24.

This annotated listing of books, services, newspapers, periodicals, and financial organizations includes over 100 recommended sources, ranging from those for the novice to others for the experienced investor.

2.131. "Meeting the Need of GM Research Laboratories." *Information Manager* 2 (Spring 1980): 21–25.

The General Motors Research Laboratories Library is profiled in terms of its collection, clientele, staffing, and services. The library's 26 professionals meet the information needs of more than 700 scientists and engineers, with a collection of over 50,000 book titles and 1,300 journal titles and with substantial use of interlibrary loan. Mechanized services include computerized literature searches and computerized circulation and acquisition. A unique feature is the System on Automotive Safety Information (SASI), a special collection containing all published information relating to automotive safety.

2.132. Melanson, Robert A. "Using the SIC in Business Reference." *RQ* 18 (Fall 1978): 16–18.

The Standard Industrial Classification (SIC) categorizes establishments by type of business activity. This numerical code is used in government statistical documents and in commercially published resources to provide a standard access point to information on particular industries, products, and services. Publications using this system include the government documents published by the Census Bureau, Dun & Bradstreet's *Million Dollar Directory, Middle Market Directory, Standard and Poor's Register of Corporations*, and *Predicasts*.

2.133. Merry, Susan A. "Inside a Major Banking and Business Library." *Canadian Library Journal* 42 (June 1985): 115-18.

Unlike academic and public libraries, a bank library collection must reflect the corporation's specific goals and objectives. The services provided by the Canadian Imperial Bank of Commerce Library are profiled.

2.134. Misinsky, Joel. "The Corporate Library: Gearing for the Late 1980s." In *Festschrift in Honor of Dr. Anulfo D. Trejo*, edited by Christopher F. Grippo, et al., eds. Tucson, AZ: University of Arizona Graduate Library School, 1984, pp. 75-82.

The sum of all knowledge is doubling every 15-18 years, and the number of journal publications is growing at an almost exponential rate. Because of this, corporate librarians of the future will need to expand their abilities to access and retrieve specific information, to be constantly aware of new technology and equipment for information access; be able to carefully justify library expenses, to develop sophisticated networking systems, and be adept at cost analysis and strategic planning.

2.135. Moyer, R. Charles, and Crockett, John H. "Academic Journals: Policies, Trends, and Issues." *Academy of Management Journal* 19 (September 1976): 489-95.

Trends in the submission of manuscripts to over 100 management, business, and economic journals were examined during 1970-74 in terms of rate of acceptance, review time, and effect of submission fees. The acceptance rates from both major and secondary journals declined significantly in the time period studied, while the lag time between submission and publication for these journals grew substantially. It was further found that journals requiring submission fees provide more substantial manuscript critiques than those that do not. There is evidence that fees have not been a hindrance to the submission of quality research.

2.136. Mueller, Bonnie. "MBA Library—An Unmined Wealth of Information." *Mortgage Banker* 37 (October 1976): 119-20.

The services of the Mortgage Bankers Association Library are reviewed. The library got requests per month for specific books, as well as information requests on specific subjects, and more than 7,000 books, journals, brochures, and periodicals were used by 350 people on a regular basis. Several cases of effective use by good users are also presented.

2.137. Mulford, Thomas W. "Discipline Resource Package: Business and Economics." In *Reference Resources: A Systematic Approach*, by James M. Doyle and George H. Grimes, pp. 120-41. Metuchen, NJ: Scarecrow, 1976.

Almost 150 citations of business reference works are presented in the systematic manner devised by Doyle and Grimes. The categories in this guide for the beginning researcher are arranged according to the "bibliographic chain": works in progress, unpublished studies, periodicals, reports and monographs, indexes and abstracting services, bibliographic lists and essays, annual review and state-of-the-art reports, books, and encyclopedia summaries.

2.138. Murphy, Marcy and Rehman, Sajjad ur. "The Reviewing of Management Literature." *Library Quarterly* 57 (January 1987): 32–60.
A bibliometric study of review literature in the area of management yielded a core of 12 journals which account for over half of all the reviews. Additionally, it was found that most literature on management is reviewed only once or not at all.

2.139. Norton, Robert, and Gautschi, David. "User Survey of an International Library: Expectations and Evaluations." *ASLIB Proceedings* 37 (April 1985): 195–206.
A survey of MBA students from 38 different nationalities at the European Institute of Business Administration found that usage and perceptions of libraries differ according to nationality. It is suggested that nationality be taken into consideration when designing library services.

2.140. ———. "User Survey of an International Library—Resource Allocation: Preferred Allocations of the Library Budget." *ASLIB Proceedings* 37 (September 1985): 371–80.
MBA students were asked to reallocate the budget of a business library in order to achieve a 10 percent cut. The majority of respondents cut expenditures for books, periodicals, and cataloging and classification while maintaining or increasing budget allocations for information on the company.

2.141. O'Connor, James P. "One Happy Hybrid." *American Libraries* 18 (April 1987): 290–92.
Kennametal Inc. (Latrobe, PA), has developed an integrated automated library system which comprises Faxon's LINX (for serials), OCLC (for cataloging and ILL), and BRS/Search (for online searching). This hybrid system is praised for its library-specific characteristics.

2.142. O'Donnell, William S. "The Vulnerable Corporate Special Library/Information Center: Minimizing the Risks." *Special Libraries* 67 (April 1976): 179–87.
The corporate information center, usually operated as a staff function and thus representing cost overhead, is particularly vulnerable in times of corporate belt-tightening like the present. This is especially true because its elimination is not seen as affecting profits in the short term. To avoid being targeted for budget reduction, it is suggested that librarians (1) establish strong ties with middle management executive users; (2) demonstrate an understanding of the library's role and a thorough knowledge of the industry and the corporation; (3) aggressively pursue the appropriate resources; (4) maintain a trained and effective staff; (5) keep management informed; and (6) relate to the users and their needs. Methods of self-assessment are also included.

2.143. Ohlson, June, and Tabuteau, Christine. "Microfiche Project on Australian Companies' Annual Reports." *Australian Academic and Research Libraries* 9 (December 1978): 215–18.

The project to microfiche 12,200 annual reports of 605 Australian companies by the Australian Graduate School of Management Library is described. The authors note the subjects of usage, company selection, fiche features, quality control, and availability of report.

2.144. Ojala, Marydee. "Public Library Business Collections and New Reference Technologies." *Special Libraries* 74 (April 1983): 138–49.
Eleven business librarians talk about the future of public library service to businesses. They are optimistic that this type of service will be in demand, and that, as long as funding for new technology is obtained, the service will grow.

2.145. O'Leary, Mick. "Probing Data Banks: The Professional Touch." *Business Computing* 2 (October 1984): 33–36.
Three case studies demonstrate how specific business information can be obtained from automated databases. Helpful tips for efficient use are also provided.

2.146. Pask, Judith M. "Bibliographic Instruction in Business Libraries." *Special Libraries* 72 (October 1981): 370–78.
The most popular methods of bibliographic instruction for graduate and undergraduate business students were identified in the responses to a survey of 61 academic libraries, including 33 separate business libraries. Although a variety of methods are employed, the most useful approach appears to be a combination of lecture and printed material, used in conjunction with regular course work. However, this type of instruction requires a cooperative relationship between the business librarian and the faculty. The librarian can provide bibliographies, give lectures, or prepare a slide tape presentation for the class.

2.147. Paterson, G. D. L. "Designing a Business Information Service for Top Management." *ASLIB Proceedings* 30 (April 1978): 142–44.
The "golden rules" for meeting the information needs of top management are: (1) make a senior library staff member available at all times; (2) disseminate news information quickly; (3) perform research quickly; (4) package information attractively; (5) keep library systems and organization simple.

2.148. Penn, Ray. "Student Use of Online Financial Databases at the AGSM." *Australia Academic and Research Libraries* 17 (June 1986): 20-22.
Business students who were taught to do their own online searching found the skills to be both very helpful and easy to master.

2.149. Pertell, Grace M. "Selling the Business Library." *Special Libraries* 72 (October 1981): 328–37.
In the corporate environment, a job well done is not necessarily good public relations. Good public relations include regular meetings with management, supplemented by written memos and reports; the acceptance of work assignments outside the library; current-awareness services; cultivation of good relations with the executive secretarial staff; serving as a public relations tool for the organization; employing competent staff; and implementing aggressive services.

2.150. Piele, Linda J., and Tyson, John C. *Materials and Methods for Business Research.* New York: Neal-Schuman Publishers Inc., 1980.

This workbook guide to business information sources is designed to be used by business students. It includes a student workbook and an instructor's manual, which teach 57 standard business resources, including major periodicals.

2.151. Popovich, Charles, J. "Business Data Bases: The Policies and Practices of Indexing." *RQ* 18 (Fall 1978): 5–18.

The state of the art of indexing in business databases was discussed at a 1977 American Library Association conference by representatives of three database vendors. Persons from *Management Contents, ABI/INFORM* and *Predicasts* summarized the features of their databases with respect to scope, purpose, content, publications index, dates covered, and accessibility. The reactions of a panel of business librarians from special, academic, and public libraries are also included.

2.152. ———. "A Bibliographic Guide to Small and Minority Business Management." *RQ* 18 (Summer 1979): 369–75.

Relevant resource materials are identified in this annotated list, an update of an earlier pamphlet, *Helping Minority Business: A List of Selected Materials.* The publications are grouped under the following categories: "Starting a Small Business," "Financing the Operation," "Managing the Business," and "Other Requirements." Addresses of associations and agencies that can provide further information are also included.

2.153. ———. "Characteristics of a Collection for Research in Business/ Management." *College and Research Libraries* 39 (March 1978): 110–17.

Citation analysis of 2,805 citations from 31 dissertations in business management was carried out. The characteristics considered were: publication form, periodical title, subject, time span, language, and publisher. The analysis revealed that 49.1 percent of the citations were to periodicals and 31.9 percent to monographs, with 78 percent of the citations to periodicals appearing in 62 titles. Monograph citations were dispersed as follows (LC classifications): 14.7 percent in Business, 11.5 percent in Economics-Labor, 10.8 percent in Economics-Production, with no other percentage higher than 10. More than 70 percent of all cited materials was 10 years old or less, and nearly 85 percent was 15 years old or less. Only four (.01 percent) of the citations were non-English-language titles. Commercial publishers were the most frequently cited (33.8 percent), followed by association publishers (29.6 percent), university publishers (24.4 percent), and government publishers (5.8 percent).

2.154. ———. "A Methodology for Categorizing International Business Literature Through Online Bibliographic Searching." *Online Review* 7 (August 1983): 341–55.

Online searching strategies that can most effectively retrieve relevant international business literature are suggested.

2.155. Prabha, Chandra G. "Some Aspects of Citation Behavior: A Pilot Study in Business Administration." *Journal of the American Society of Information Science* 34 (May 1983): 202–06.

A survey of business faculty at the University of Illinois to determine the reasons authors cite certain sources and not others concluded that: (1) less than one third of cited sources are considered essential by those who cited them; (2) cited items of critical importance are likely to be owned by the authors; and (3) cited items of critical importance may not be used heavily by authors.

2.156. Preston, Jenny. "Starting a Library at McDonnell Douglas Automation Company." *Show-Me Libraries* 32 (July 1981): 14–18.
The special library at McDonnell Douglas emphasizes selection in the areas of computers and data processing, with secondary emphasis on management, business planning and forecasting, finance and accounting, marketing, purchasing, and building design. Collection development is by a combination of acquisition and interlibrary loan, facilitated by liberal use of OCLC and an internal, automated catalog.

2.157. Prickett, Jeanine, et al. "Monsanto's Company-Wide On-Line Catalog." In *Conference on Integrated Online Library Systems.* 2nd, 1984. Edited by David C. Genaway. Atlanta, GA; Genaway and Associates, 1984, pp. 291–305.
A detailed description is given of development, implementation, and specifications of the online catalog at the Monsanto Research Center in St. Louis.

2.158. Quinn, Karen Takle. "The Information Center—Another Perspective." *Online* (July 1982): 11–23.
Suggestions for integrating the traditional special library with the data-processing information center are illustrated with examples from the IBM Santa Teresa Laboratory's Information/Library/Learning Center.

2.159. Reid, Christine. "Business Information Needs in Scotland." *ASLIB Proceedings.* 38 (February 1986): 51–64.
A survey of public, university, and college libraries in Scotland found that Scotland has a considerable wealth of business information which is, unfortunately, scattered throughout the country. Library resource sharing, frequent meetings of business librarians, fees for service to industry, marketing of business information services, and a national centralized business information center are all cited as necessary improvements.

2.160. ——. "Information Services to Business and Industry." *SLA News* 192 (March/April 1986): 3–6.
Even though no library can collect all the business resources needed by business and industry, every library can direct the businessperson directly to the appropriate information resources. Librarians must be careful, however, not to promote a service to a level beyond their libraries' abilities to provide it.

2.161. de Rivaz, P. et al. "The Use of CAIRS in an Industrial Library and Information Department." *Journal of Information Science* 4 (August 1982): 193-201.
The Computer Assisted Information Retrieval System (CAIRS) was designed to collect, index, retrieve, and disseminate scientific literature, as well as to maintain in-house catalogs. The system's implementation at one industrial library is described, as are its benefits to the library.

2.162. Rohmiller, Thomas D. "Through the Bull to the Bear Facts: A Comparison of the Library Packages of Moody's and Standard and Poor's." *Reference Services Review* 9 (January 1981): 27–32.

The two library packages are compared in terms of patron use, internal arrangement of information, coverage, value to users, statistics, and price. The author does not recommend one over the other.

2.163. Rose, Robert. "Identifying a Core Collection of Business Periodicals for Academic Libraries." *Collection Management* 5 (Spring/Summer 1983): 73–87.

A study which employed the correlation of business indexes and databases as well as citation analysis identifies 244 major business periodicals. A smaller list of 66 titles is recommended for large public libraries.

2.164. Rowley, J. E. "Local Current Awareness Services in Industrial Libraries." *ASLIB Proceedings* 31 (October 1979): 476–84.

A survey of 147 British industrial libraries and information centers indicated that a wide range of current-awareness services are offered, including circulation of bulletins and publications, scanning, and distribution of current contents of appropriate journals. The majority of libraries engage in in-house services rather than those commercially produced. Only 21 percent of the libraries used automation in current-awareness activities.

2.165. Ruokonen, Kyllikki. "Survey of Economic and Business Libraries in Scandinavia." *UNESCO Bulletin for Libraries* 31 (September 1977): 277–85.

Information about economic and business libraries in Finland, Denmark, Norway, and Sweden is presented, including hours, collections, microforms, periodicals, newspapers, special depositories, subject fields, services, publications, automated operations, and personnel. Collectively this information not only provides profiles of individual countries, but also forms a picture of general conditions.

2.166. Russell, Ann N. "Tri-County Regional Library Serves Special Needs of Business Community." *Georgia Librarian* 17 (February 1980): 10.

The business library of the Tri-County Regional Library of Rome, Georgia, helps meet the specific information needs of business and industry in its service area. The library has several promotional programs, including a series of workshops on business topics and a video production entitled "Minding Your Business."

2.167. Russell, J. Thomas, and Martin, Charles H. "Sources of Scholarly Publications in Marketing, Advertising, and Public Relations." *Journal of Advertising* 5 (Summer 1976): 29–34.

Articles published in the fields of advertising and marketing from January 1970 to December 1974 in *Journal of Marketing Research, Journal of Marketing, Journal of Advertising, Journal of Advertising Research, Public Relations Journal,* and *Journalism Quarterly* were examined in terms of vocation of author, specific universities and departments represented, content of articles, and citation sources used by each publication. The majority of authors were from departments of marketing (almost 60 percent were academicians), and seven of the 165 universities represented in the study accounted for 15 percent of the articles.

2.168. Ryans, Cynthia C., and Ryans, John K., Jr. "The Role and Functions of the Company Librarian." *Research Management* 20 (March 1977): 38–40.

As the business library should be a continuation of the company's functioning departments, so there is no one simple pattern for corporate library organization and function. The report of results of a survey of 96 firms listed in *Fortune's* 100 largest companies identifies some of the similarities between corporate libraries.

2.169. Sable, Martin H. "Industrial Espionage/Trade Secrets: Bibliographic Reflections on a Burgeoning Activity." *Behavioral and Social Sciences Librarian* 4 (Fall 1984): 1– 93.

A study of international periodical literature from 1907 to 1984 indicates that industrial espionage to acquire trade secrets is a "rapidly growing characteristic of twentieth-century civilization, whether capitalist or communist." A lengthy bibliography cites relevant articles for the time period surveyed.

2.170. Salter, B. T. "Economics Libraries in the United States." *INSPEL* 12 (1977): 113–24.

Strong economics collections are often held by five types of libraries: company; college and university; public; government agencies; and non-profit organizations, institutions, and associations. Brief background information is given for each group, and some of the stronger collections are discussed. A solid growth in economics libraries has been fostered by a growing economy, and library cooperation has become a highlight of special collections. A lack of development in the area of information retrieval may have to be remedied with international efforts.

2.171. Sardella, Mark. "A Bull Market Library." *Bay State Librarian* 68 (Fall 1979): 7–9.

The special Stock Advisory Information Library, developed by Donald Bye, is geared to the interests of stock investors. Operated on a subscription basis, its patrons share the cost of acquiring very expensive and esoteric investment services publications. The collection, which includes stock advisory aids such as the *Wall Street Transcript* and *Forbes Special Situation Service*, serves as a supplement to public library resources.

2.172. Schlessinger, Bernard S., et. al., "A Core Collection for a Brokerage Firm Library." *Current Studies in Librarianship* 12 (1988): 1–7.

Statistical sources, directories, indexes, handbooks, biographical sources, dictionaries, encyclopedias, bibliographies, and periodicals are included.

2.173. "Scientific, Technical, Medical and Business Books." *Library Journal* [Year].

Each year, *Library Journal* provides a list of forthcoming books in the areas indicated in the article title. Usually, 200-400 business titles are included, in subject areas such as taxes, mathematics, statistics, real estate, marketing, management, law economics, computers, communications, education, banking, finance, investment, advertising, public relations, accounting, reference, and general business topics.

2.174. Seabrooks, N. "Detroit Library Network." *Library Journal* 102 (May 15, 1977): 1123-27.

The dimensions of cooperation in Detroit's library community are reviewed, with business one of the noted participants. Mentioned in this connection are the Detroit Public Library's collections and its information service to business and industry (the library has over 400 "company card" holders), and such participants as the Wayne State University Library, the Campbell-Ewald Reference Center Advertising Agency Library, and the General Motors Public Relations Library.

2.175. Selby, Karen; Lutz, Linda; and Maxwell, Roberta. "IMS and STAIRS: An Answer to a Corporate Library's Online System." In American Society for Information Science. Meeting. (46th: 1983: Washington, DC). *Productivity in the Information Age: Proceedings of the 46th ASIS Annual Meeting, Washington, DC, October 2-6, 1983.* White Plains, NY: Knowledge Industry Publications, 1983, pp. 217-224.

The development and implementation of Texas Instrument's automated library system is described in detail.

2.176. Seng, Mary. "Reference Service Upgraded Using Patrons' Reference Questions." *Special Libraries* 69 (January 1978): 21-28.

Reference questions evaluated over a three-year period by the staff in the Business Administration Economics Library at the University of Texas at Austin fell into three broad categories: directional, information-related, and general reference. Typical questions in each category are described. Analysis of the data identified improvements that could be made in such areas as graphics, publicity, and staff training to reduce the number of directional and information questions and to maximize staff availability for answering reference questions.

2.177. Sharp, Geoffrey. "Online Business Information." *Online* 2 (January 1978): 33-40.

Information is an essential resource to support business decision making, and it can be successfully retrieved through the use of online business databases. The 13 principal online business databases—surveyed for identification of subject coverage, the essential characteristics, time periods available, and vendors—are: ABI/Inform; Management Contents; the Predicasts Terminal System (Market Abstracts, F&S Indexes, U.S. Statistical Abstracts, International Statistical Abstracts, U.S. Time Series, U.S. Regional Series, International Time Series, and EIS Plants); Chemical Industry Notes (CIN); P/E News; and the Pharmaceutical News Index (PNI).

2.178. Shaver, Nancy B. "Suggested Bibliography for Prospective Franchisees—1979." *Unabashed Librarian* 30 (1979): 14.

The following titles on franchising are listed: *International Franchise Association Classified Directory of Members, Investigate Before Investing, Facts on Selecting a Franchise, Federal Trade Commission Consumer Bulletin No. 4—Franchise Business Risks, Franchise/Index Profile, Franchise Opportunities Handbook, Franchised Distribution, Franchising in the Economy* and *Securities and Exchange Commission "10K" Reports.* Information on how to obtain the publications and brief descriptions of their contents are included.

2.179. Sheridan, Jean. "Teaching Tough Stuff: Teaching Part-Time MBAs to Use a Library." *Research Strategies* 3 (Fall 1985): 184–90.

Traditional library bibliographic instruction has been found to be inadequate for business students. Instead, immediate instruction in the use of business reference sources is more appropriate, more useful, and much more heavily attended.

2.180. Shorthill, Rachel R. "Unexpected Online Sources for Business Information." *Online* 9 (January 1985): 68–78.

A study of PsychINFO, ERIC, Health Planning and Administration, and the Public Affairs Information Service databases reveals that all four are good sources for business information. It is concluded that these and other nonbusiness databases should be regarded as valuable supplemental tools for online business searchers. An appendix lists major business journals and identifies nonbusiness databases which index them.

2.181. Shupe, Barbara. "Maps for Business." *Special Libraries* 73 (April 1982): 118–34.

The National Cartographic Information Center is recommended as the first place to consult in obtaining specialized maps. Other agencies which can help are described, and appendixes list maps published by government agencies and addresses and telephone numbers for major map publishers and distributors.

2.182. Sieck, Steven K. "Business Information Systems and Databases." *Annual Review of Information Science and Technology* 19 (1984): 311–27.

This bibliographic essay considers recent literature that focuses on information about business.

2.183. Slater, Margaret. *Non-Use of Library-Information Resources at the Workplace.* London: ASLIB, 1984.

A survey of chemists, engineers, and insurance staff who do not use libraries revealed that underuse of information services is proportional to library/information professionals' enthusiasm for their services.

2.184. Sligo, F. X. "Managing Information for Managers." *Australian Library Journal* 31 (May 1982): 41– 45.

Research shows that managers rely more heavily on oral information than on information received from print sources. This is in contrast to librarians, who depend mostly on print resources. It is suggested that librarians pay more attention to oral communication as a mode of reference service in corporations.

2.185. Smith, Gerry M. "The Demand for Business Information in an Academic Library: An Analysis of the Library Inquiry Service of the City University Business School." *ASLIB Proceedings* 28 (November/ December 1976): 392–99.

The nature of the reference service and the suitability of the collection in the City University Business School Library in London was studied by analyzing reference requests according to subject, originator, source, and frequency of requests. The need for a staff with extensive knowledge of the subject was indicated by the preponderance of requests centered on management and business functions, practices, and techniques. Patrons are equally divided among students, faculty, and alumni, and it was found that outsiders are more likely to ask for information in person than by telephone or mail. Only a small proportion of reference sources, primarily bibliographical tools, is consulted, and a low number of requests are recorded. Results should help in formulation of future collection development policies.

2.186. ———. "Keybooks in Business and Management Studies: A Bibliometric Analysis." *ASLIB Proceedings* 29 (May 1977): 174–87.

Heavily used monographs from British business school libraries were bibliometrically analyzed in terms of authorship, type of book, subject, nationality, publisher, language, and date of publication. Results showed that the books are written primarily by academics, are predominately textbooks and monographs, and cover a wide range of subjects. Approximately 150 publishers are active in this field, although 70 percent of the material is published by only 30 publishers. Use is evenly split between British and American materials, and 90 percent of the material used is 10 years old or less.

2.187. Smith-Burnett, Letitia. "A Public Information Service to the Offshore Service Industry: The Commercial and Technical Department of Aberdeen City Libraries." *SLA News* 192 (March/April 1986): 20–23.

A small core collection of materials on the oil industry for use by public libraries is annotated in this bibliographic essay.

2.188. Spencer, J. *Business Information in London: A Study of the Demand and Supply of Business Information in Thirteen London Business Libraries.* London: ASLIB, 1976.

This three-part study looks at the use of London business libraries, subject coverage at each library, and staff views at two of the libraries. A summary, an attempt to place the conclusions into some type of theoretical structure, is provided.

2.189. Spindler, Donald C. "Management Looks at the Corporate Library." *Special Libraries* 73 (October 1982): 251–53.

Corporate management expects the corporate librarian to be knowledgeable about relevant literature and databases, as well as to develop rapport with employees and make external contacts in the business world. The corporate librarian must also use good judgment, be actively engaged in public relations, and anticipate needs.

2.190. Steininger, Ellen. "An Advertising and Public Relations Agency Library." *Illinois Libraries* 62 (March 1980): 272–74.

The special library of a large advertising and public relations agency maintains subscriptions to 3,000 serials, but keeps each for only six months. The book collection is small, with major emphasis on almanacs, fact books, and directories. Extensive picture files, annual reports from other companies, and internal research reports are important to the collection, as are liberal use of online searching, interlibrary loan, and informal contacts with Special Library Association members. Users expect speed and a high hit rate from the library.

2.191. Sterngold, Arthur. "Marketing for Special Libraries and Information Centers: The Positioning Process." *Special Libraries* 73 (October 1982): 254–59.

In order to acquire adequate financial resources, special librarians must "position" their services so that they are aligned with the parent institution's actual goals and activities as opposed to stated goals and activities. Even though this process ignores some users, it is essential for successful internal marketing of the library.

2.192. Stoakley, Roger J. "Why Should Our Users Pay Twice?" *Library Association Record* 79 (April 1977): 170+.

Continuation of free library service in Great Britain is advocated. The author considers questions such as whether we already pay for library service through taxes; whether fees charged should go into general coffers; for what services the public should be charged; and whether fees might be charged for entertainment or business.

2.193. Strader, Charlotte. "The Big Business of Business Newspapers." *Serials Review* 8 (Summer 1982): 33–35.

Five newspapers that are critical to providing business information are described in detail. Annotations include a short history of each publication, description of format, availability of access, and general content.

2.194. Suydam, Bill. "Tapping Electronic Libraries for Business Data." *Business Computing* 2 (October 1984): 24–32.

In this review of business databases, Dow Jones News/Retrieval Service, Predicast, Nexis, Newsnet, Dialog, The Source, and Compuserve are described. Specific uses for businesses are detailed.

2.195. Ternberg, Milton G. "BI for Accounting Students." *College and Research Library News* 46 (June 1985): 293–94.

One hundred twenty-five accounting undergraduates participated in an instruction module in which they used online searching to complete a class assignment. Although the students reported that they were impressed with the ease of online information retrieval and its usefulness, most indicated that they would not be willing to spend their own money on the service.

2.196. ———. "Business Basics: A Guide to Selection Sources." *Collection Building* 5 (Spring 1983): 22–27.

The annotated listing of selection tools for business collection development includes basic tools, sources for keeping up with new publishing developments, sources for specialized or esoteric materials, business journals, and important publishers' catalogs.

2.197. ———. "Library Orientation for Business Students: A Case Study." *College and Research Library News* 44 (April 1983): 14–15.

The Louisiana State University Library has developed special bibliographic instruction for undergraduate and graduate business students. Instruction includes a specially produced videotape which introduces business sources; it is supplemented with a series of printed guides to the library's business resources. Additionally, special two-hour library orientations are provided on demand to graduate students in the business school.

2.198. Trott, Fiona. "Information for Small Firms—The Relevance of Public Information Services." *Library Association Record* 87 (July 1985): 259.

A two-year study of the information needs of small businesses in Britain revealed that businesspeople do not consider the public library as a source of technical information, but that once they realize the benefits of using the public library, they are willing to pay for services. The importance of publicizing the public library as a business information source and the library's telephone reference services are highlighted.

2.199. Trott, Fiona, and Martyn, John. "An Information Service for Small Firms from a Public Library Base." *ASLIB Proceedings.* 38 (February 1986): 43–50.

A survey of manufacturing and service industries in Suffolk County, England, concluded that 1) most requested information from industry is technical; 2) local information resources must be backed up by the resources of the British Library; and 3) marketing the library increases its use by industry and business.

2.200. Trubkin, Loene. "Building a Core of Business Management Periodicals: How Databases Can Help." *Online* 6 (July 1982): 43–49.

A study of business database coverage indicates that not only do databases provide specific information on business topics, but they can also be used to develop an overall picture of what a particular journal contains. Additionally, database producers often offer translation services and full-text retrievals, as well as evaluations of the business and management literature when they decide what to include in the database. The author cites these attributes as very helpful in collection-building decisions.

2.201. Tufts, Aileen. "Vancouver Public Library's Business and Economic Division." *Canadian Library Journal* 34 (April 1977): 87–89.

Important considerations of policies and practices employed by the Business Information Service at the Vancouver Public Library are presented to provide information on a successful special library service in a public library setting.

2.202. Varma, D. K. "Increasing Subscription Costs and Problems of Resource Allocation." *Special Libraries* 74 (January 1983): 61–66.

A study of 100 major business periodicals to which most academic libraries subscribe found that subscription prices for U.S. periodicals went up 76.2 percent over a seven-year period while the price of Canadian journal subscriptions increased 86.4 percent. These figures must be taken into account when librarians allocate monies for resources.

2.203. Venett, Anthony J. "Technology Transfer for Industry and Business through the University Library." *Special Libraries* 72 (January 1981): 44–50.

PENNTAP, the Pennsylvania Technical Assistance Program, provides free information assistance to business, industry, and local governments. Originally funded by the State Technical Service Act (PA 89–192), it is now supported by the state department of commerce and Pennsylvania State University. The center answers a wide variety of technical questions from clients. Access to the comprehensive library collection of the Pennsylvania State Libraries and the corporation of the university, faculty, library staff, and federal private sources have been instrumental in the center's success.

2.204. Vernon, K. D. C. "Classification of Business and the Business of Classification." *Catalog and Index* 57 (Summer 1980): 8–12.

The beginnings, use, and revision of the *London Classification of Business Studies* are discussed. The classification's continuing popularity is demonstrated by sales of 300 copies of the second edition and its use by 50 libraries in the United Kingdom and 30 libraries elsewhere. The author notes reclassification, the future of the system, and the major changes in the second edition. These include abandonment of a completely hierarchical notation, provision of some alternate locations, incorporation of a thesaurus in the schedules, introduction of five classes, restructuring of four classes, and the addition of 500 terms.

2.205. ———. *Information Sources in Management and Business.* Boston: Butterworths, 1984.

The literature of business is described in a discussion that includes accounting, corporate finance, organization studies, marketing, strategic management and planning, operations management, quantitative business analysis, and business law. Materials described cover management, the library as an information source, abstracts, indexes, current-awareness sources, periodicals, newspapers, reference works, bibliographies, company information, online services, and unpublished materials.

2.206. Walker, Clare M. "Making Information Services Pay." *South African Journal of Information Sciences* 53 (June 1985): 55–58.

Bell's cutback management techniques and Gulick's POSDCORB management principles are reviewed in terms of their relevance to special libraries.

2.207. Walker, Mary Ann. "Business Directory Databases." *Reference Services Review* 11 (Fall 1983): 43–45.

The annotated listing of six business databases describes and compares each database in relation to its competitors.

2.208. Warden, Carolyn L. "Use or Evaluation of a Corporate Library Online Search Service." *Special Libraries* 72 (April 1981): 113–17.

An evaluative questionnaire, given to 233 first-time users of the online search service available at General Electric Corporation's Research and Development Library, requested information on the relevancy and benefits of the service. It was found that, overall, a high percentage of useful citations are retrieved. Interactions between the searcher and the patron yield a greater number of relevant titles than does a search done solely by the librarian. Significant benefits in time savings and cost-effectiveness were identified.

2.209. Webb, Sylvia P. *Creating an Information Service.* Dorchester, England: ASLIB, 1985.

A core reference collection for a British business library is presented, as well as materials on the internal structure and external environment of corporate libraries. The author includes valuable information about researching British business.

2.210. ———. "What's So Special About the Special Librarian?" *ASLIB Proceedings* 37 (September 1985): 341–44.

Corporate librarians cannot fit the stereotype of the remote, passive librarian because they must constantly justify their existence within the corporation. Communication skills are critical in order to adequately represent the library and the corporation. Thorough knowledge of the business, as well as the ability to make external contacts for the business, is also critical. It is further suggested that simplicity, efficiency, and the ability to meet deadlines are keys to successful corporate librarianship.

2.211. "Weeding and Replacement Ordering Guidelines—Real Estate." *Unabashed Librarian* 57 (1984): 3–4.

A brief list of criteria for weeding in the subject area of real estate is presented.

2.212. White, Herbert S. "Special Libraries and the Corporate Political Process." *Special Libraries* 75 (April 1984): 81–86.

Special libraries are often overlooked in budget increases but are just as often the first for budget cuts. Users who do not know what good library service is accept poor service from the library, preferring to use alternative information sources. The library budget, part of the corporation's overhead, is accordingly expected to be low, and the image of the librarian is one of passivity rather than of innovation or competence. Specific solutions to these problems and the budget problems to which they contribute are suggested.

2.213. Wilkinson, W. A. "Monsanto Company Information Center: Twenty-Five Years of Accelerating Change." *Show-Me Libraries* 37 (January 1986): 5-10.

After 25 years of operation, Monsanto's Information Center is successfully providing business and technical information, 24–hour access, online searching, an automated catalog, and a variety of interlibrary loan services. These types of services are identified as constituting the future of business librarianship.

2.214. Wood, Elizabeth J. "How the International Business Directories Compete: A Comparative Review." *Reference Services Review* 8 (July/September 1980): 54–58.

Four reference sources on international or multinational businesses are compared: *Kelly's Manufacturers and Merchants Directory, The Who Owns Whom (WOW) Directory, Bottin International: International Business Register,* and *Principal International Businesses.* While the purpose and content of each are similar, scope and ease of use differ. Prices and suggested audiences are also discussed.

2.215. ———. "Stalking the Private Company: How Good is Dun & Bradstreet's Third Volume?" *Reference Services Review* 10 (Spring 1982): 35–42.

In a comparison of the *Million Dollar Directory, Standard and Poor's Register of Corporations, The Top 1500 Private Companies, EIS Industrial Plants, EIS Non-Manufacturing Establishments,* the *Colt Microfiche Library,* and *50,000 Leading US Corporations,* the *Million Dollar Directory* is rated the highest.

2.216. Wood, Frances K. "Business and Industrial Needs: Special Libraries Are Willing to Share Resources." *Wisconsin Library Bulletin* 76 (May/June 1980): 109–10.

The state of Wisconsin has from 50 to 60 business and industrial libraries, located throughout the state, most in the Milwaukee area. The major subject areas covered by these libraries are: banking, paper making, packaging, plastics technology, motor machinery of all types, insurance, pension planning, pollution control, electric-power generation, food technology, household products, batteries, and law. The staff members in these libraries are receptive to public requests for information and welcome library tours.

2.217. Wooding, Geoffrey. "Corporate Intelligence Networks." *ASLIB Proceedings* 38 (September 1986): 285–95.

Management Information Systems are merely (according to the author) transaction records which provide information for use in established decision models. Essential to business management is a corporate intelligence network which utilizes decision support systems to provide early warnings of changes in the business environment.

2.218. Yates, Joanne. "Internal Communication Systems in American Business Structures: A Framework to Aid Appraisal." *American Archivist* 48 (Spring 1985): 141–58.

Different methods of appraising business records for archival purposes must be utilized since corporate organizational structures differ. Suggestions are made for adequate appraisal of traditional, functionally departmentalized, and multidivisional companies.

2.219. Zimmerman, Anne R. "Library Services for Members: How the FHL Banks Can Help." *Federal Home Loan Bank Board Journal* 11 (September 1978): 13–16.

The Federal Home Loan Bank System Library of Seattle was initiated by management to provide efficient access to research and reference materials. The collection consists of a wide range of information on financial institutions and the savings and loan industry. Staffed by a professional librarian and a clerical assistant, the library provides patrons with an appraisal of current activities in the field, assists in research and planning projects, and provides access to information otherwise unavailable. The Seattle library is also open to the public by appointment.

PART III

Business Reference
Sources and Services:
Essays

Databases for Online Access to Business Information

by Janice F. Sieburth

Databases are sources of vast amounts of information on current business events, companies, industries, the labor force, economic predictions, and other important subjects of interest to the business community. A request for the latest financial report on a company, a list of articles on foreign investment in the United States, or a survey of the competition providing a particular type of product can be quickly satisfied by going "online." The capability to access remote databases of business information provides the smallest information center with the same resources as a very large library. All that is needed for this electronic connection is a terminal or computer, modem, telephone, and the passwords for a variety of databases. The optimal utilization of these electronic files as a part of business information services, however, requires training and experience. Librarians must know what resources are available, when an online database is an appropriate source, and how to retrieve needed information.

ADVANTAGES OF SEARCHING ONLINE DATABASES

A quick search of the Moody's Corporate Profiles database can provide a description of a public company and financial information that includes data on earnings, dividends, sales, and last week's news release about the expansion of a specific product line. This file is updated every week. Other databases of interest may include yesterday's news or a list of companies that is revised yearly. An online database is much easier to keep up-to-date than a book and can be searched in many different ways. The number of employees, zip code, primary and secondary SIC codes, year of incorporation, gross sales,

Janice F. Sieburth heads the Pell Marine Science Library, University of Rhode Island, Narragansett, RI. All data in this essay were updated as of August 1988 by Alice Johnson, Texas Woman's University Library, Denton, TX.

product or trade name, ticker symbol or D-U-N-S number can all be used to retrieve names of companies, which can then be sorted into various lists. The financial status of a company, its major stockholders and competitors, and its recent business successes can be determined in a single online search, along with the latest news on mergers and acquisitions; or a bibliography of recent articles on international trade restrictions can be limited to countries of interest, specific products, or the economic implications of tariffs.

The computer provides powerful flexibility and control for the searcher. A quick search can retrieve a specific bit of data, or a carefully composed strategy can be used to probe a complex problem or to assemble more comprehensive information. The advantages of searching online for information include:

- Faster and more efficient information retrieval than is usually possible in printed sources.
- The currentness of business news.
- The ability to combine different facets of a subject in a single search statement.
- The interactive search process that provides a means of adjusting search strategy until the desired information is found.
- The ease of searching several databases in sequence to produce a comprehensive survey of the available literature.
- The increased number of access points for standard reference sources.
- The growing amount of information accumulating in databases (which can be quickly scanned by the computer).
- The ability to retrieve data and store them on a disk for later editing and manipulation of figures.

The versatility and speed of computerized access to a broad scope of information resources are essential factors for meeting today's needs of the business community.

Online Resources

Databases cover a wide variety of business subjects, from management and personnel relations to marketing research and advertising. Publishers of major printed information sources such as Dun & Bradstreet, Moody's, Predicasts, and Standard & Poor's have also produced databases that are the electronic equivalent of their printed directories or indexes. Other databases contain information that is only available online. The Thomas Register Online corresponds to the *Thomas Register of American Manufacturers* and is supplemented by two other online files—the Thomas Regional Industrial Suppliers and the Thomas New Industrial Products—to cover local suppliers of products and services and to provide information on new products, respectively. Other databases include information on British, German, or Canadian companies; over 600,000 trademarks registered in the United States; potential government contracts and contract awards; foreign trade opportunities; and high and low stock prices for public companies. It is possible to search a database and to print out:

- Citations and abstracts of articles on a specific subject.
- A listing of companies in a particular industry and location.
- The full text of a recent news article.
- A time series of price indexes on a specific commodity.
- A forecast of sales for an industry or product.
- Current information on market trends.
- Comprehensive financial data on a company.

Each entry in a database or file is a single record, and there may be more than a million records contained in a database. The contents of a record will depend on the type of database, but may include a company's financial statement; a citation, abstract, and indexing for a magazine article; a directory listing or the complete text of a press release or newspaper article. New records are added to the database monthly, weekly, daily, or at some other interval. The different types of databases are:

Bibliographic. Databases such as Business Periodicals Index provide references to articles in periodicals, and others such as PTS Promt also contain abstracts of other types of material—investment reports, newspaper articles, local business publications, newsletters, and government publications.

Directory. Listings of companies include databases such as Standard & Poor's Corporate Descriptions (11,000 public U.S. companies), ICC British Company Directory (1.9 million British companies) and the Hoppenstedt Directory of German Companies (36,000). Other directory databases may list trademarks, products in catalogs, government contracts, company executives, or export opportunities.

Company Financial. Data on companies may come from reports filed with government agencies or from annual reports to stockholders. Disclosure, for example, provides information on 10,000 U.S. companies and D&B—Dun's Financial Records contains 700,000 U.S. companies.

Numerical. Figures available from numerical databases include price indexes on specific commodities, such as those from the BLS (Bureau of Labor Statistics) Producer Price Index, demographic data for consumer marketing research in D&B—Donnelly Demographics, and economic forecasts of production or sales from PTS U.S. Forecasts.

News. Databases including the latest developments may cover opportunities for government contracts, updated daily in the Commerce Business Daily; business news from press releases, updated every 15 minutes in Businesswire; or banking news, added daily to the American Banker News.

Full-Text. Complete articles are searchable and can be printed out from the Bond Buyer or Financial Times Fulltext databases, which correspond to those newspapers, or from the McGraw-Hill Business Backgrounder, which contains complete articles from business magazines.

Other databases of interest that are not included in this discussion of business sources are those listing patents, technical developments, government statistics, and regulations; those covering subjects such as energy, the environment, and occupational safety; and indexes to general newspapers, news services, and magazines.

SOURCES OF DATABASES

While some databases are marketed by the producer, most are made available by online database vendors who offer a selection of both common and unique files. Securing a contract with a vendor allows access to a group of databases with one password, one command language, and one monthly bill. Nearly 300 different databases on a variety of subjects are available from DIALOG Information Services. DIALOG is the leading vendor of business databases, which include information collections, such as directories of company information in D&B—Dun's Electronic Yellow Pages, literature abstracts in Biobusiness, financial and stock information in the Media General Databank, or full-text newspaper and magazine articles in Business Dateline.

Other major vendors of business databases are BRS and Pergamon, which recently purchased the ORBIT system. BRS's holdings include the Investors Rateline for daily news of jumbo CD rates, and Fairbase, a directory of trade fairs and exhibitions to the year 2010. The Pergamon InfoLine has a number of different databases with emphasis on the United Kingdom. Infocheck, for example, concentrates on financial ratings of U.K. companies, while the U.K. Standard Industrial Classification and British Trademarks are additional resources.

The databases which are covered in detail in this chapter include 91 DIALOG databases, 28 on BRS, 14 from Pergamon InfoLine, seven from the ORBIT system, and the Business Periodicals Index from H. W. Wilson. Two databases are available through three of the systems, and 20 can be obtained from two separate vendors, while the other 94 are unique files available from a single vendor. Sixty-nine of these unique files come from Dialog, 13 from Pergamon, 10 from BRS, two from ORBIT, and one from Wilsonline.

Additional online database vendors which make significant business information available include Dow Jones News/Retrieval, with business and investor services, Mead Data Central's NEXIS, for full-text sources, NewsNet with over 300 online newsletters, and VU/TEXT for full-text newspaper databases.

THE SEARCH PROCESS

Searching an online database can be a relatively simple procedure of typing a word, pushing a "send" button to communicate with the distant computer, and then reading the response, which is usually the number of records where this subject term can be found. This technique can be used to secure groups of records on different aspects of a topic. The groups are then combined by the searcher to provide a final set of records that contain all the subject elements needed. For instance, the SIC industry code can be used to restrict a study of employment patterns of minorities to a particular industry.

Terminology is an important aspect of online searching. Words in the database may come from a structured thesaurus, an abstract in a publication, the jargon of the business world, company or personal names, or geographic locations. Each database can have different components and vocabulary, so it is important to know the contents and source, and to understand the language of the database environment. A successful searcher must also recognize variant spellings or the differing use of words in international databases. Numeric codes may be used in some files for more general access to industry, product, or location. For example, Predicasts has developed uniform codes for its various databases, with numbers (or numbers and letters) for products, events, and countries or geographic areas. In the Predicasts databases, a product code of 1082000 is used for beer and other malt beverages; a geographic code of 1906, for California; and an event code of 44, for facilities and equipment. A search with a combination of these three codes could result in a list of articles on the facilities and equipment used by California beer companies, or data and forecasts for this segment of the beverage industry.

Careful planning of a search strategy will provide information that is both comprehensive and precise, and several databases can be searched in sequence to increase the scope of information recovery. The records identified in a search can be ordered for offline printing and mailing, can be typed immediately, or transferred to a disk (downloaded). Arrangements can be made for SDI (Selective Dissemination of Information), in which the search strategy is stored and run automatically against each new update to a database.

Search results can be printed with the most recent information first, sorted for an alphabetical listing by author, or used to print names and addresses from a directory database on mailing labels. DIALOG has developed a report feature, principally utilized with business databases, to facilitate the transfer of database information to most personal computer spread-sheet analysis programs. The procedure for formating search results from selected databases can also be used to prepare tables of data; lists of companies with addresses and telephone numbers; or arrangements of company information by sales, location, number of employees, stock exchange, and other elements of the records.

REQUIREMENTS FOR EFFECTIVE ONLINE SEARCHING

While basic search techniques are easy to learn, effective searching to find specific bits of data or comprehensive coverage of information on a subject requires a mastery of the search process; a knowledge of available databases, their coverage, and organization; consideration of the terminology of the field; an understanding of the needs of the individual seeking information; and enough mechanical skill to type on a keyboard and fix paper jams in a printer.

Each of the database vendors provides a manual for search language and procedures. Usually chapters of these manuals contain additional information about each database, the content, characteristics, and access points. In addition, each vendor offers training for new searchers and advanced sessions on business topics. Other supporting materials, such as thesauri, journal lists, and manuals from the producers of the databases, may be important for effective searching of complex databases. A competent searcher must have good training, adequate support material, enough practice, and experience in working with individuals who are seeking information.

While librarians are usually trained to search databases for their patrons, increasingly they are called on to advise individuals who wish to do their own searching. There are a number of simplified systems for easy access by a novice searcher. Systems such as CompuServe, InfoMaster, Knowledge Index (DIALOG), and BRS AfterDark have been designed for the businessperson, the executive, or the personal-computer owner at home. In addition, software is available for microcomputers which will guide an untrained searcher using the major vendor systems. These packages serve as an effective intermediary assisting in the selection of databases and providing a menu of choices for carrying out the search. They are excellent systems for simple questions and strategies.

DIALOG has recently introduced the "Business Connection," designed specifically to help business professionals find information. The menu-based system is divided into five sections, which can be scanned for corporate intelligence, financial screening, products and markets, sales prospectuses, and travel planning. The sign-up fee of $145 allows access to the information from a selected group of databases at a special rate of $84/connect hour plus telecommunications and some data charges.

COSTS OF ONLINE ACCESS

While there may be some password or sign-up fees, charges for online searching are generally based on connect time with the host computer, which varies with the database being used, combined with a charge for the citations or records which represent the information received. These connect-time and citation charges are the database vendor fees and the royalty charges of the database producer. Connect time usually costs between $45 and $120 per hour, and full record charges generally range between $0.25 and $2. Company financial statements can also be obtained, with costs varying from $13 for lengthy records from Disclosure on BRS, to $85 for up to three years of a company's financial statements from D&B Dun's Financial Records on Dialog. Charges change frequently, may vary between vendors, and may be reduced by various contract arrangements, prepaying the online vendor for access, or subscribing to the corresponding print source.

These direct search costs are highly variable and mainly depend on:

- The amount of time spent online.
- The speed of the search equipment.
- The skill of the searcher.
- The complexity of the topics searched.
- The specific databases utilized.
- The amount of information retrieved.
- Any additional charges for mailing printouts, formating reports or producing mailing labels.

Budgeting and projecting costs are very difficult since the total charges depend on so many factors. Other cost elements that must be considered when composing a budget or financial report include those for equipment, telephone charges, telecommunications, personnel time and training, manuals and support material, plus the indirect costs of space, furniture, and overhead.

NEW TECHNOLOGIES

The use of microcomputers instead of computer terminals for searching has increased the speed and efficiency of accessing databases. A microcomputer with software such as Pro-Search offers the searcher a choice of direct command searching for top efficiency and precision, or a menu-driven, assisted procedure for novice searchers. With this software the online connect time can be reduced by preparing the search strategy offline and then uploading (sending to the host computer in one step), and the results can be typed immediately or downloaded (transferred to a disk). Downloading, which must follow copyright regulations, allows the results to be edited, transferred to a different electronic file, or sent to another location by electronic mail.

CD-ROM (Compact Disk-Read Only Memory) has begun to make an impact on the variety of online resources that are available. By attaching a CD-ROM player to a microcomputer, one can search databases that have been purchased on compact disks. While the initial costs are high, the disk can be searched repeatedly and the results printed out or transferred to another disk without incurring connect-time fees. This type of access is especially appropriate when the database usage is very high. Software accompanying CD-ROMs usually provides access to the information via menus, for simplified searching. This makes them ideal for students, businesspeople, or library patrons who wish to do their own searching. A subscription is necessary in order to receive updated disks at regular intervals. A major advantage of providing information by CD-ROM is the ability to budget for the subscription cost. A disadvantage is the need to supplement the information with online access to the equivalent database to retrieve the most up-to-date information.

CD-ROM has generated new products, such as CD/Corp Tech by Datext, Inc., which has combined information from seven different databases to provide up to seven years of extensive data on 12,000 private and public domestic companies. The disks, which are updated quarterly, have an annual subscription fee of $7500. Compact Disclosure is a CD-ROM product derived from the Disclosure databases which contains complete profiles on 10,000 public companies. The disks are updated quarterly for a nonprofit-organization fee of $3,200.

Improving technology and increased competition will cause many changes in the field of online information, but should result in the availability of more databases which contain greater amounts of data. The large number of combinations of microcomputers, CD-ROM, and software that can assist searchers without training has made these resources readily available to the "end user," the information consumer. The information specialist who only searches occasionally can also benefit from these simplified systems. However, for comprehensive, precise, and efficient searching, an expert, well-trained and experienced searcher is needed. The primary challenges for the future will continue to be (1) keeping up with new developments, (2) maintaining an awareness of the range and depth of information that is available online, and (3) developing effective and efficient procedures for retrieving information.

THE DATABASES

The following list of 120 databases of business information is available from BRS, DIALOG, ORBIT, Pergamon, and Wilsonline. Information includes the number of records in the database, dates of coverage, the maximum access rates, and the availability of SDI. The database description gives any corresponding print publication, the scope of the subjects covered, sources of information, and significant contents of the records.

The appendix provides eight tables of databases, which have been compiled according to the type of database or the information included. Table 1 lists business news sources, primarily those updated daily and weekly. The company directories listed in Table 2 each include between 11,000 and 8 million public and private companies, divisions, and subsidiaries. Thirteen databases in Table 3 provide company financial information. Table 4 lists business information directories which include computer software, products in catalogs, trademarks, and business contacts outside the United States. The numerical databases in Table 5 cover time series, demographic data, economic figures, and price indexes. Full-text databases are listed in Table 6, and the information on bibliographic databases in Table 7 includes the number of records in each database and the years of coverage. The databases in Table 8 concentrate on specific industries, such as agriculture, biotechnology, chemicals, computers, food, health, pharmaceuticals, defense, and textiles.

Database Information

ABI/INFORM. Data Courier, Louisville, KY. 1971 to present. 337,000 records. Weekly updates, Dialog; monthly updates, BRS.

Bibliographic databases of journal literature on business administration and management. Subject areas include accounting, advertising, financial management, data processing, marketing, personnel, and international trade. Approximately 580 journals are represented, mostly English-language.

Availability:

Dialog: $105/connect hour, $1.30/full record printed offline, $0.80/full record typed or displayed. SDI available for $9.95/update.

BRS: $62/connect hour, $0.77/full records printed offline, $0.57/full record typed or displayed. SDI available for $4/update plus print charges.

ORBIT: $81/connect hour, $0.60/full record printed offline, $0.50/full record typed or displayed. SDI available for $5.45/update.

Abstracts of Working Papers in Economics. Cambridge University Press, New York, NY. 1982 to present. 3,000 records. Monthly updates.

Provides bibliographic information with lengthy abstracts of working papers produced by over 50 prominent research and academic organizations. Important for following trends in finance, investments, economic theory, and government policy. Expected to expand to 5,000 records and will be limited to papers not more than three years old.

Availability:

BRS: $42/connect hour, $0.25/full record printed offline, $0.35/full record typed or displayed.

Accountants. American Institute of Certified Public Accountants. 1974 to present. 150,000 records. Quarterly updates.

Corresponds to the *Accountants Index.* Covers international literature from English-language books, pamphlets, government documents, and journals. Accounting subjects include auditing, data processing, investments, financial management, and taxation.

Availability:

ORBIT: $85/connect hour, $0.30/full record printed offline, $0.25/full record typed or displayed online.

Agribusiness U.S.A. Pioneer Hi-Bred International, Inc. Johnston, IA. 1985 to present. 40,000 records. Biweekly updates.

Broad perspective on agricultural business and the industries that carry products to the consumers. Subjects include crops and livestock, agricultural chemicals, biotechnology, farm equipment manufacturing, and agricultural statistics. Coverage of more than 300 agricultural business journals and government

documents. Includes full-text narratives of government reports since January 1986 and abstracts of the other articles. Complete tables of statistical data can be printed.
Availability:
    Dialog: $96/connect hour, $0.60/full record printed offline, $0.50/full record typed or displayed online. SDI available for $6.95/update.

American Banker Full Text. American Banker-Bond Buyer, New York, NY. 1981 to present. 66,000 records. Daily updates.
    Provides the complete text of articles appearing in *American Banker*. Covers all phases of domestic banking and financial services, including articles about federal and state legislation. Articles may be textual or tabular. Also includes the full text of regulations affecting the industry as well as articles and speeches by industry leaders. Additional articles and regulations selected by the *American Banker* staff are included. Does not include stories and commentaries from other news services that have appeared in the newspaper. Features Key Word in Context and Highlite display features.
Availability:
    Dialog: $120/connect hour.
    BRS: $45/connect hour.

American Banker News. American Banker, New York, NY. Current day plus last five days. Daily updates.
    Menu-driven database providing full text of the most important stories in the *American Banker*. Headlines can be scanned and then complete article read. Current day online (by 6:00 A.M.) before newspaper delivery to subscribers. Menu provides choice of daily news, previous day's news, events and major developments in Washington affecting finance, executive job changes, major speeches, opinions, and analysis.
Availability:
    Dialog: $120/connect hour.
    BRS: $45/connect hour.

Arthur D. Little/Online. Arthur D. Little Decision Resources, Cambridge, MA. 1977 to present. 1,101 records. Monthly updates.
    Index to consulting firm's reports and newsletters, industry forecasts, planning documents, and development reports on new technologies. Broad range of subjects, from chemical products to health care.
Availability:
    Dialog: $114/connect hour, $0.50/full record printed offline, $100/full record plus complete text of executive summary.

Biobusiness. BioSciences Information Service, Philadelphia, PA. 1985 to present. 64,966 records. Monthly updates.
    References from two databases: BIOSIS and Management Contents, with additional subject indexing to provide current information on the business aspects of biological and biomedical research. Subject areas include agriculture, biotechnology, food and beverages, and pharmaceuticals. Coverage includes journal articles, research communications, review articles, and conferences. Abstracts are included for about three-fourths of the records.
Availability:
    Dialog: $129/connect hour, $0.43/full record printed offline, $0.40/full record typed or displayed online. SDI available for $9.95/update.

BioCommerce Abstracts. BioCommerce Data Ltd., Slough, UK. 1981 to present. 18,000 abstracts representing 70,000 articles. Semi-monthly updates.

Corresponds to printed *Abstracts in BioCommerce*, with some material added. Covers the business aspects of biotechnology and the biological sciences, including biological control, fermentation, genetic engineering, industrial enzymes, monoclonal antibodies, and recombinant DNA. Brief abstracts of articles from over 100 English-language publications, including newsletters, newspapers, trade periodicals, and scientific journals.
Availability:
Dialog: $90/connect hour, $0.50/full record printed offline or typed or displayed online. SDI available for $9.95/update.

BIS Infomat. Business Intelligence Services, Wallingford, UK. 1983 to present. 400,000 records. Updated daily.

Provides summaries of business news, along with figures on market opportunities, activities of competitors, trends in consumption, political and economic activity, and international trade. Sources are newspapers, journals, newsletters, conferences, wire services, and corporate reports.
Availability:
InfoLine: $100/connect hour, $0.60/full record printed offline or typed or displayed online.

Bond Buyer. The Bond Buyer, Inc., New York, NY. 1982 to present. 61,000 records. Daily updates.

Full-text file of the daily newspaper, covering the bond and credit markets. Some statistical tables are included, as well as information on bond offerings, municipal bonds, interest rates, federal regulations, credit, and debt.
Availability:
Dialog: $120/connect hour, $0.25/full record printed offline. SDI available for $5.95/update.
BRS: available soon.

British Trademarks. U.K. Patent Office. Current. 450,000 records.

Provides details of all trademarks in the United Kingdom which are active, pending, or lapsed since January 1976. Record includes name and address of owner, class of the item, and the specifications.
Availability:
InfoLine: $125/connect hour, $0.50/full record printed offline, or $0.45/full record typed or displayed online.

Business Dateline. Data Courier, Louisville, KY. 1985 to present. 20,000 records. Weekly updates.

Full text of articles on regional activities of local companies, their products, and executives. Source publications are 110 regional business magazines and newspapers in the U.S. and Canada. Topics include mergers, acquisitions, expansions, and business failures; competitive strategies; and economic conditions in selected cities, states, or regions.
Availability:
Dialog: $114/connect hour, $4.50/full record printed offline, $4/full record typed or displayed online.

Business Periodicals Index. H. W. Wilson Co., New York, NY. 290,000 records. 1982 to present. Semi-weekly updates.

Corresponds to *Business Periodicals Index.* Indexes 300 English-language business periodicals. Subjects include accounting, advertising, banking, economics, finance, industrial relations, international business, business regulation, real estate, marketing, and personnel.
Availability:
   Wilsonline: $65/connect hour, $0.20/full record printed offline (reduced rate for subscribers).

Business Software Database. Information Sources, Inc., Berkeley, CA. Current. 8,231 records. Quarterly reloads.
   Index to available software packages for mini- and microcomputers. Business applications covered include accounting, inventory control, database management, word processing, graphics, marketing, and economic analysis. Records contain description of software, manufacturer, price and number of packages sold, availability, and information on machine compatibility, program language, associated documentation, and customer services from manufacturer.
Availability:
   Dialog: $90/connect hour, $0.90/full record printed offline or typed, or displayed online.
   BRS: $57/connect hour, $0.55/full record printed offline or typed, or $0.60/displayed online.

BusinessWire. BusinessWire, San Francisco, CA. 1986 to present. 29,400 records. Updated every 15 minutes as received.
   Full text of business news items, with about 500 press releases added per day. Broad coverage of American industries. Sources are 5,000 corporations, universities, research institutes, government agencies, trade associations, hospitals, and other noncorporate organizations. Recap records are produced at intervals to summarize stories.
Availability:
   Dialog: $96/connect hour, $0.60/full record printed offline. SDI available weekly for $3.95/update.

Canadian Business and Current Affairs. Micromedia Ltd. 1980 to present. 656,000 records. Monthly updates.
   Corresponds to *Canadian Business Index* and *Canadian News Index* and covers more than 170 Canadian business periodicals and 10 newspapers, including the *Financial Post, Financial Times,* and *Globe and Mail.* Provides information on Canadian companies, products, industries, and business leaders. Includes national, provincial and local news, government activities, labor, mergers, acquisitions, and other aspects of current business news.
Availability:
   Dialog: $72/connect hour, $0.20/full record printed offline. SDI available for $6.95/update.

Catalyst Resource on the Work Force and Women Database. Catalyst Information Center, New York, NY. 1963 to date. 8,400 records. Quarterly updates.
   Index, with abstracts, of materials in the Catalyst Information Center, a major national clearinghouse for information on career and family issues, and working women. Subjects include child care, maternity and parental leave, employee benefits, affirmative action, corporate women, women in manage-

ment, pay equity, working mothers, and other aspects of women in business. Materials covered include books, journal and newspaper articles, pamphlets, papers, government reports.
Availability:
BRS: $42/connect hour, $0.35/full record printed offline or typed, or $.40/ displayed online.

CENDATA. U.S. Bureau of the Census, Washington, DC. Current. 1,497 records. Daily updates.
Statistical data, press releases, and product information from the Bureau of the Census covering current economic and demographic news. Data include surveys of retail trade, manufacturing, shipments, inventories, orders of manufactured products, international and foreign trade. Limited data on more than 200 countries. CENDATA can be accessed by command searching or by a menu option.
Availability:
Dialog: $36/connect hour, $0.20/full record printed offline.

Chemical Business Newsbase. Royal Society of Chemistry, Nottingham, England. 1984 to present. 55,750 records. Weekly updates.
Abstracts of business news of the worldwide chemical industry, with emphasis on Europe. Indexing terms are in English, French, and German. Sources (70 percent European, the rest from the U.S. and Japan) include journals, press releases, company reports, newsletters, and books. Some statistical data included.
Availability:
Dialog: $155/connect hour, $0.80/full record printed offline, $1.05/full record typed or displayed online. SDI available for $12.50/update.
InfoLine: $110/connect hour, $1/full record printed offline or typed or displayed online.

Chemical Industry Notes. Chemical Abstracts Service, Columbus, OH. 1974 to present. 630,700 records. Biweekly updates.
Corresponds to *Chemical Industry Notes*, with emphasis on the business literature of the chemical processing industry, including pharmaceutical products, petroleum, paper and pulp, agriculture, and food. Abstracts over 80 international journals and newspapers.
Availability:
Dialog: $115/connect hour, $0.50/full record printed offline, $0.33/full record typed or displayed online. SDI available for $11.95/update.
ORBIT: $120/connect hour, $0.45/full record printed offline, $0.33/full record typed or displayed online. SDI available for $4.95/update.

Coffeeline. International Coffee Organization, London. 1973 to present. 16,500 records. Bimonthly updates.
Corresponds to *International Coffee Organization Library Monthly Entries* and covers all aspects of coffee farming, processing, production, and marketing. Sources include more than 5,000 journals, books, patents, reports, and theses. Records after 1980 include abstracts.
Availability:
Dialog: $65/connect hour, $0.20/full record printed offline or typed or displayed online.

Commerce Business Daily. U.S. Department of Commerce, Chicago, IL. 1982 to present. 1,480,000 records. Daily and monthly updates.

Full text of *Commerce Business Daily*, announcing products and services wanted or offered by the U.S. government. Includes procurements by civilian and military agencies, federal contract awards (including those for the Department of Defense), surplus government property sales, and notification of the government's interest in particular research and development programs. One file contains most recent 60 to 90 days and is updated weekly. Older material is transferred to the other file monthly.

Availability:

Dialog: $54/connect hour, $0.25/full record printed offline. SDI available at $5.95/update.

Computer Database. Information Access Company, Belmont, CA. 1983 to present. 192,000 records. Biweekly updates.

Provides information on products, companies, and people in computers, related electronics, and telecommunications. Abstracts over 530 journals, newsletters, books, and conference proceedings. Includes industry information, business applications, product evaluations, and new products.

Availability:

Dialog: $108/connect hour, $0.95/full record printed offline. $0.90/full record typed or displayed online. SDI available for $11.95/update.

Corporate Affiliations. National Register Publishing Company, Wilmette, IL. Current. 42,500 records. Quarterly reloads.

Corresponds to *Directory of Corporate Affiliations*, covering about 3,100 public and 800 private U.S. parent companies and their 38,000 divisions, subsidiaries, branch offices, sales offices, and other associated units. Includes corporate structure, address and telephone number, ticker symbol, stock exchange, key personnel, up to 20 SIC codes, number of employees, total assets, sales, and net worth. File will be expanded to include international corporate affiliations.

Availability:

Dialog: $84/connect hour, $1.50/full record printed offline or typed or displayed online.

Corporate and Industry Research Reports Online Index. JA Micropublishing Inc., Eastchester, NY. 1982 to present. 45,300 records. Monthly updates.

Corresponds to *Corporate and Industry Research Reports Index*, providing index access to company and industry research reports issued by major U.S. and Canadian securities and institutional investment firms. Reports indexed analyze industry trends, public financial information, and the company's philosophy, management, research and development, competitive position, and projected strategies.

Availability:

BRS: $44/connect hour, $0.89/full record printed offline or typed, or $0.94/displayed online.

D&B—Canadian Dun's Market Identifiers. Dun & Bradstreet Canada Ltd., Toronto, ON. Current. 350,000 records. Quarterly reloads.

Directory of approximately 350,000 public and private Canadian companies. All companies have five or more employees and include branches or subsidiaries. Each record provides address and telephone number, chief executive's name and title, major line of business, up to five U.S. and Canadian funds, number of employees, age of company, manufacturing facilities, geographical area, and headquarters or parent company.

Availability:
Dialog: $100/connect hour, $2/full record printed offline or typed and displayed.

D&B—Donnelley Demographics. Donnelley Marketing Services, Mountain Lakes, NJ. Current. 62,220 records. Annual reloads.

The data derived by Donnelley from the 1980 census, current-year estimates, and five-year projections provide demographics on a wide range of units, as well as a U.S. summary. Figures include age, sex, and race; marital status, household size, housing, and income; and industry, occupations, and employment. Includes market areas as defined by Arbitron's Areas of Dominant Influence (ADI), A. C. Nielsen's Designated Market Areas (DMA), and Selling Areas Marketing, Inc. (SAMI).

Availability:
Dialog: $60/connect hour, $12/full record printed offline, $10/full record typed or displayed online.

D&B—Dun's Financial Records. Dun's Marketing Services, Mountain Lakes, NJ. Current. 742,763 records. Quarterly reloads.

Provides access to detailed financial records of more than 700,000 U.S. private and public companies. Up to three years of a company's financial statements are included, along with a brief description of the history and operation of the company and up to 14 business ratios which deal with solvency, efficiency, and profitability. Applications of the information include competitive and performance analysis, determination of merger or acquisition potential, financial ranking within the industry, and changes over previous years.

Availability:
Dialog: $135/connect hour, $85/full record printed offline or typed or displayed online.

D&B—Dun's Market Identifiers. Dun's Marketing Services, Mountain Lakes, NJ. Current. 1,980,346 records. Quarterly reloads.

Provides detailed information on more than 2 million U.S. companies which have 10 or more employees or annual sales of $1 million or more. Extensive coverage of all types of establishments, including both public and private companies. Each record includes address, names of executives, corporate structure, products, financial and marketing information. About one-third contain the same comprehensive financial data as that in D&B—Dun's Financial Records.

Availability:
Dialog: $100/connect hour, $2.50/full record printed offline or typed or displayed online.

D&B—Electronic Yellow Pages. Dun's Marketing Services, Mountain Lakes, NJ. Current. Quarterly reloads.

Provides directory information for approximately 8.5 million businesses and professionals in the United States. A full directory listing is provided for each entry, including address, telephone number, SIC codes and descriptions, and employee size range. Coverage includes both public and private companies and is indexed as industry groups in fourteen broad business categories: agriculture, business services, communication, construction, finance, insurance, manufacturing, mining, professional services, real estate, retail, transportation, utilities, wholesale.

Availability:

Dialog: $72/connect hour, $0.30/full record typed, displayed, or printed. Mailing labels available at $0.12/each.

D&B—International Dun's Market Identifiers. Dun's Marketing Services, Mountain Lakes, NJ. Current. 502,330 records. Quarterly updates.

Corresponds in part to *Principal International Business Directory*, and provides information on more than 500,000 non-U.S. public and private companies from 133 countries. Selection is determined by volume of sales in local and U.S. currency, national prominence, and international interest. Record includes address, sales, number of employees, type of company, and parent company.

Availability:

Dialog: $100/connect hour, $2/full record printed offline or typed or displayed online.

D&B—Million Dollar Directory. Dun's Marketing Services, Mountain Lakes, NJ. Current. 160,000 records. Annual reloads.

Corresponds to the *Million Dollar Directory*. Lists over 160,000 public and private U.S. companies with assets of $500,000 or more. Information in the record includes full address, sales, primary and secondary SIC codes, number of employees, and up to 25 executives.

Availability:

Dialog: $100/connect hour, $2/full record printed offline or typed or displayed online.

DIALOG Quotes and Trading. Trade*Plus, Palo Alto, CA. Daily updates (20-minute delay).

Delivers stock and options quotes from the New York and American Stock Exchanges, NASDAQ, and the four major options exchanges. Order entry allows the purchase or sale of any stock or option listed in the *Wall Street Journal*. Up to 75 portfolios can be set up with the value of the portfolio's securities updated to reflect current market prices, the capability to track gains and losses, and to project the dividend income of a portfolio. Tax records maintained on the service can include stocks, securities, mutual funds, options, and bonds. It can reflect all stocks and options sold. The file offers quantitative tools to evaluate stock option transactions.

For this file, DIALOG acts as a gateway to Trade*Plus. Searches are automatically transferred to the Trade*Plus system after logging in. The service operates with prompted menus.

Availability:

Dialog: $36/connect hour, offline record printing not available.

Directory of American Research and Technology. R. R. Bowker Company, New York, NY. Current. 11,000 records.

Corresponds to printed directory with same title, listing research and development facilities of 6,000 parent corporations and 5,000 subsidiaries in the U.S. Includes privately financed and non-profit organizations which carry out industrial research. Record includes address, divisions or parent company, key personnel, staffing, and research specialties.
Availability:
InfoLine: $95/connect hour, $0.50/full record printed offline, $0.35/full record typed or displayed online.

Disclosure. Disclosure Information Group, Bethesda, MD. Current. Records vary. Weekly updates.
The Disclosure Online Database from BRS contains lengthy records of over 10,000 public companies. The information is taken from reports filed with the Securities and Exchange Commission. Each record includes address, officers and directors, subsidiaries, SIC codes, exchange, balance sheets, ratio analysis, pricing, earnings and dividends, five-year summary, and corporate events. Dialog's database is a single file as well.
Availability:
Dialog: $45/connect hour, $11.80/full record printed offline, $8/full record typed or displayed online.
BRS: $22/connect hour, $15/full record printed offline, $13/full record typed or displayed online.

Disclosure/History. Disclosure Information Group, Bethesda, MD. 1978 to present. Semi-annual updates.
Records from the Disclosure database are added to this file for historical data. Each of the more than 10,000 American and non-U.S. public companies has a separate record for each year. Information comes from 10-K, 10-Q, and 8-Q reports; annual reports to stockholders; and proxy and registration statements. The record includes an annual balance sheet, sales, profits, income tax, outstanding shares, and debts.
Availability:
BRS: $22/connect hour, $8.35/full record printed offline, $7.37/full record typed or displayed online.

Disclosure/Spectrum Ownership. Disclosure Information Group, Bethesda, MD. Current. 5,400 records. Quarterly updates.
Contains stock ownership information for over 5,000 publicly held companies, with data taken from stockholder reports filed with the Securities and Exchange Commission. Record contains corporate name, exchange, ticker symbol, SIC codes, and market value of stock. Stock ownership section lists institutional holders, 5-percent owners, and inside owners, with the number of shares and date of last trade.
Availability:
Dialog: $60/connect hour, $25/full record printed offline, or typed or displayed online.
BRS: $47/connect hour, $33/full record printed offline, $28/full record typed or displayed online.

DMS Contract Awards. DMS Inc., Greenwich, CT. 1981 to present. 1,000,000 records. Quarterly updates.

Provides details on nonclassified contracts awarded by the federal government in excess of $25,000. Agencies covered include Department of Defense, General Services Administration, National Aeronautics and Space Administration, and the Department of Energy. The record for each award includes amount of funding, company receiving the contract, any defense program involved, awarding agency, date, and contract number.
Availability:
Dialog: $84/connect hour, $0.35/full record printed offline, or $0.35/full record typed or displayed online.

DMS Contractors. DMS Inc., Greenwich, CT. Current. 22,000 records. Reloaded weekly.
Directory of contractors working on projects listed in the DMS Market Intelligence Reports databases, including all contractors and subcontractors working on particular projects. The source is *DMS Market Intelligence Report.* Each record gives program title, company and division names, location, and a brief summary of the company's activities on the project.
Availability:
Dialog: $174/connect hour, $.30/full record printed offline (controlled access).

DMS Market Intelligence Reports. DMS Inc., Greenwich, CT. Current. 3,200 records. Reloaded weekly.
Full-text data and analysis of the aerospace and defense industry. Includes information on military equipment, weapons systems, defense funding, production quantities, recent activities, and forecasts of future government requirements and funding potential. Sources include *DMS Market Intelligence Reports,* government documents, defense journals and field interviews.
Availability:
Dialog: $174/connect hour, $6.00/full record printed offline (controlled access).

ECONOBASE. Interactive Data Corporation, Bala Cynwyd, PA. 1984 to present. 12,000 records. Reloaded monthly.
Numerical file which includes both two-year forecasts and historical data back to 1948 of key financial market indicators. Economic and demographic figures cover U.S. Standard Metropolitan Statistical Areas, more than 400 industries, and 40 countries. Time series data can be used to indicate market or industry trends for planning and assessing business conditions.
Availability:
Dialog: $75/connect hour, $1/format 5 record printed offline or typed or displayed online, $5.00/format 9 record printed offline or typed or displayed online.

Economic Literature Index. American Economic Association, Pittsburgh, PA. 1969 to present. 123,757 records. Quarterly updates.
Corresponds to the index section of the *Journal of Economic Literature* and to the annual *Index of Economic Articles.* Indexes journal articles and book reviews from 260 economics journals. About one-quarter since 1984 have abstracts.
Availability:
Dialog: $75/connect hour, $0.15/full record printed offline.

Economics Development and Education. Commonwealth Agricultural Bureaux International, Slough, England. 1980 to present. 40,000 records. Monthly updates.

Corresponds to three sections of CAB Abstracts database: *World Agricultural Economics and Rural Sociology Abstracts, Rural Development Abstracts,* and *Rural Extension, Education and Training Abstracts.* Provides information on developing countries, Third World development, agricultural economics, and farm management. International coverage includes journals, books, dissertations, government and business reports, international agency documents, and conferences.
Availability:
BRS: $41/connect hour, $0.32/full record printed offline, or $0.37/full record typed or displayed online.

Fairbase. Internationale Arbeitsgruppe fuer Technologreberatung, Hannover, West Germany. 1986 to 2010. 10,800 records. Updates every six weeks.

Directory of trade fairs, exhibitions and conferences to be held up to 2010. Covers all important events scheduled in the U.S. and 100 other countries. Record includes organizer, telephone number, beginning and ending date, and location. Some records also include a contact person, exhibit space and number of exhibitors, and number of visitors expected.
Availability:
BRS: $82/connect hour, $0.75/full record printed offline, or $0.80/full record typed or displayed online.

Financial Times Company Abstracts. Financial Times Business Information, Ltd., London. 1981 to present. 114,000 records. Weekly updates.

Summaries of every article about companies in the London and the international editions of the newspaper. Includes complete text of articles under 120 words. Covers more than 30,000 companies, both large and small, and subsidiaries. Offers a European perspective on international business.
Availability:
Dialog: $72/connect hour, $0.85/full record printed offline, or $0.80/full record typed or displayed online.

Financial Times Fulltext. Financial Times Business Information, Ltd., London. 1986 to present. 30,000 records. Weekly updates.

Full text of all articles published in the London and international editions of *Financial Times,* a well-known newspaper for international business, finance, companies, markets and world trade. Provides complete articles for all the abstracts in the Financial Times Company Abstracts database.
Availability:
Dialog: $96/connect hour, $1.60/full record printed offline.

FINDEX: The Directory of Market Research Reports, Studies, and Surveys. National Standards Association, Bethesda, MD. 1977 to present. 12,255 records. Reloaded quarterly.

Corresponds to *FINDEX: The Directory of Market Research Reports, Studies and Surveys.* Abstracts industry and market research studies produced by U.S. and worldwide publishers, plus reports by investment research firms. Provides analyses of markets, industries, and companies.

Availability:
Dialog: $105/connect hour, $0.75/full record printed offline, or $1.50/full record typed or displayed online.

FINIS: Financial Industry Information Service. Bank Marketing Association, Chicago, IL. 1982 to present. 50,000 records. Biweekly updates, Dialog; bimonthly updates, BRS.

Provides information on organizations in the financial services industry, with emphasis on marketing. Includes activities of banks, brokers, credit unions, insurance companies, investment houses, real estate firms, thrift institutions and relevant government agencies. Sources include journals, books, press releases, newsletters, newspapers, and reports.
Availability:
Dialog: $78/connect hour, $0.30/full record printed offline, or $0.20/full record typed or displayed online. SDI available at $9.95/update.
BRS: $52/connect hour, $0.40/full record printed offline, or $0.48/full record typed or displayed online.

Foods Adlibra. General Mills, Minneapolis, MN. 1974 to present. 124,000 records. Monthly updates.

Corresponds to print title of the same name. Covers all aspects of the food industry, including new food products since 1974, international food marketing, commodities, statistics and news. Sources include 250 periodicals, government publications, the *Federal Register* and news releases.
Availability:
Dialog: $63/connect hour, $0.15/full record printed offline, or $0.10/full record typed or displayed online.

Foreign Trade and Econ Abstracts. Netherlands Foreign Trade Agency, The Hague. 1974 to present. 175,000 records. Monthly updates.

Corresponds to portions of *Economic Titles/Abstracts.* Provides information on industries, market trends, international economics, import regulations, and foreign trade. Sources include 1,800 journals, books, directories, and reports.
Availability:
Dialog: $78/connect hour, $0.30/full record printed offline, or $0.25/full record typed or displayed online. SDI available for $7.95/update.

Foreign Traders Index. U.S. Department of Commerce, Washington, DC. Current four years. 65,000 records. Reloaded three times a year.

Directory of business contracts in 130 countries outside the U.S. The manufacturers, service organizations, retailers, wholesalers, distributors, and cooperatives which are included import merchandise from the U.S. or are interested in representing U.S. exporters. Record includes company and personal names, nature of business, size of firm, number of employees, date of establishment, product or service handled. Restricted to U.S. use.
Availability:
Dialog: $54/connect hour, $0.25/full record printed offline, or typed or displayed online.

Harvard Business Review. John Wiley & Sons, Inc., New York, NY. 1971 to present. 2,780 records. Bimonthly updates.

Full-text of the *Harvard Business Review* since 1976, plus abstracts of articles from 1971 to 1975. This outstanding management journal includes coverage of accounting, automation, business policy and ethics, industry analysis, human relations, marketing, and trade.
Availability:
BRS: $67/connect hour, $0.55/page printed offline, or $0.37/full record typed or displayed online.
Dialog: $96/connect hour, $0.20/complete text printed offline.

Health Planning and Administration. U.S. National Library of Medicine, Bethesda, MD. 1975 to present. 358,700 records. Monthly updates.
Corresponds to *Hospital Literature Index*, with the addition of some records from MEDLINE. Covers non-medical aspects of health care. Provides abstracts of literature on health care planning and facilities, health insurance, hospital management, financing, and personnel administration.
Availability:
BRS: $13/connect hour, $0.11/full record printed offline, or $0.14/full record typed or displayed online. SDI available for $4/update plus print charges.
Dialog: $36/connect hour, $0.20/full record printed offline, or $0.05/full record typed or displayed online. SDI available for $5.25/update.

Hoppenstedt Directory of German Companies. Hoppenstedt Wirtschaftsdatenbank, Darmstadt, West Germany. Current. 36,000 records. Reloaded quarterly.
Corresponds to directories *Handbuch der Grossunternehmen* and *Handbuch der Mittlestaendischen Unternehmen*. Lists 36,000 important German companies with sales over 2 million DM or at least 20 employees. Record includes company name, address and telephone number, executives, subsidiaries and branches, industry, and ownership. Searching may be done in either English or German and the record may be secured in either language.
Availability:
Dialog: $105/connect hour, $2.60/full record printed offline, or typed or displayed online.

ICC British Company Directory. Inter Company Comparisons Ltd., London. Current. 1,909,237 records. Weekly updates; reloaded quarterly.
Listing of every limited liability company registered in England, Scotland, Wales, Northern Ireland, and the Republic of Ireland, along with about 500,000 British companies that have dissolved. Information includes address, company history, incorporation date, and dates of latest returns and accounts.
Availability:
Dialog: $72/connect hour, $0.25/full record printed offline, or typed or displayed online.

ICC British Company Financial Datasheets. Inter Company Comparisons, Ltd., London. Latest four years. 82,000 records. Weekly updates.
Detailed financial information on 44,000 public and private British companies with annual sales of more than one million pounds sterling, plus abridged records for many smaller companies. Data include sales, profits, assets, current liabilities and up to 29 business ratios.

Availability:
Dialog: $96/connect hour, $4/format 5 record printed offline or typed or displayed online.

IHS Vendor Information Database. Information Handling Services, Englewood, CO. 30,000 records. Current. Monthly updates.

Index to information in catalogs from more than 30,000 vendors of industrial products, with emphasis on architectural engineering products, plant engineering, transportation and materials handling. Also includes equipment and supplies in the medical, electrical, construction, and marine fields. Record includes name, address, and brand or trade name.
Availability:
BRS: $57/connect hour, $0.31/full record printed offline, or $0.16/full record typed or displayed online.

Index to Frost & Sullivan Market Research Reports. Frost & Sullivan, Inc., New York, NY. 1980 to present. 700 records. Monthly updates.

Abstracts of F&S research reports. Documents concern product development, market share, forecast by market size and distribution, and projected international markets. Industries covered include data processing, communication, electronics, defense, and health.
Availability:
BRS: $12/connect hour, $0.10/full record printed offline, or $0.15/typed or displayed online.

Industrial Market Locations. Market Locations, Ltd., Warwickshire, UK. Current. 140,000 records.

Directory of more than 130,000 United Kingdom industrial establishments. Record includes name, address, telephone number, activities and details of facilities.
Availability:
InfoLine: $85.00/connect hour, $2.25/full record printed offline or typed or displayed online.

Industry Data Sources. Information Access Company, Belmont, CA. 1979 to present. 119,000 records. Monthly updates.

Corresponds to *Directory of Industry Data Sources.* Indicates sources of financial and marketing data for 65 major industries worldwide, including apparel, chemicals, energy, food and retail trade. Summarizes the kind of information found in market research reports, statistics, investment studies, journal articles and special issues, economic forecasts, directories, yearbooks, newsletters, and databases.
Availability:
BRS: $49.50/connect hour, $0.03/full record printed offline, or $0.15/full record typed or displayed online.
Dialog: $96/connect hour, $.040/full record printed offline, or $0.60/full record typed or displayed online.

Infocheck. Infocheck, Ltd., London. Current, with up to four years' data. 1,260,000 records. Weekly updates.

Directory of financial and credit ratings on all corporations registered in the United Kingdom, with some overseas status reports also available. Includes both fully analyzed reports on over 150,000 British companies and basic reports on others. Record is a company profile that includes capital, distribution of shares, accounts, ratios, trends, and credit summation report, including credit limit recommendation.

Availability:
InfoLine: $100/connect hour, $12.50/full record printed offline, or $12/full record typed or displayed online.

Insider Trading Monitor. Invest/Net, Inc., North Miami, FL. 1984 to present. 450,000 records. Daily updates.

Contains the transaction details of all insider trader filings (ownership changes) received by the U.S. Securities and Exchange Commission. It tracks the activities of over 100,000 officers, directors, and beneficial owners (those owning more than ten percent of a company's stock) of more than 8,500 public companies. All New York Stock Exchange, American Stock Exchange, and over-the-counter companies are included. Used primarily by investors, money managers, analysts, attorneys, marketers, and fund raisers.

Availability:
Dialog: $84/connect hour, $0.75/full record typed, displayed, or printed.

Insurance Abstracts. University Microfilms International, Ann Arbor, MI. 1979 through 1984. 68,912 records. Closed file.

Corresponds to *Life Insurance Index* and *Property and Liability Index.* Abstracts the insurance literature for life, property and liability insurance, financial planning and risk management. Sources include newsletters and journals. Coverage primarily of the U.S. and Canada.

Availability:
Dialog: $55/connect hour, $0.15/full record printed offline.

Investext. Business Research Corporation, Boston, MA. 1982 to present. 284,158 records. Weekly update.

Full-text company and industry research reports from analysts of leading investment banking concerns in the U.S., Europe, Canada, and Japan. The database has both regional and international coverage. Reports cover about 1,000 of the largest U.S. public corporations, 500 smaller and newer companies and around 1,000 large firms listed on prominent foreign stock exchanges. Records include comprehensive company analysis, including financial data, management, marketing and future outlook. Industry reports include market conditions, competition, market share, and product potential.

Availability:
Dialog: $96/connect hour, $4.50/full record printed offline, or typed or displayed online. SDI available for $3.50/update.
BRS: $89/connect hour, $4.75/page for full-text printed offline or typed or displayed online.

Investors Daily. JA Micropublishing, Inc., Eastchester, NY. 1986 to present. 3,300 records. Monthly updates.

Abstracts of articles in the financial newspaper, *Investor's Daily.* Covers U.S. stock market news, stock quotes and financial graphs. Record includes company names, personnel, location, products and the type of report.

Availability:
BRS: $32/connect hour, $0.95/full record printed offline, or $1/typed or displayed online.

Investors Rateline. Investors Rateline, Inc., Roswell, GA. Current. Daily updates.
Provides the latest rates for jumbo CDs ($100,000). Also includes financial information on banks and savings and loan associations, with menu-driven database access. Record on financial institutions includes telephone number, location, type of federal insurance, term, and asset-to-equity ratio.
Availability:
BRS: $150/connect hour.

Japan Economic Newswire Plus. Kyodo News International,Inc., New York. 1984 to present. 52,675 records. Daily updates.
Contains all English-language newswires reported by Kyodo News Service, Tokyo, Japan. Includes general and business news from Japan and international news which relates to Japan.
Availability:
Dialog: $96/connect hour, $0.60/full record printed offline. SDI: $3.95/update (weekly).

Japan Technology. Japan Technical Information Service, University Microfilms, Ann Arbor, MI. 1985 to present. 75,000 records. Monthly updates.
Corresponds to *Japanese Technical Abstracts.* Covers more than 600 Japanese journals published by societies, corporations, universities and government and commercial publishers. Includes business and technical information with broad subject coverage in electronics, robotics, automobile manufacturing, textiles, aerospace, and other fields. Mentions new products, industry trends and economic conditions.
Availability:
Dialog: $120/connect hour, $0.95/full record printed offline, or $0.80/full record typed or displayed online (reduced rate for subscribers). SDI available for $9.95/update.

Jordanwatch. Jordan & Sons Ltd., London. Current. 1,600,000 records. Weekly updates.
Directory of both British and foreign public and private companies registered in the United Kingdom. Record includes name and name changes, address, and date of incorporation. Executives, number of employees, assets, capital, SIC codes, and other detailed financial information are given for 130,000 companies.
Availability:
InfoLine: $120/connect hour, $12.60/full record printed offline, or typed or displayed online.

Key British Enterprises. Dun & Bradstreet Ltd. Current. 20,000 records. Monthly updates.
Directory of the top 20,000 British companies. Record lists address, telephone number, executives, parent company, number of employees, SIC codes, sales, markets, and trade names.

Availability:
InfoLine: $130/connect hour, $1.10/full record printed offline, or $3.60/full record typed or displayed online.

Labor Law. U.S. Library of Congress. Washington, DC. 1968 to present. 2,746,138 records. Monthly updates.

Provides summaries of decisions and references to the textual source of decisions relating to labor relations, fair employment, occupational safety and health, and wages and hours. The database has seven major subfiles: Labor relations (1966-present); Labor Arbitration Reports (1969-present); Fair Employment Practice Cases (1938-present); Wage and Hours Cases (1961-present); Occupational Health and Safety Cases (1972-present); Mine Safety and Health Cases (1970-present); Individual Employment Rights Cases (1986-present).
Availability:
Dialog: $120/connect hour, $0.70/free record print offline, $0.60/free record typed or displayed.

Labordoc. International Labour Organisation. 1965 to present. 100,800 records. Monthly updates.

Corresponds to *International Labour Documentation.* Based on acquisitions of the International Labour Organisation, this database covers international book and journal literature with emphasis on labor and labor-related materials. Subjects include industrial relations, economic and social development, labor law, employment, working conditions, and vocational training.
Availability:
ORBIT: $110/connect hour, $0.50/full record printed offline, or $0.25/full record typed or displayed online. SDI available for $5.50/update.

M&A Filings. Charles E. Simon & Company. Washington, DC April 1985 to present. 13,335 records. Updated daily.

Contains detailed abstracts of every original and amended merger and acquisition document released by the Securities and Exchange Commission since early 1985. M&A information available on publicly traded companies includes company name; SIC code; state of incorporation; state of headquarters; ticker symbol; Cusip number; filing type; amendment number; date of filing; reporting person, name, country, city and state; approximate deal value; synopsis sentence for the deal; expiration and withdrawal information; dealer manager; depositary; information agent; purpose of the transaction; summary abstract of the filing, including description of transaction, persons retained, employed, or compensated; material filed as exhibits; and keywords associated with each filing. Also available as menu-driven mergers.
Availability:
Dialog: $84/connect hour, $4/full record printed offline, $3/full record typed or displayed $0.25/report element, $1/per filing used in a preformatted REPORT.

Management and Marketing Abstracts. Paper & Board, Printing & Packaging Industries Research Association. 1976 to present. 26,500 records. Biweekly updates.

Covers worldwide literature on theoretical and practical aspects of international marketing, advertising, economics, administration, forecasting, research, and development.

Availability:
InfoLine: $105/connect hour, $0.40/full record printed offline, or $0.25/full record typed or displayed online.

Management Contents. Information Access Company, Belmont, CA. 1974 to present. 253,000 records. Monthly updates.

Abstracts of articles in over 120 international journals, conferences, newsletters and research reports. The subject emphasis on management and administration also includes accounting, finance, industrial relations, marketing, operations research, organization behavior, and public administration.
Availability:
BRS: $54/connect hour, $0.40/full record printed offline, or typed or displayed online. SDI available for $4/update plus print charges.
Dialog: $96/connect hour, $0.80/full record printed offline, or $0.75/full record typed or displayed online. SDI available for $9.95/update.
ORBIT: $90/connect hour, $0.55/full record printed offline, or $0.48/full record typed or displayed online. SDI available for $5.95/update.

Materials Business File. American Society for Metals, Metals Park, OH. 1985 to present. 20,000 records. Monthly updates.

Corresponds to *Steels Alert, Polymers/Ceramics/Composites Alert,* and *Nonferrous Alert.* Provides abstracts of commercial news of polymers, ceramics, composites, steels, and nonferrous metals and materials. Covers international journals, financial reports, dissertations and conferences. Current news, environmental issues, management, and industry developments are included.
Availability:
Dialog: $90/connect hour, $0.45/full record printed offline, or $0.40/full record typed or displayed online.
ORBIT: $90/connect hour, $0.45/full record printed offline, or $0.40/full record typed or displayed online. SDI available for $3.95/update.

McGraw-Hill News. McGraw-Hill Information Network, New York, NY. June 18, 1987 to present. 18,679 records. Updated every 15 minutes.

Provides the complete text of current news stories on the top business events worldwide. Coverage includes company and industry news, activity on U.S. and foreign stock markets, economic indicators and forecasts, U.S. government news pertaining to daily business operations, and political and general news significantly affecting the business community. With updates every 15 minutes, stories are available as soon as they are written.
Availability:
$96/connect hour, $0.60/full record printed offline. SDI: $3.95/update (weekly).

McGraw-Hill Publications Online. McGraw-Hill, Inc., New York, NY. 1985 to present. 33,000 records. Weekly updates.

Provides full-text coverage of 17 McGraw-Hill business magazines and newsletters. Publications covered include: *Business Week, Byte, Chemical Week, Commercial Space, Electronics, Data Communications, Nuclear Fuel, Inside NRC,* and *Securities Week.* Subjects include general business and developments in major industries.
Availability:
Dialog: $96/connect hour, $1.80/full record printed offline. SDI available for $3.50/update.

Media General Plus. Media General Financial Services, Richmond, VA. Latest seven years. 4,831 records. Reloaded weekly.
Detailed financial and trading information on 4,400 public companies. Covers seven years of weekly, quarterly and annual high and low stock prices and volumes. Sources are company reports, press releases, SEC forms and news wire services. Balance sheets, profit statements, and ratios given for each company, along with summary industry information.
Availability:
Dialog: $72/connect hour, $4/full record printed offline, or $3/full record typed or displayed online.

Moody's Corporate News—International. Moody's Investor Services, Inc., New York, NY. 1983 to present. 19,000 records. Weekly updates.
Corresponds to *Moody's International News Reports*, and includes business news and financial data on about 3,900 major companies from 100 countries. Information comes from company reports, news releases, prospectuses, periodicals, and news wire services. Includes both descriptive and numerical information.
Availability:
Dialog: $96/connect hour, $0.25/full record printed offline, or typed or displayed online.

Moody's Corporate News—U.S. Moody's Investor Services, Inc., New York, NY. 1983 to present. 187,240 records. Weekly updates.
Covers current news and financial data on more than 13,000 public U.S. companies. Records include both descriptive and numeric information. Sources are business periodicals, company reports, regulatory reports, and news wire services.
Availability:
Dialog: $75/connect hour, $0.25/full record printed offline, or typed or displayed online.

Moody's Corporate Profiles. Moody's Investor Services, Inc., New York, NY. Current. 4,227 records. Weekly updates.
Descriptive and financial information on more than 900 U.S. public companies includes current business news and data on earnings, dividends, sales and financial ratios from quarterly and annual reports, news releases, proxy statements, periodicals and news wire services. Record includes description of the business, capitalization, summary of quarterly developments and an analysis of the outlook, earnings, and balance sheets for up to five years.
Availability:
Dialog: $60/connect hour, $4/full record printed offline, or typed or displayed online.

Newswire ASAP. Information Access Company, Belmont, CA. PR Newswire January 1985 to present; Kyodo July 1987 to present; Reuters June 1987 to present. 196,884 records. Daily updates.
Provides the complete text and indexing of news releases and wire stories from PR Newswire, Kyodo, and Reuters. It offers current and retrospective information on companies, industries, products, economics, and finance. PR Newswire (available as a database on Dialog) records cover more than 10,000 companies, government agencies, and other agencies and include announcements of new products and services, quarterly earnings reports, and S&P Credit Wire ratings. Kyodo's Japan Economic Newswire (available as a separate

database on Dialog) covers Japanese Finance, industry, government, high technology, and companies. Reuter's Financial Report (also available as a separate DIALOG database) provides international business and financial news and analysis. Stories cover mergers, trade, commodities, stock markets, world news, and political events.

Use of this file is restricted to DIALOG customers in North America.
Availability:
Dialog: $96/connect hour, $0.20/Format 5 record printed offline, $0.10/Format 5 record typed or displayed online; $2/Format 9 offline print, $1/Format 9 record typed or displayed online. (Format 9 contains the complete text.)

PAIS International. Public Affairs Information Service, Inc., New York, NY. 1972 to present (*PAIS Foreign Language Index*) and 1976 to present (*PAIS Bulletin*). 270,000 records. Monthly updates.

Index to public policy aspects of business, economics, finance, and international trade. Sixty percent of the sources are in English, and sources include articles, books, government documents, pamphlets, and reports of public and private organizations. Records may contain very brief contents notes.
Availability:
BRS: $47/connect hour, $.35/full record printed offline, or $.35/full record typed or displayed online. SDI available for $4/update plus print charges.
Dialog: $75/connect hour, $0.40/full record printed offline, or $.30/full record typed or displayed online. SDI available for $8.95/update.

P/E News. American Petroleum Institute, New York, NY. 1975 to present. 407,000 records. Weekly updates.

Corresponds to *Petroleum/Energy Business News Index.* Fully indexes 16 major petroleum and energy publications including *Energy Asia, International Petroleum Finance, Lundberg Letter, Oil and Gas Journal,* and others. Important source of information on the energy industries. Record includes citation, and about 10 percent of the records have abstracts.
Availability:
Dialog: $96/connect hour, $0.35/full record printed offline, or $0.30/full record typed or displayed online.
ORBIT: $95/connect hour, $0.25/full record printed offline, or $0.20/full record typed or displayed online (reduced rates for subscribers).

Pharmaceutical News Index. Data Courier, Louisville, KY. 1974 to present. 189,000 records. Monthly updates.

Indexes newsletters and reports in the pharmaceutical, cosmetic, medical-device and related health fields. Sources include *Applied Genetic News, Biomedical Business International, Health Devices, Pharma* and the *Washington Drug and Device Letter.* Information includes government regulations, corporate and industry sales, mergers, and court action.
Availability:
Dialog: $139/connect hour, $0.735/full record printed offline, or $0.60/full record typed or displayed online. SDI available for $9.95/update.

PR Newswire. PR Newswire Association Inc., New York, NY. May 1, 1987 to present. 38,300 records. Updated every 15 minutes.

Contains the complete text on news releases prepared by companies, public relations agencies, trade associations, city, state, federal, and foreign government agencies as well as other sources. About 80% of the records available are business/financial. The complete text of a news release usually contains details

or background information not published in newspapers. Each release gives a name and telephone number of an individual who can be contacted for additional information. News releases cover the following topics: dividends, mergers and acquisitions, earnings, new products, executive changes, new securities offerings, hostile takeovers, repurchases of stock, leveraged buyouts, restructuring, litigation, and write-offs.
Availability:
    Dialog: $96/connect hour, $0.60/full record printed offline. SDI: $3.95/update (weekly).

PTS Aerospace/Defense Markets & Technology. Predicasts, Cleveland, OH. 1982 to present. 123,000 records. Weekly updates.
    Abstracts major defense journals and selected defense-related articles from other business periodicals, newspapers, press releases, and government reports. All major defense contracts awarded by the U.S. Department of Defense are included. Records include contract number, awarding agency, contractor, and amount.
Availability:
    Dialog: $150/connect hour, $0.78/full record printed offline, or $0.68/full record typed or displayed online (reduced rates for subscribers). SDI available for $5.45/update.

PTS Annual Reports Abstracts. Predicasts, Cleveland, OH. Current. 152,000 records. Monthly updates.
    Coverage of annual reports of over 3,000 public U.S. and selected international companies. Includes abstracts of management statements, organizational changes, products and markets. Financial information is derived from annual reports and 10-K statements.
Availability:
    BRS: $77/connect hour, $.75/full record printed offline, or $0.80/full record typed or displayed online.
    Dialog: $126/connect hour, $0.78/full record printed offline, or $0.68/full record typed or displayed online.

PTS F&S Indexes. Predicasts, Cleveland, OH. 1972 to present. 2,769,000 records. Weekly updates.
    Corresponds to *Predicasts F&S Index United States, F&S Index Europe,* and *F&S Index International.* Abstracts of international publications, providing country, company, product, and industry information. Information includes corporate acquisitions and mergers, new products, analyses of companies, and forecasts of future economic changes. A subfile, Source Directory, is a bibliography of the more than 5,000 publications indexed by the various Predicasts files.
Availability:
    BRS: $77/connect hour, $0.32/full record printed offline, or typed or displayed online. SDI available for $4/update plus print charges.
    Dialog: $114/connect hour, $0.33/full record printed offline, or $0.28/full record typed or displayed online. SDI available for $7.95/update.

PTS International Forecasts. Predicasts, Cleveland, OH. 1971 to present. 585,000 records. Monthly updates.

Corresponds to *Worldcasts.* Provides both short- and long-range forecasts of leading foreign economic indicators and for industries outside the U.S. References to sources of statistics include government publications, statistical reports of foreign industries, trade and international association publications, newspapers, and journals.
Availability:
    Dialog: $114/connect hour, $0.48/full record printed offline, or $0.38/full record typed or displayed online.

PTS Marketing & Advertising Reference Service (MARS). Predicast, Cleveland, OH. 1984 to present. 85,000 records. Weekly updates.
    Provides abstracts, tables, and statistics from publications on the marketing and advertising of consumer goods and services. Sources include consumer and advertising magazines, journals, newsletters, and advertising columns of major newspapers.
Availability:
    Dialog: $150/connect hour, $0.68/full record printed offline, or $0.58/full record typed or displayed online. SDI available for $4.95/update.

PTS New Product Announcements. Predicasts, Cleveland, OH. 1985 to present. 38,000 records. Weekly updates.
    Provides full text of news releases issued by manufacturers, distributors, or their marketing representatives. Includes information about products, distribution, sales or licensing agreements, new technologies or production facilities, and prices. Records include company contacts and telephone numbers.
Availability:
    Dialog: $126/connect hour, $1.90/full record printed offline, or $0.80/full record typed or displayed online. SDI available for $7.94/update.

PTS PROMT. Predicasts, Cleveland, OH. 1972 to present. 1,164,000 records. Weekly updates.
    Provides broad coverage of business and industry information. Abstracts local, regional, national, and international activities. Subjects include new products and new technologies; local activities of large companies; small, growing companies and industries; market data; and international trade. Sources include journals, newspapers, local business publications, investment reports, government documents, bank letters, and newsletters.
Availability:
    BRS: $82/connect hour, $0.62/full record printed offline, or $0.67/full record typed or displayed online.
    Dialog: $126/connect hour, $0.73/full record printed offline, or $0.63/full record typed or displayed online.

PTS Promt Daily. Predicasts, Cleveland, OH. Records in file for one week, then transferred to other Predicasts files. 750 to 4,000 records. Daily updates.
    Abstracts of articles are available within 48 hours of publication in major business and trade journals, newspapers, government reports, bank letters, brokerage reports, news releases, and special reports. Includes information on companies, products, markets, and industries. After a week, records are transferred to PTS PROMT, PTS Aerospace Defense Markets and Technology, and PTS Marketing and Advertising Reference Service (MARS). Subjects include new technologies, acquisitions and mergers, marketing, and new products.

Availability:
Dialog: $132/connect hour, $0.78/full record printed offline, $0.68/full record typed or displayed online. SDI available for $4.95/update.

PTS U.S. Forecasts. Predicasts, Cleveland, OH. 1971 to present. 585,000 records. Monthly updates.
Corresponds to *Predicasts Forecasts.* Provides forecasts with historical data for economic indicators and industries and products in the United States. Citations are provided for the source document, which may be a journal, newspaper, government document, or special study. Data include the *Census of Manufacturers* for 1967, 1972, and 1977. Records contain figures from the historical base period, a short-term forecast, and a long-term forecast.
Availability:
Dialog: $114/connect hour, $0.48/full record printed offline, or $0.38/full record typed or displayed online.

PTS U.S. Time Series. Predicasts, Cleveland, OH. Years variable back to 1957. 45,086 records.
Quarterly updates to *Basebook* records with replacement annually; quarterly replacements for *Composites* records. The numeric file is divided into two parts. *Predicasts Basebook* provides annual data from 1957 on nearly 47,000 series that include U.S. production, consumption, prices, trade, agriculture, mining, manufacturing, wages, and distribution for a wide variety of industries, services, and products. *Predicasts Composites* include about 500 time series beginning with 1975 and including predictions through 1990. Subjects include population, GNP, income, employment, energy, construction, industrial production, and prices.
Availability:
Dialog: $114/connect hour, $0.40/full record printed offline, or $0.35/full record typed or displayed online.

Reference Book of Corporate Managements. Dun's Marketing Services, Mount Lakes, NJ. Current. 78,000 records. Annual updates.
Name, address, and biographical information on the executives and directors of more than 12,000 U.S. companies. Includes professional history, educational background, and military service.
Availability:
InfoLine: $98/connect hour, $2.25/full record printed offline, or typed or displayed online.

Research Index. Business Surveys Ltd., Surrey, England. 1985 to present. 97,000 records. Biweekly updates.
Index to business and financial news in over 100 international journals and British newspapers.
Availability:
InfoLine: $130/connect hour, $0.40/full record printed offline, or $0.25/full record typed or displayed online.

Reuters. Reuters U.S., Inc., New York, NY. January 1987 to present. 198,800 records. Updated every 15 minutes.
Contains the complete text of news releases from the Reuter Financial Report and the Reuter Library Service newswires. The file provides access to current information on business and international news. News "flashes" are added throughout the day before the complete story is written, then eliminated

every evening. Reuter Financial Report, with a two-hour embargo, includes news on publicly traded companies which could affect their stock, as well as government statistics on unemployment, gross national product, international trade, and news from Washington affecting the economy.

Use of Reuters is restricted to DIALOG customers in the United States and Canada.

Availability:

Dialog: $96/connect hour, $0.60/full record printed offline. SDI: $3.95/update (weekly).

Standard & Poor's Corporate Descriptions. Standard & Poor's Corporation, New York, NY. Current. 12,141 records. Biweekly updates.

Corresponds to *Standard & Poor's Corporation Records.* Includes both descriptive and financial information on more than 11,000 public companies. Provides brief company history, description of products and markets, subsidiaries and divisions, stock and bond data, earnings, and finances. Sources include stockholder and government reports, wire service and newspaper articles, and stock-exchange releases.

Availability:

Dialog: $85/connect hour, $3.50/full record printed offline, or typed or displayed online.

Standard & Poor's News. Standard & Poor's Corporation, New York, NY. 1979 to present. 517,000 records. Daily updates.

Corresponds to *Standard & Poor's Corporation Records Daily News.* Provides current news and financial information on more than 11,000 public companies.

Availability:

Dialog: $96/connect hour, $0.25/full record printed offline. SDI available for $5.95/update.

Standard & Poor's Register—Biographical. Standard & Poor's Corporation, New York, NY. Current. 71,127 records. Reloaded semiannually.

Corresponds to *Standard & Poor's Register of Corporations, Directors, and Executives,* Vol. 2. Provides biographical information on selected executives and directors of companies listed in the companion database Standard & Poor's Register—Corporate. Includes personal, educational, and professional facts, current position, and address.

Availability:

Dialog: $84/connect hour, $1.50/full record printed offline, or typed or displayed online.

Standard & Poor's Register—Corporate. Standard & Poor's Corporation, New York, NY. Current. 46,238 records. Reloaded quarterly.

Corresponds to *Standard & Poor's Register of Corporations,* Vol. 1. Provides business information on about 45,000 public and private companies with sales over $1 million. Primarily U.S. companies. Record includes subsidiaries, divisions, and affiliates; financial and marketing information; officers and directors.

Availability:

Dialog: $84/connect hour, $1.50/full record printed offline, or typed or displayed online.

Standards and Specifications. National Standards Association, Inc., Bethesda, MD. 1950 to present. 116,239 records. Updated monthly.

Provides access to all government and industry standards, specifications, and related documents which specify performance rating, terminology, safety, materials, products, or other requirements and characteristics of interest to a specific industry or technology. To identify standards and specifications the database contains the following: issuing organization, Federal Supply Classification code, whether documents have been cancelled or superseded, if adopted by a U.S. government agency, designated an American National Standard, and for international standards, whether approved for use by an agency of the U.S. government. Suppliers of services and products conforming to standards and specifications are also provided. Most standards and specifications in the database have been issued since 1950, but some date from as early as 1920.
Availability:
Dialog: $65/connect hour, $0.30/full record printed offline, $0.20/full record typed or displayed online.

Tax Notes Today. Tax Analysts, Arlington, VA. January 1987 to present. 31,631 records. Updated daily.
Contains analytical summaries combined with full text of all important legislative, judicial, regulatory, and policy documents regarding federal taxation. It also includes state tax notes. The news stories are written by tax attorneys, tax accountants, public finance economists, and journalists on staff at *Tax Analysts.* Documentary material is obtained from government agencies, then processed during the day, and transmitted to DIALOG that night.
Availability:
Dialog: $96/connect hour, $4/full record printed offline, or typed or displayed online, $0.10/report element.

Thomas New Industrial Products. Thomas Publishing Company, Inc., New York, NY. 1985 to present. 18,640 records. Weekly updates.
Corresponds primarily to *Industrial Equipment News.* Provides information on all types of new products as announced in press releases. Data include manufacturer, specifications, properties, applications, components, and trade names.
Availability:
Dialog: $96/connect hour, $0.50/full record printed offline, or typed or displayed online.

Thomas Regional Industrial Suppliers. Thomas Publishing Company, New York, NY. Current. 306,946 records. Reloaded quarterly.
Corresponds to 14 versions of the *Regional Industrial Purchasing Guide.* Emphasis on local suppliers of industrial products and services. Lists more than 325,000 public and private companies, with contract information and products and services offered.
Availability:
Dialog: $84/connect hour, $0.45/full record printed offline, or $0.40/full record typed or displayed online.

Thomas Register Online. Thomas Publishing Company, New York, NY. Current. 140,734 records. Reloaded annually.

Corresponds to *Thomas Register of American Manufacturers.* Covers about 133,000 U.S. companies, over 50,000 groups of products, and 106,000 trade or brand names. Records include street and cable address, company officers, number of employees, asset rating, parent company or subsidiaries and divisions, up to 50 products, trade names in use, and cross references to name changes.
Availability:
   Dialog: $100/connect hour, $1.50/full record printed offline, or typed or displayed online.

Trade & Industry ASAP. Information Access Company, Belmont, CA. 1983 to present. 304,000 records. Monthly updates.
   Complete text and indexing of major articles from over 85 selected journals from the Trade & Industry Index database and from news releases from *PR Newswire.*
Availability:
   BRS: $85/connect hour, $2/full record printed offline, or $1/full record typed or displayed online.
   Dialog: $96/connect hour, $0.20/full record printed offline, or typed or displayed online.

Trade & Industry Index. Information Access Company, Belmont, CA. 1981 to present. 1,472,000 records. Monthly updates.
   Provides abstracts of over 300 trade and industry journals and more than 1,200 additional publications, including newspapers, newsletters, wire reports, and local and regional publications. Some records are full-text. Subjects include agriculture, banking, manufacturing, public utilities, securities, taxation, and trade.
Availability:
   BRS: $73/connect hour, $0.20/full record printed offline, or $1/full record typed or displayed online.
   Dialog: $90/connect hour, $0.40/full record printed offline, or $0.20/full record typed or displayed online for format 5. Full-text records are printed offline, or typed or displayed online.

Trademarkscan. Thomson & Thomson, North Quincy, MA. 1884 to present. 1,177,000 records. Weekly updates.
   Contains records of over 600,000 active trademarks registered in the U.S., and those with pending applications. Includes serial number or registration number, the U.S. classification of goods and services, owner's name, and other pertinent information. When trademarks have been abandoned, cancelled, or the registration has expired, they remain in the database and the latest information on their status is listed.
Availability:
   Dialog: $120/connect hour, $0.60/full record printed offline, or $0.35/full record typed or displayed online. SDI available for $12.95/update.

Trademarkscan—State. Thomson & Thomson, North Quincy, MA. 1986 to present. 500,000 records. Biweekly updates.
   Contains records of trademarks registered with secretaries of state of the 50 states and Puerto Rico. Trademarks represent products and services that are marketed commercially. The record includes description of trademark, state of registration, U.S. and international class numbers, registration number, name of owner, and current status.

Availability:
Dialog: $120/connect hour, $0.60/full record printed offline, or typed or displayed online. SDI available for $8.95/update.

Trinet Company Database. TRINET, Inc., Parsippany, NJ. Current. 230,364 records. Quarterly updates.

Directory of U.S. private and public companies, manufacturing and non-manufacturing, with 20 or more employees. Emphasis on overall company information. Sources are U.S. Census Bureau statistics, state and industrial directories, corporate reports, journals and clipping services, plus direct response from the companies. Records include U.S. and non-U.S. sales, sales by industry, number of branches, and locations.

Availability:
Dialog: $90/connect hour, $1.60/full record printed offline, or typed or displayed online.

Trinet Establishment Database. TRINET, Inc., Parsippany, NJ. Current. 384,890 records. Quarterly updates.

Directory of U.S. establishments with 20 or more employees. Emphasis on branch locations. Provides address, parent company, SIC codes, revenues, number of employees, and other financial information. Reports on the line of business and share of the market can be produced.

Availability:
Dialog: $90/connect hour, $0.50/full record printed offline, or typed or displayed online.

U.K. Standard Industrial Classification. Pergamon Press Ltd., London. Current. 650 records.

Directory of 5-digit SIC codes maintained by the United Kingdom Central Statistical Office. Provides description of each classification and lists specific industries included.

Availability:
InfoLine: $40/connect hour, $0.40/full record printed offline.

U.S. Standard Industrial Classification. U.S. Department of Commerce, Office of Federal Statistical Policy and Standards, Washington, DC. Current. 1,253 records.

Directory of U.S. SIC codes corresponding to the 1972 manual and the 1977 supplement. Covers major industry classifications, includes descriptive abstract and specific industries in each group.

Availability:
InfoLine: $45/connect hour, $0.40/full record printed offline, or $0.15/full record typed or displayed online.

Who Owns Whom. Dun & Bradstreet Ltd., London. Current. 300,000 records. Monthly updates.

Directory of international company structures, covering 25,000 parents and 275,000 subsidiaries. Record includes parent company, with names of subsidiaries, affiliates, and divisions. Changes in ownership are indicated when file is updated. Data on individual companies and ownership information are included.

Availability:
InfoLine: $198/connect hour, $40/full record printed offline. SDI available for $6/update.

World Textiles. Shirley Institute, Manchester, England. 1970 to present. 141,900 records. Monthly updates.

Corresponds to *World Textile Abstract.* Includes economics, consumption, production, management, and international trade in the textile industry. Sources include journals, patents, books, conferences, and statistical publications.
Availability:
Dialog: $55/connect hour, $0.10/full record printed offline.

Database Vendors

BRS Information Technologies
1200 Rt. 7
Latham, NY 12110

DIALOG Information Services, Inc.
3460 Hillview Avenue
Palo Alto, CA 94304

Pergamon Orbit InfoLine, Inc.
8000 Westpark Drive
McLean, VA 22101

H. W. Wilson Company
950 University Avenue
Bronx, New York, NY 10452

APPENDIX

TABLE 1. BUSINESS NEWS DATABASES

Name of Database	Vendor*	Update	Subject Emphasis
AMERICAN BANKER NEWS	D,B	Daily	Banking, finance from daily newspaper
BIS INFOMAT	I	Daily	General business, marketing
BOND BUYER	D,B	Daily	Bonds, credit from daily newspaper
BUSINESS & INDUSTRY NEWS	D	Daily	New information for Predicasts databases
BUSINESSWIRE	D	15 min.	Business news from press releases
COMMERCE BUSINESS DAILY	D	Daily	Government contracts
DIALOG QUOTES AND TRADING	D	Daily	Stock quotations
INVESTORS DAILY	B	Monthly	Finance from daily newspaper
INVESTORS RATELINE	B	Daily	CD rates
MOODY'S CORPORATE NEWS—INTERNATIONAL	D	Weekly	Major international companies

*D—Dialog, B—BRS, I—InfoLine, O—Orbit, W—Wilsonline

TABLE 1. BUSINESS NEWS DATABASES (cont.)

Name of Database	Vendor*	Update	Subject Emphasis
MOODY'S CORPORATE NEWS—U.S.	D	Weekly	Public U.S. companies
PTS NEW PRODUCT ANNOUNCEMENTS	D	Weekly	New products
RESEARCH INDEX	I	Biweekly	International finance
STANDARD & POOR'S NEWS	D	Daily	Public companies
THOMAS NEW INDUSTRIAL PRODUCTS	D	Weekly	New products
TRADE OPPORTUNITIES WEEKLY	D	Weekly	Export information

TABLE 2. COMPANY DIRECTORIES

Name of Database	Vendor*	Update	Number of Companies
CORPORATE AFFILIATIONS	D	Quarterly	3,100 public U.S. 800 private U.S. 38,800 divisions
D&B CANADIAN DUN'S MARKET IDENTIFIERS	D	Quarterly	350,000 Canadian public/ private
D&B DUN'S ELECTRONIC YELLOW PAGES	D	Quarterly	8,383,425 U.S.
D&B MILLION DOLLAR DIRECTORY	D	Annual	160,000 public/private U.S.
HOPPENSTEDT DIRECTORY OF GERMAN COMPANIES	D	Quarterly	36,000 German
ICC BRITISH COMPANY DIRECTORY	D	Weekly	1,900,000 British
JORDANWATCH	I	Weekly	1,600,000 British
KEY BRITISH ENTERPRISES	I	Monthly	20,000 British
STANDARD & POOR'S CORPORATE DESCRIPTIONS	D	Biweekly	11,000 public U.S.
STANDARD & POOR'S REGISTER—CORPORATE	D	Biweekly	11,000 public U.S.
THOMAS REGIONAL INDUSTRIAL SUPPLIERS	D	Quarterly	325,000 public/private U.S.
THOMAS REGISTER ONLINE	D	Annual	133,000 U.S.
TRINET COMPANY DATABASE	D	Quarterly	230,000 public/private U.S.
TRINET ESTABLISHMENT DATABASE	D	Quarterly	380,000 U.S.
WHO OWNS WHOM	I	Monthly	25,000 parents 275,000 subsidiaries international

TABLE 3. COMPANY FINANCIAL INFORMATION

Name of Database	Vendor*	Update	Number of Companies
D&B DUN'S FINANCIAL RECORDS	D	Quarterly	700,000 public/private U.S.
D&B DUN'S MARKET IDENTIFIERS	D	Quarterly	2,000,000 public/private U.S.

*D—Dialog, B—BRS, I—InfoLine, O—Orbit, W—Wilsonline

TABLE 3. COMPANY FINANCIAL INFORMATION (cont.)

Name of Database	Vendor*	Update	Number of Companies
D&B INTERNATIONAL DUN'S MARKET IDENTIFIERS	D	Quarterly	500,000 non-U.S.
DISCLOSURE	D,B	Weekly	10,000 public U.S.
DISCLOSURE/HISTORY	B	Semiannual	10,000 public U.S.
ICC BRITISH COMPANY FINANCIAL DATASHEETS	D	Weekly	82,000 public/private British
INFOCHECK	I	Weekly	1,260,000 registered in U.K.
INVESTEXT	D	Weekly	2,500 public U.S., foreign
MEDIA GENERAL DATABANK	D	Weekly	4,400 public U.S.
MOODY'S CORPORATE PROFILES	D	Weekly	900 public U.S.
MOODYS CORPORATE NEWS—INTERNATIONAL	D	Weekly	3,900 from 100 countries
MOODY'S CORPORATE NEWS—US	D	Weekly	13,000 public U.S.
PTS ANNUAL REPORTS ABSTRACTS	D,B	Monthly	3,000 public U.S. international

TABLE 4. BUSINESS INFORMATION DIRECTORIES

Name of Database	Vendor*	Update	Applications
BRITISH TRADEMARKS	I	—	British trademarks
BUSINESS SOFTWARE DATABASE	D,B	Quarterly	Software packages
DIRECTORY OF AMERICAN RESEARCH & TECHNOLOGY	I	—	Research & development facilities
DISCLOSURE/SPECTRUM OWNERSHIP	D,B	Quarterly	Stockholders
DMS CONTRACT AWARDS	D	Quarterly	U.S. government contracts
DMS CONTRACTORS**	D	Weekly	U.S. government contractors
FAIRBASE	B	6 weeks	Trade fairs, exhibitions
FINDEX: THE DIRECTORY OF MARKET RESEARCH REPORTS, STUDIES, AND SURVEYS	D	Quarterly	Markets, industries, companies
FOREIGN TRADERS INDEX***	D	3 times/yr	Business contacts outside U.S.
IHS VENDOR INFORMATION DATABASE	B	Monthly	Products in catalogs
INDUSTRIAL MARKET LOCATIONS	I	—	British establishment activities & facilities
INDUSTRY DATA SOURCES	D,B	Monthly	Sources of industry information
INTERNATIONAL LISTING SERVICE	D	Irregular	International investment and sales
REFERENCE BOOK OF CORPORATE MANAGEMENTS	I	Annual	Executives of U.S. companies
S&P'S REGISTER— BIOGRAPHICAL	D	Semiannual	Executives of U.S. companies
THOMAS NEW INDUSTRIAL PRODUCTS	D	Weekly	New products
TRADE OPPORTUNITIES	D	Quarterly	Export opportunities

*D—Dialog, B—BRS, I—InfoLine, O—Orbit, W—Wilsonline
**—Controlled access
***—Restricted to U.S. use

TABLE 4. BUSINESS INFORMATION DIRECTORIES (cont.)

Name of Database	Vendor*	Update	Applications
TRADEMARKSCAN	D	Weekly	600,000 U.S. trademarks
TRADEMARKSCAN—STATE	D	Biweekly	Trademarks registered in states
UK STANDARD INDUSTRIAL CLASSIFICATION	I	Quarterly	SIC codes in United Kingdom
US STANDARD INDUSTRIAL CLASSIFICATION	I	—	SIC codes in United States

TABLE 5. NUMERICAL DATABASES FOR BUSINESS-RELATED INFORMATION

Name of Database	Vendor*	Update	Data Provided
BLS CONSUMER PRICE INDEX	D	Monthly	Consumer prices
BLS EMPLOYMENT, HOURS AND EARNINGS	D	Monthly	Employment, Hours, Earnings
BLS PRODUCER PRICE INDEX	D	Monthly	Producer, Industry Price Indexes
CENDATA	D	Daily	Economic, demographic data
CHASE ECONOMETRICS	D	Monthly	Market indicators, time series, economic, demographic data
D&B DONNELLEY DEMOGRAPHICS	D	Annual	Census, market areas
PTS INTERNATIONAL FORECASTS	D	Monthly	Foreign economic forecasts
PTS US FORECASTS	D	Monthly	Economic forecasts, U.S.
PTS US TIME SERIES	D	Quarterly	Economic time series

TABLE 6. FULL-TEXT BUSINESS DATABASES

Name of Database	Vendor*	Update	Subject Emphasis
AGRIBUSINESS USA	D	Biweekly	Government reports on agriculture
AMERICAN BANKER	D,B	Daily	Bank, finance newspaper
BOND BUYER	D,B	Daily	Bonds, credit newspaper
BUSINESS DATELINE	D	Weekly	Company regional activities
BUSINESSWIRE	D	15 min.	Business press releases
COMMERCE BUSINESS DAILY	D	Daily	Government contracts
DMS MARKET INTELLIGENCE REPORTS**	D	Weekly	Aerospace, defense
FINANCIAL TIMES FULLTEXT	D	Weekly	International business newspaper
HARVARD BUSINESS REVIEW	D,B	Bimonthly	General business, management
INVESTEXT	D	Weekly	Company/industry research reports
McGRAW-HILL BUSINESS BACKGROUNDER	D	Weekly	Business magazines, newsletters
PTS NEW PRODUCT ANNOUNCEMENTS	D	Weekly	News releases on new products
TRADE & INDUSTRY ASAP	D,B	Monthly	Articles from 85 journals; news releases, PR Newswire

*D—Dialog, B—BRS, I—InfoLine, O—Orbit, W—Wilsonline
**—Controlled access

TABLE 7. BIBLIOGRAPHIC DATABASES OF BUSINESS INFORMATION

Name of Database	Vendor*	Dates Covered	No. of Records	Updates****	Subject Emphasis
ABI/INFORM	D,B,O	1981-	1,472,000	W/M	General business, management
ABSTRACTS OF WORKING PAPERS IN ECONOMICS	B	1982-	3,000	M	Economics, finance
ACCOUNTANTS	O	1974-	150,000	Q	Accounting
ADTRACK	D	1980-	390,000	IR	Advertisements
AGRIBUSINESS USA	D	1985-	40,000	BiW	Agriculture related business
ARTHUR D. LITTLE/ ONLINE	D	1977-	1,101	M	Analysis, forecasts
BIOBUSINESS	D	1985-	64,966	M	Biological, biomedical
BIOCOMMERCE ABSTRACTS	D	1981-	70,000	S-M	Biotechnology
BIS INFOMAT	I	1983-	400,000	D	Marketing, trade
BUSINESS PERIODICALS INDEX	W	1982-	290,000	S-W	General business
CANADIAN BUSINESS AND CURRENT AFFAIRS	D	1980-	656,000	M	Canadian business
CATALYST RESOURCE ON THE WORK FORCE AND WOMEN DATABASE	D	1963-	8,400	Q	Working women
CHEMICAL BUSINESS NEWSBASE	D,I	1984-	55,750	W	International chemical industry
CHEMICAL INDUSTRY NOTES	D,O	1974-	630,700	BiW	Chemical processing industry
COFFEELINE	D	1973-	16,500	BiM	Coffee industry
COMPUTER DATABASE	D	1983-	192,000	BiW	Computers
CORPORATE AND INDUSTRY RESEARCH REPORTS ONLINE INDEX	B	1982-	45,300	M	Company, industry financial standing
DMS MARKET INTELLIGENCE RE-PORTS**	D	current	3,200	W	Aerospace/defense industry
ECONOMIC LITERATURE INDEX	D	1969-	123,757	Q	Economics
ECONOMICS DEVELOPMENT AND EDUCATION	B	1980-	40,000	M	Third world, rural development
FINANCIAL TIMES COMPANY ABSTRACTS	D	1981-	114,000	W	International business, European companies

*D—Dialog, B—BRS, I—InfoLine, O—Orbit, W—Wilsonline
**—Controlled access
***—Restricted to U.S. use
****—IR—Irregular, M—Monthly, Q—Quarterly, S—Semi, W—Weekly

TABLE 7. BIBLIOGRAPHIC DATABASES OF BUSINESS INFORMATION (cont.)

Name of Database	Vendor*	Dates Covered	No. of Records	Updates****	Subject Emphasis
FINIS: FINANCIAL INDUSTRY INFORMATION SERVICE	D,B	1982-	50,000	BiW/BiM	Financial services industry
FOODS ADLIBRA	D	1974-	124,000	M	Food industry
FOREIGN TRADE AND ECON ABSTRACTS	D	1974-	175,000	M	Foreign trade
HEALTH PLANNING AND ADMINISTRATION	D,B	1975-	358,700	M	Health care
INDEX TO FROST & SULLIVAN MARKET RESEARCH REPORTS	B	1980-	700	M	Markets
INDUSTRY DATA SOURCES	D,B	1979-	119,000	M	Industry data
INSURANCE ABSTRACTS	D	1979-84	68,912	—	Insurance—U.S./ Canada
JAPAN TECHNOLOGY	D	1985-	75,000	M	Japanese business
LABORDOC	O	1965-	100,800	M	Labor, industrial relations
MANAGEMENT AND MARKETING ABSTRACTS	I	1976-	26,500	BiW	Marketing
MANAGEMENT CONTENTS	D,B,O	1974-	253,000	M	Management-related business subjects
MATERIALS BUSINESS FILE	D,O	1985-	20,000	M	Steel, non-ferrous materials
PAIS INTERNATIONAL	D,B	1972-	270,000	M	Business, economics, trade
P/E NEWS	D,O	1975-	407,000	W	Petroleum, energy industry
PHARMACEUTICAL NEWS	D	1974-	189,000	M	Pharmaceuticals industry
PTS AEROSPACE/ DEFENSE MARKETS & TECHNOLOGY	D	1982-	123,000	W	Defense industry
PTS F&S INDEXES	D,B	1972-	2,769,000	W	Company, industry
PTS MARKETING & ADVERTISING REFERENCE SERVICE	D	1984-	85,000	W	Marketing consumer goods
PTS PROMT	D,B	1972-	1,164,000	W	Business, industry
TRADE & INDUSTRY INDEX	D,B	1981-	1,472,000	M	Industry, trade
WORLD TEXTILES	D	1970-	141,900	M	Textile industry

*D—Dialog, B—BRS, I—InfoLine, O—Orbit, W—Wilsonline
**—Controlled access
***—Restricted to U.S. use
****—IR—Irregular, M—Monthly, Q—Quarterly, S—Semi, W—Weekly

TABLE 8. DATABASES FOR SPECIFIC INDUSTRIES

Name of Database	Vendor*	Dates Covered	No. of Records	Subject Emphasis
AGRIBUSINESS USA	D	1985-	40,000	Agriculture
BIOBUSINESS	D	1985-	64,966	Biological, biomedical industries
BIOCOMMERCE ABSTRACTS	D	1981-	70,000	Biotechnology
CHEMICAL BUSINESS NEWSBASE	D,I	1984-	55,750	International chemical business
CHEMICAL INDUSTRY NOTES	D,O	1974-	630,700	Chemical processing
COFFEELINE	D	1973-	16,500	Coffee
COMPUTER DATABASE	D	1983-	192,000	Computers
FOODS ADLIBRA	D	1974-	124,000	Food
HEALTH PLANNING AND ADMINISTRATION	D,B	1975-	358,700	Health care
P/E NEWS	D,O	1975-	407,000	Petroleum, energy
PHARMACEUTICAL NEWS INDEX	D	1974-	189,000	Pharmaceuticals
PTS AEROSPACE/ DEFENSE MARKETS & TECHNOLOGY	D	1982-	123,000	Aerospace/defense
WORLD TEXTILES	D	1970-	141,900	Textiles

*D—Dialog, B—BRS, I—InfoLine, O—Orbit, W—Wilsonline

Access to U.S. Government Information: Recommended Bibliographies, Indexes, and Catalogs

by Melody S. Kelly and Frank Lee

As a collective body of departments, agencies, offices, printing offices, etc., the U.S. government is almost certainly the most prolific disseminator of printed publications in the world. While numerous individual federal agencies publish, print, and distribute their own publications, two major government bodies print, warehouse, and distribute government publications: the U.S. Government Printing Office and the National Technical Information Service.

VOLUME OF PUBLICATION

The Government Printing Office (GPO) is the official printing organ of the U.S. government. During the fiscal year 1987, it sent 22.7 million copies of the 58,143 paper titles available for free distribution to the federal depository libraries. That same year 13.1 million copies (58% of the titles) were distributed in microfiche rather than in paper. Many of these same publications were also available for sale through the GPO sales branch. The publications ranged from the annual *Franchise Opportunities Handbook* (C61.31; 98; S/N 003–009–00528–1) to the essential periodical, *Commerce Business Daily* (C1.76; yr./no.; S/N 703–013–00000–7) to the informative Congressional hearing, *Impact of Tax Reform on Small Business* (Y4.Sml:T19/11.)

Melody S. Kelly is Head of Government Documents, North Texas State University, Denton, TX. Frank Lee is Library Director, Jones-Day, Dallas, TX.
Editor's Note: The original version of this essay in the first edition of *The Basic Business Library* was written by Roberta A. Scull, librarian, Louisiana State University, Baton Rouge.

The National Technical Information Service (NTIS), still an agency of the Department of Commerce as of August 1988, is probably the world's largest collector and distributor of government-sponsored research-and-development reports. NTIS has well over one million titles on file and adds approximately 70,000 reports each year. Titles in this collection have been available for purchase in paper or microfiche. The future role of NTIS as a government agency is presently under review. The Office of Management and Budget has decided that the Department of Commerce should plan to allow greater private-sector involvement in NTIS operations, with the government retaining control over overall policy direction. How this will affect the cost and availability of the NTIS backfile of research reports, and the international agreements governing the foreign documents in its collection is still uncertain at this writing (August 1988).

It is estimated that 80,000 government publications escape the bibliographic control of both the GPO and the NTIS each year. However, millions of publications, both current and retrospective, are included in these programs. Easily accessible through standard bibliographic tools, a selected number are described below.

BIBLIOGRAPHIC TOOLS (COMMERCIAL)

Government regulations require that many types of social, demographic, business, regulatory, trade, technical, and statistical information be gathered. It is not surprising, therefore, that the government generates studies and statistics on government operations as well as on consumer finances; banks and other financial institutions; construction and housing; various price and wage indexes; foreign and domestic trade; management, labor, and personnel problems; manufacturers, retailers, wholesalers, and services; the environment and energy, etc. Some of the government's publishing efforts may seem frivolous, but there is much of value. It is imperative that one survey the government literature when preparing economic and statistical analyses for forecasts, developing product designs or marketing reports, making management decisions, surveying business opportunities, conducting technical evaluations, writing grant proposals, or engaging in countless other business activities. Users of business information know that if the public or business is considering a problem, the government is probably studying it, or has already studied it.

In recognition of the value of government information, numerous commercial bibliographic tools have been developed. Listed below are some of the best and most valuable of those that are available.

Chen, Morris L., and Robert C. Berring. *How to Find the Law*. 8th ed. St. Paul, MN: West Publishing Co., 1983. $8.95; Jacobstein, Myron, and Roy Mersky. *Fundamentals of Legal Research*. 3rd ed. Mineola, NY: Foundation Press, 1986. $22.95.

Chen and Morris's and Jacobstein and Mersky's books are two texts invaluable for legal research in the business environment. Both can serve as teaching and student guides.

Delphos, William A., ed. *Washington's Best Kept Secrets: A U.S. Government Guide to International Business.* New York: John Wiley, 1983. $40.85.

Elias, Stephen. *Legal Research.* 2nd ed. Berkeley: Nolo Press, 1986. $14.95.
A popular entry into legal literature is offered by Elias.

Garner, Diane L., and Diane H. Smith. *The Complete Guide to Citing Government Documents: A Manual for Writers and Librarians.* Bethesda, MD: Congressional Information Service, 1984. $9.95.
The Government Documents Round Table of the American Library Association has developed this standard citation manual for government materials.

Government Information Quarterly: An International Journal of Resources, Services, Policies and Practice. Peter Hernon, ed. Greenwich, CT: JAI Press, 1984–. $30, individuals; $45, institutions; *Government Publications Review: An International Journal of Issues and Information Resources.* Steven Zink, ed. New York: Pergamon Press, 1974–. $175.
These two major journals should be used to stay abreast of the currents in government information flow and publishing.

Hoel, Arline Alchian, et al. *Economics Sourcebook of Government Statistics.* Lexington, MA: Lexington Books, 1983. $23.

Lesko, Matthew. *Information U.S.A.* Rev. ed. New York: Penguin, 1986. $22.95 (paper).
An informational rather than bibliographical tool, Lesko's emphasis is on where to find help in specific situations, such as starting a business or locating government bookstores or vendors.

Morehead, Joseph. *Introduction to the United States Public Documents.* 3rd ed. Littleton, CO: Libraries Unlimited, 1983. $28.50/$19.50.
Morehead is the standard textbook in the field of federal documents. Virtually all library-related courses use it. It should be on every reference librarian's shelf.

Robinson, Judith Schiek. *Subject Guide to U.S. Government Reference Sources.* Littleton, CO: Libraries Unlimited, 1985. $40.
Robinson's selective guide to significant government resources on specific subjects, such as economics and business, is the first revision of Sally Wynkoop's 1972 edition.

———. *Tapping the Government Grapevine: The User-Friendly Guide to U.S. Government Information Sources.* Phoenix, AZ: Oryx Press, 1988. $36/$24.40.
Robinson is a recent excellent alternative to Morehead, which includes valuable information on print sources, microforms, databases, AV materials, and clearinghouses.

Schwarzkopf, LeRoy C., comp. *Government Reference Books 84/85: A Biennial Guide to U.S. Government Publications.* 9th ed. Littleton, CO: Libraries Unlimited, 1986. $47.50.

Schwarzkopf may know more about federal publications over the past 30 years than any living librarian. The focus is on books in four broad subject areas: general library resources, social sciences, science and technology, and humanities. Serials are included in a new title, *Government Reference Serials.* Englewood, CO: Libraries Unlimited, 1988. $45.

————. *Guide to Popular Government Publications.* Littleton, CO: Libraries Unlimited, 1986. $29.50.

If one basic guide to core materials published by the U.S. government is to be selected, this is it. Subjects are broken down, from citizenship to social security, with the federal sources noted.

Sears, Jean L., and Marilyn K. Moody. *Using Government Publications, Volume 1: Using Government Publications, Volume 2: Finding Statistics and Using Special Techniques.* Phoenix, AZ: Oryx Press, 1986. *Searching by Subjects and Agencies, Finding Statistics and Using Special Techniques.* Phoenix, AZ: Oryx Press, 1985; 1986. $74 each.

This 1986 ALA Reference Books of the Year selection serves as a basic reference guide to the types of materials available and how to use them. More importantly, it suggests specific strategies for locating different types of information.

INDEXES (COMMERCIAL)

A number of commercial indexes also provide access to U.S. government publications. The most outstanding are the *American Statistics Index* (ASI), the *Congressional Information Service Index* (CIS), the *Index to United States Government Periodicals*, and the *CIS Federal Register Index.*

American Statistics Index: Comprehensive Guide and Index to the Statistical Publications of the United States Government. Washington, DC: Congressional Information Service, 1975–. Monthly with quarterly annual, and quinquennial cumulative indexes. $810, small public libraries; $2,180, large academic libraries.

American Statistics Index first became available in 1975. The first volume includes retrospective statistical sources from 1960 through 1974. Subsequent volumes cover materials released during successive one-year periods. Virtually every statistic available to the public through the depository library program, the sales program, or directly from the federal agencies, in monographic or serial report, is referenced. Accompanying the bibliographic citation for each document is a lengthy abstract that details the statistics covered, allowing the researcher to assess the potential usefulness of the material. All publications mentioned are available in printed or microfiche formats from the GPO or *ASI*. In addition to the standard subject and title indexes, *ASI* provides indexes arranged by categories, including geographic area and demographic characteristics. These additional access points help to make this service the most important bibliographic source for federally produced statistical information. DIALOG offers this index online as File 102.

CIS Annual. Washington, DC: Congressional Information Service, 1970–. Monthly, with quarterly, annual, and quinquennial cumulative indexes. $825, small public libraries; $3,250, large academic libraries.

Congressional hearings, prints, documents, reports, public laws, and the reports of special commissions and committees are indexed by subject, personal name, individual business, title, and legislative number. Frequently, congressional publications contain unique and valuable statistics and studies on business or economic topics. These would be inaccessible without this index/abstracting service. All materials indexed are sold on microfiche by CIS and are also available from the GPO or the respective congressional committee.

CIS Federal Register Index. Bethesda, MD: Congressional Information Service, Inc. 1984–. Weekly, with quarterly and semiannual cumulations. $400.

Federal regulatory agencies, through their rules, proposed rules, regulations, and notices, affect every aspect of professional and personal lives. The activities of all federal regulatory agencies must be published in the daily *Federal Register*. In this excellent index, CIS has produced a tool that far surpasses the government's own index to the *Federal Register*. Access is provided by subject, geographic area, federal agency names and programs, names of companies, organizations, individuals, and popular names of legislation. Special indexes allow access by *Code of Federal Regulation* section numbers, agency docket numbers, and a calendar of effective dates with comment deadlines.

Index to United States Government Periodicals. Chicago: Infordata International, 1970–. Quarterly with annual cumulations. $408.

Almost 200 of the most popular government periodicals are indexed here, in an arrangement similar to that of the *Reader's Guide to Periodical Literature*. Although some of the periodicals covered are also indexed in *Business Periodicals Index*, the majority of titles are not indexed elsewhere. The subject coverage is comprehensive.

In addition to the indexes/bibliographies noted above, one should also be aware of a new set of tools available in the past few years, the microfilm or CD-ROM catalogs based on the Government Printing Office MARC cataloging records for the *Monthly Catalog of U.S. Government Publications.* Two of these COM catalogs are the Brodart *Federal Publications Catalog* and the Autographics *Government Documents Catalog Service.* Each differs in type of equipment, in arrangement of the bibliographic entries, and in advantages and disadvantages for the user. The principal advantage of both these COM catalogs over the printed *Monthly Catalog* is their coverage of a far greater number of years indexed for each search point. The greater availability of CD-ROM products in the future will increase the advantage of these commercial products over the *Monthly Catalog.*

SELECTED INDEXES AND CATALOGS (GOVERNMENT)

The government issues many recurring bibliographic tools that are essential for locating current government and nongovernment publications, articles, and additional bibliographies of interest to the business and technical communities. Each of the indexes listed here is currently available for sale from the Superintendent of Documents, Government Printing Office, Washington, DC 20402. The citations include the S/N (stock number) and the SuDoc (Superintendent of Documents) classification number to assist the user in either placing an order or using one of the many federal depository library collections. Prices given are for 1986/87.

Government Periodicals and Subscription Services, Price List 36. Washington, DC: GPO. Quarterly. Free. SuDoc# GP3.9:36/no.

Available upon request, this quarterly publication provides current ordering information for approximately 500 periodicals and loose-leaf and irregular subscription services of the federal agencies. Stock number, price, and SuDoc number are included for each title. All titles are available for selection by federal depository libraries.

Government Reports Announcements and Index. Springfield, VA: National Technical Information Service. 1975–. Biweekly with annual indexes. $398 per year from the agency. SuDoc# C51.9/3:vol./no.

Government Reports Announcements and Index (*GRA&I*) and its earlier titles provide access to the technical report literature of projects that were funded or performed by government agencies. Although originally intended to index only scientific and technical literature, *GRA&I* now includes reports from the humanities and social science fields. Materials included in this index are generally not indexed by the *Monthly Catalog* and are generally not available for selection by the federal depository libraries. All materials indexed remain available for sale upon request. International as well as U.S. studies are included in the NTIS files under treaty agreements with a variety of foreign countries. All subject fields are covered, including business topics and problem solving information for state and local governments. Over 70,000 reports are added each year. DIALOG offers this index online as File 6, covering 1964 to the present.

GPO Sales Publications Reference File (microfiche ed.) Washington, DC: GPO. Six issues each year with monthly supplements. $100 per year. S/N 721–002–00000–4; SuDoc# GP3.22/2:date.

Each issue of the file supersedes the previous one and contains more than 16,000 books, maps, posters, and periodicals. Indexes are provided by subject, agency, S/N, title, and SuDoc and report numbers. All publications listed are available for sale and were available for selection by federal depository libraries. DIALOG offers this index online as File 166.

Monthly Catalog of U.S. Government Publications. Washington, DC: GPO, 1895–. Monthly with semiannual, annual, and quinquennial cumulative indexes. $166. S/N 721–014–00000–2; SuDoc# GP3.8: date.

Prepared since July 1976 from machine-readable cataloging (MARC) records, this is the primary index for documents available to libraries and the general public. Included are publications sold by the Superintendent of Documents, those only available for official use, and those available for selection by federal depository libraries. DIALOG offers this index online as File 66, which covers the years 1976 to the present.

U.S. Government Books. Washington, DC: GPO, 1982–. Quarterly. Available upon request. SuDoc# GP3.17/5:vol./no.

An illustrated mail-order catalog representing a cross-section of new and popular publications available for sale from the GPO, *U.S. Government Books* covers a wide range of subject areas. All of the publications covered are also listed in the *GPO Sales Publication Reference File.* All subject areas are included.

In addition to the general indexes noted above, index/abstracts for special fields are also available. *Energy Research Abstracts* (S/N 761–005–00000–6) SuDoc# E1.17:vol./no. and *Scientific and Technical Aerospace Reports, An Abstract Journal* (S/N 733–003–00000–6) SuDoc# NAS1.9/4:vol./no. are two examples. Many of these are available through *Government Periodicals and Subscription Services, Price List 36.*

Special catalogs from various federal agencies are also available, including the items listed below.

Census Catalog and Guide: 1987. Washington, DC: GPO, 1947–. Currently an annual publication. $21. (S/N 003–024–06637–8) SuDoc# C3.163/3:date.

Published by the Bureau of the Census with various titles, frequencies, and SuDoc numbers, and covering 1790 through the current year, this catalog serves as an excellent source of information for census publications. Each abstract includes the subject, time period covered, geographic area, frequency, S/N, SuDoc number, length, format, and price. Hundreds of products are listed in each issue. Paper, microfiche, and data files are a few of the many formats available. To keep up-to-date throughout the year, the Bureau offers a newsletter, *Monthly Product Announcement* (available free upon request; SuDoc# C3.163/7:date/no.).

Directory of Computer Software. Springfield, VA: NTIS, 1987. PB87–143236; $48. Available from NTIS. SuDoc# C51.11/2:date.

Subject-arranged abstracts for 1,300 machine-readable computer programs available for purchase from more than 100 federal agencies or their contractors are included here.

Directory of Computerized Data Files. Springfield, VA: NTIS, 1987. PB87–181574. $48. Available from NTIS. SuDoc# C51.11/2–2:date.

A companion to the computer software directory above, this offers subject-arranged abstracts of more than 1,000 data files available for public purchase from 50 agencies.

Directory of Federal and State Business Assistance. Springfield, VA: NTIS, 1986-1987. PB86–100344/CAU. $19. SuDoc# C51.19/2:date.

More than 180 federal agencies and 400 state programs are included in this edition, planned to be updated in late 1988.

Directory of Federal Laboratory and Technology Resources. Springfield, VA: NTIS, 1988–89. PB88–100011/CALL. $36. Available from NTIS. SuDoc# C51.19:L11.

This directory is designed to alert private industries to the hundreds of federal facilities available to assist them with their research needs in both the expertise and equipment areas. Arranged by subject, each abstract describes the facility or service and lists a contact person.

Index to Information. Washington, DC: GPO, [1980-]. Available upon request from the agency. SuDoc# PM1.44:date.

Publications from the Office of Personnel Management available under the Freedom of Information Act, as well as other publications of general interest, are included in this catalog. Topics covered generally relate to management and employee issues. Ordering information is included.

Media Resource Catalog. Washington, DC: National Audiovisual Center. [Annual.] Available upon request from the agency. SuDoc# AE1.110:14:986.

This National Audiovisual Center catalog features more than 2,700 videotapes, films, and multimedia lists on a variety of topics, many with business applications for beginning or advanced personnel. The center serves as a clearinghouse for federal agency media products. Ordering information is included. The latest edition is 1986.

Other catalogs that may be helpful to those interested in U.S. government information are easily identified through the *Monthly Catalog,* the *GPO Sales Publication Reference File,* and *Government Periodicals and Subscriptions Services, Price List 36.*

Access to U.S. Government Information: Selected Federal Documents on Business Topics

by Melody S. Kelly and Frank Lee

As pointed out in the preceding essay, government information for and about business is abundant. Knowledge and use of the indexes, bibliographies, and catalogs included in that essay can open the door to public resources to which all citizens are entitled. This essay provides a selected list of recommended federal documents for a business collection. It is divided into four main subject oriented sections: Statistics, Domestic Business, International Business, and Law. Prices and S/N listed are for paper copies of each document and are taken from the April 21, 1988, *GPO Sales Publications Reference File* and *Government Periodicals and Subscription Services, Price List 36*, Spring 1988.

STATISTICS (HANDBOOKS)

County and City Data Book, 1983. Bureau of the Census. Washington, DC: GPO, 1983. 697 pp. $24. S/N 003–024–05833–2; SuDoc# C3.134/2:C83/2/983.

A variety of statistical information is presented, arranged by state, county, and city. Topics covered range from economic census data to demographics from the population census. A companion to the *Statistical Abstract* and the *State and Metropolitan Area Data Book, 1986*, each edition is abstracted in *American Statistics Index*.

Melody S. Kelly is head of government documents, North Texas State University, Denton, TX. Frank Lee is library director, Jones-Day, Dallas, TX.

County Business Patterns, 1985. Bureau of the Census. Washington, DC: GPO, 1987. 200 pp. Price and S/N varies with each title. SuDoc# C3.204/3-#:985.

Arranged by SIC number, each publication in this series gives employment, payroll, number, and size of establishments by detailed industry number within each county. The individual publications for each state and Puerto Rico, as well as a U.S. summary, are abstracted in *American Statistics Index.*

Economic Report of the President, 1988. Executive Office of the President. Washington, DC: GPO, 1987. 368 pp. $10. S/N 040-000-00523-4; SuDoc# Pr40.9:988.

This annual is a statement of presidential domestic policy, together with supporting statistical information from the Council of Economic Advisors. Each edition is abstracted in *American Statistics Index.*

Handbook of Cyclical Indicators, 1984: A Supplement to the Business Conditions Digest. Bureau of Economic Analysis. Washington, DC: GPO, 1984. 195 pp. $5.50. S/N 003-010-01027-5; SuDoc# C59.9/3:In2/984.

A compilation of historical tables showing 300 economic time series from the monthly *Business Conditions Digest,* this handbook is an essential one-volume reference tool.

Handbook of Economic Statistics, 1986. National Foreign Assessment Center. Washington, DC: GPO, 1986. 242 pp. $19. S/N 041-015-00165-5; SuDoc# PrEx3.10/7:CPAS-10002.

Statistics from the Central Intelligence Agency on all communist countries and selected noncommunist countries are arranged in easy-to-use tables for each country.

Handbook of Labor Statistics. Bureau of Labor Statistics. Washington, DC: GPO, 1985. 461 pp. $16. S/N 029-001-02846-6; SuDoc# L2.3/5:985.

The *Handbook of Labor Statistics* is a compilation of major statistical series from the Bureau of Labor Statistics on the labor force and employment in the U.S. The *Handbook* is abstracted in *American Statistics Index.*

Historical Statistics of the United States, Colonial Times to 1970. Bureau of the Census. Washington, DC: GPO, 1975. 2 vols., 1,060 pp. $35.00 per set. S/N 003-024-00120-9; SuDoc# C3.134/2:H62/789-970/pt.1,2.

Historical Statistics presents historical tables containing information parallel to that found in the annual *Statistical Abstract.* Each subject section has an introductory chapter explaining statistical methodology for each table. Each part is abstracted in *American Statistics Index.*

Local Area Personal Income, 1979-84. Bureau of Economic Analysis. Washington, DC: GPO, 1986. In 9 vols. Example: *Southwest Region,* $7. S/N 003-010-00171-2; SuDoc# C59.18:979-84/v.7.

This series present the Bureau's estimates of total and per capita personal income by type and major industry with reference to region and county. Each volume is abstracted in *American Statistics Index.*

State and Metropolitan Area Data Book, 1986. Bureau of the Census. Washington, DC: GPO, 1986. 751 pp. $28. S/N 003–024–0633–4; SuDoc# C3.134/5:986.

This *Data Book* presents a variety of information on states, metro areas, and central cities in the U.S. Both economic and demographic data are covered. A companion to the *Statistical Abstract* and the *County and City Data Book*, each edition is abstracted in *American Statistics Index.*

Statistical Abstract of the United States, 1988. Bureau of the Census. Washington, DC: GPO, 1988. 973 pp. $25. S/N 003–024–06707–2; SuDoc# C3.124:987.

Hundreds of subjects are represented in this essential one-volume annual abstract of statistical information covering both the United States and foreign countries. If only one statistical handbook can be purchased, this should be the one. Each edition is abstracted in *American Statistics Index.*

Statistics of Income—Corporation Income Tax Return, 1984. Internal Revenue Service. Washington, DC: GPO, 1987. 168 pp. $8.50. S/N 048–004–02256–7; SuDoc# T22.35/5:984.

An annual publication presenting data by industry, and giving assets, liabilities, etc. by size of company, *Statistics of Income* includes data not covered in other government publications. Each edition is abstracted in *American Statistics Index.*

STATISTICS (PERIODICALS)

Business Conditions Digest. Bureau of Economic Analysis. Washington, DC: GPO. 1979–. Monthly. $44 per year. S/N 703–012–00000–1; SuDoc# C59.9:

Business Conditions Digest regularly covers 500 economic indicators in an easy-to-use form for analysis. Included in each issue are the national income model and the leading indicators, as well as other basic economic data. Each issue is abstracted in *American Statistics Index.*

CPI Detailed Report. Bureau of Labor Statistics. Washington, DC: GPO, 1974–. Monthly. $16 per year. S/N 729–002–00000–3; SuDoc# L2.38/3:date/no.

CPI charts statistics on consumer prices for all urban consumers and wage earners and is often cited as the basis for data on the inflation rate. Each table is abstracted in *American Statistics Index.*

Current Business Report Series. Bureau of the Census. Washington, DC: GPO, 19–. Monthly; Annual. S/N and price vary for each series. SuDoc# varies for each series. (See *Government Periodicals and Subscription Services, Price List 36* for specific information.)

This series of reports on retail and wholesale business is available in monthly and annual publications and provides national trade figures. Each series is abstracted in *American Statistics Index.*

Current Industrial Reports Series. Bureau of the Census. Washington, DC: GPO, 19–. Monthly; Quarterly; Annual. S/N and price vary for each series. SuDoc# C3.158: (See *Government Periodicals and Subscriptions Services, Price List 36* for specific information.)

A series of 36 individual reports on U.S. industries, each issue has statistics on total shipments, production, and consumption based on surveys of manufacturers. Each series is abstracted in *American Statistics Index.*

Economic Indicators. U.S. Congress. Joint Economic Committee. Washington, DC: 1948–. Monthly. S/N 752–004–00000–5. $27 per year. SuDoc# Y4.Ec7:Ec7/date/no.

Each issue of *Economic Indicators* gives a variety of economic information covering prices, wages, CPI, production, business activity, purchasing power, credit, money, and federal financial status. The tables are abstracted in *American Statistics Index.*

Employment and Earnings. Bureau of Labor Statistics. Washington, DC: GPO, 1969–. Monthly with annual supplement. $22 per year. S/N 729–004–00000–6; SuDoc# L2.41/2: date/no.

Employment and Earnings provides current data on employment hours and earnings for U.S. states and 200 local areas. The annual supplement issue contains revised data, with a survey of business establishment statistics. The tables are abstracted in *American Statistics Index.*

Producer Price Indexes. Bureau of Labor Statistics. Washington, DC: GPO, 1985–. Monthly with annual supplement. $21 per year. S/N 729–009–00000–8; SuDoc# L2.61:date/no.

Each issue of *Producer Price Indexes* reports on price movements at the primary market level. The tables are abstracted in *American Statistics Index.*

Quarterly Financial Report of Manufacturers, Mining, and Trade Corporations. Bureau of the Census. Washington, DC: GPO, 1979–. Quarterly. $20 per year. S/N 703–083–00000–5; SuDoc# C3.267:date/no.

The *Quarterly* presents "balance sheet" information showing financial characteristics and operating results for categories of U.S. manufacturing corporations by industry. Each issue covers the current quarter as well as the four previous quarters and is abstracted in *American Statistics Index.*

Treasury Bulletin. Treasury Department. Washington, DC: GPO, 1945–. Quarterly. $20 per year. S/N 748–007–00000–8; SuDoc# T1.3:date/no.

A synopsis of Treasury Department activities, the *Bulletin* covers financial operations, budget receipts, expenditures, debt, cash transactions, etc. of the U.S. government. Rates of interest on "T-bills" is an example of the detailed information given. The *Bulletin* is abstracted in *American Statistics Index.*

DOMESTIC BUSINESS (HANDBOOKS, DIRECTORIES, ETC.)

Catalog of Federal Domestic Assistance. Office of Management and Budget. Washington, DC: GPO, 1987. Loose-leaf with updates. 1,384 pp. $38. S/N 941–001–00000–9; SuDoc# PrEx2.20:986.

The only one-volume directory of all federal programs, projects, services, and activities offering assistance to individuals and groups, the listing gives all necessary information for applicants to determine which program meets their need, the amount of assistance offered, conditions of grant, and time and reporting requirements. This is essential for any collection.

Congressional Directory, 100th Congress, 1987/88. U.S. Congress. Washington, DC: 1987. $25. S/N 052–070–06241–0; SuDoc# Y4.P93/1:1/100.

The official directory of Congress provides biographical information on its members, committee memberships, and special listings of the official press corps, government agencies, foreign diplomatic corps, and many other groups associated with the activities of Congress. It is essential for any collection.

Domestic Mail Manual. Postal Service. Washington, DC: 1986. Looseleaf with updates. $46. S/N 939–002–00000–6; SuDoc# P1.12/11:986.

The *Manual* provides an official listing of postal regulations and information on rates, postage, classes of mail, and mailing requirements.

Franchise Index Profile, a Franchise Evaluation Process. Small Business Administration. Washington, DC: GPO, 1986. 59 pp. $2. S/N 045–000–00231–4; SuDoc# SBA1.12:35.

This Small Business Administration handbook gives basic information for individuals considering franchise investing.

Franchise Opportunities Handbook, 1988. International Trade Administration. Washington, DC: GPO, 1988. 303 pp. $16. S/N 003–009–00528–1; SuDoc# C61.31:988.

Now in its 21st edition, the *Franchise Opportunities Handbook* lists equal opportunity franchise companies and gives a brief description of each company with its franchise requirements.

Franchising in the Economy, 1986–88. International Trade Administration. Washington, DC: GPO, 1988. 102 pp. $4.75. S/N 003–009–00525–6; SuDoc# C61.31/2:986/88.

Results of the sixteenth annual survey of franchisors, representing 99 percent of business-format franchising sales and operations in the U.S., are reported.

General Information Concerning Patents. Patent and Trademark Office. Washington, DC: GPO, 1986. 45 pp. $2. S/N 003–004–00626–9; SuDoc# C21.26/2:986.

A brief introduction to patents and how to apply for them is presented in easy-to-understand language.

General Information Concerning Trademarks. Patent and Trademark Office. Washington, DC: GPO, 1986. 25 pp. $1.50. S/N 003–004–00625–1; SuDoc# C21.26:986.

Information on trademarks and how to apply for them is included in this short publication.

Government Depository Libraries: The Present Law Governing Designated Depository Libraries. U.S. Congress. Joint Committee on Printing. Washington, DC: GPO, 1984. 148 pp. Free from the agency. SuDoc# Y4.P93/1:D44/984.

The current law on the depository library system and the rules for participating libraries is included in this official directory of libraries receiving free government documents on deposit.

Handbook for Analyzing Jobs. Department of Labor. Washington, DC: GPO, 1986–. 351 pp. S/N 029–000–00131–6; SuDoc# L1.7/2:J57/6.

The Department of Labor offers an explanation of procedures used by the U.S. Employment Service to analyze jobs. This is especially useful for private industry concerned with recruitment, training, and personnel utilization.

Handbook of Job Analysis for Reasonable Accommodation. Office of Personnel Management. Washington, DC: GPO, 1984. 16 pp. $1. S/N 060–000–01304–0; SuDoc# PM1.28:720–B.

The job analysis process which can be used to plan and select procedures for accommodating disabled persons in specific job and work environments is discussed.

National Five Digit ZIP Code and Post Office Directory. U.S. Postal Service. Washington, DC: GPO, 1988. 2,480 pp. $13. S/N 039–000–00274–4; SuDoc# P1.10/8:988.

A complete information source on Postal Service operations and the five-digit ZIP codes, the directory has lists of ZIP codes arranged by state, city, and street. City information often includes a separate list of government offices, universities, hospitals, and military installations.

Small Business Management Series. Small Business Administration. Washington, DC: GPO. S/N, price, and length vary with each document. Generally priced at $5. SuDoc# SBA1.12:nos.

The Small Business Administration provides this series of 45 publications on basic management techniques. One example is "Employee Suggestion Systems for Small Companies."

Small Business Self-Instructional Booklet Series. Small Business Administration. Washington, DC: GPO. S/N, price, and length vary with each document. Generally priced at $5. SuDoc# SBA1.19:CT.

This series of 23 booklets covers basic aspects of business management. One example of a specific booklet topic is "Capital Planning."

Standard Industrial Code Manual, 1987. Office of Management and Budget. Washington, DC: NTIS, 1987. $24. S/N 041–001–00314–2; SuDoc# REX 2.6/2:In27/987.

This is the long-awaited new edition of the directory of classification code numbers assigned to U.S. industries and reflecting the composition and structure of the economy. The class system allows for aggregate data on industries to be collected and for comparisons to be made between companies by primary function and products. Divided into manufacturing, wholesale, retail, and service industries, this is the basic manual for classification of industries, used by most commercial business reference services.

Treasury Department Telephone Directory. Treasury Department. Washington, DC: GPO, 1988. Loose-leaf with updates. 146 pp. $6 per year. S/N 848-001-00004-0; SuDoc# T1.28:988-no.

A simple directory of agency offices and personnel, this is essential for business establishments wishing to contact an office within the Internal Revenue Service. Other government agency directories should be considered in addition to this one and the one immediately below.

U.S. Department of Commerce Telephone Directory. Department of Commerce. Washington, DC: 1987. 264 pp. $12. S/N 003-000-00649-2; SuDoc# C1.37:987.

A complete listing of the agencies within the department, this directory also includes field offices. For business, this is one of the essential telephone directories.

U.S. Government Manual, 1986/1987. Office of the Federal Register. Washington, DC: GPO, 1987. 900pp. $20. S/N 069-000-00006-1; SuDoc# AE2.108/2:1987/88.

The *U.S. Government Manual* is the directory of federal agencies, quasi-official agencies, international organizations, boards, commissions, and committees. Each agency listing includes a summary of its mission, history, and programs. Also included is a list of the principal officials, with phone numbers and mailing address.

U.S. Government Printing Office Style Manual. Government Printing Office. Washington, DC: GPO, 1984. 448 pp. $15. S/N 021-000-00121-0; SuDoc# GP1.23/4:St9/984.

The official source for the government's accepted rules for good language usage and custom in printing, the *Style Manual* includes rules on grammar and forms of address.

U.S. Government Purchasing and Sales Directory. Small Business Administration. Washington, DC: GPO, 1984. 199 pp. $5. S/N 004-000-00026-8; SuDoc# SBA1.13/3:984.

This directory is a major aid to small businesspeople wanting to sell to or buy from the U.S. government. It also includes information on services of the Small Business Administration.

U.S. Industrial Outlook, 1988. International Trade Administration. Washington, DC: GPO, 1988. 643 pp. $24. S/N 003-009-00522-1; SuDoc# C61.34:988.

The 28th edition of the *U.S. Industrial Outlook* gives the prospects for over 350 industries. Each chapter is arranged by SIC number and covers the economic assumptions, highlights of past years, and trends. Some specific companies are mentioned, but statistics are for each industry as a whole. This important business reference source is abstracted in *American Statistics Index.*

DOMESTIC BUSINESS (PERIODICALS)

Commerce Business Daily. Commerce Department [1978]- . Daily, Monday through Friday. $243 per year. S/N 703-013-00000-7; SuDoc# C1.76:date/month/day.
   A daily listing of government procurement, sales, and contract awards is contained in this important periodical. Each notice indicates closing dates for bidding or transacting business.

Federal Reserve Bulletin. Board of Governors of the Federal Reserve. Washington, DC: Federal Reserve Board of Governors. Monthly. $20 per year. Available from the agency. SuDoc# FR1.3:vol./no.
   The official journal of the Federal Reserve Board reports its policies and decisions. Also included in each issue are tables and articles on monetary movements, economic issues, and financial statistics of member banks. It is abstracted in *American Statistics Index* and indexed by *Business Periodicals Index.*

Monthly Labor Review. Bureau of Labor Statistics. Washington, DC: GPO, 1918-. Monthly. $16 per year. S/N 729-007-00000-5; SuDoc# L2.6:
   One of the best-known periodicals issuing from the government, this monthly includes articles on the labor force, wages, prices, productivity, economic policy, and employment issues. It is indexed by *Business Periodicals Index*, abstracted in *American Statistics Index*, and included in the *Index to U.S. Government Periodicals.*

Survey of Current Business. Bureau of Economic Analysis. Washington, DC: GPO. 1921-. Monthly. $46 per year (priority). S/N 703-036-00000-7; SuDoc# C59.11:
   The *Survey* is an excellent source of information on trends in industry, the business situation, economic outlook, and other economic issues. It is indexed in *Business Periodicals*, abstracted in *American Statistics Index*, and included in the *Index to U.S. Government Periodicals.*

INTERNATIONAL BUSINESS (HANDBOOKS, DIRECTORIES, ETC.)

Background Notes on Various Countries of the World. Department of State. Washington, DC: GPO. Loose-leaf. $14 per year. S/N 844-002-00000-9; SuDoc# S1.123:CT.
   Background Notes are individual reports published irregularly on many world countries. Each report covers land area, demographics, history, government, and the economy. Most reports average four to six pages.

Basic Guide to Exporting. International Trade Administration. Washington, DC: GPO, 1986. 158 pp. $8.50. S/N 003-009-00487-0; SuDoc# C61.8:Ex7/3/986.
   Export profitability is the focus of this title.

Commercial News USA Annual Directory. International Trade Administration. Washington, DC: International Trade Administration, 1986. 222 pp. For copies inquire Room H-2106, Export Promotion Services, ITA, Washington, DC 20230. SuDoc# C61.10/2:985.

Arranged by broad product areas, this directory lists U.S. companies in a way that allows interested foreign importers to make contact with potential suppliers.

Country Studies. Department of the Army. Washington, DC: GPO. S/N and prices vary for each country. SuDoc# D101.22:550/nos.

The Area Handbook series is an excellent basic reference source prepared at the American University. Individual monographs are published on over 80 countries, with chapters discussing geography, history, culture, politics, economics, etc. The specific studies are listed in the *GPO Sales Publication Reference File.*

Export Trading Company Guidebook. International Trade Administration. Washington, DC: GPO, 1987. 144 pp. $8. S/N 003-009-00523-0; SuDoc# C61.8:Ex7/4.

A new edition, this guidebook is designed to assist those considering starting an exporting business or expanding their current exporting activities through an export trading company.

Foreign Business Practices Materials on Practical Aspects of Exporting, International Licensing, and Investing. International Trade Administration. Washington, DC: GPO, 1985. 96 pp. $3.50. S/N 003-009-00460-8; SuDoc# C61.2:P88/985.

Practical information on foreign agents, distributors, treaties, foreign licensing, and joint ventures in foreign countries are covered by this International Trade Administration handbook.

Foreign Consular Offices in the U.S., November, 1987. Department of State. Washington, DC: GPO, 1987. 93 pp. $4.50. S/N 044-000-02210-9; SuDoc# S1.69/2:987-2.

The complete official list of foreign consular offices in the U.S., with their jurisdictions and recognized consular officers, is included in this directory.

Foreign Economic Trends. International Trade Administration. Washington, DC: GPO. Irregular. $49 per year. S/N 803-006-00000-8; SuDoc# C61.11:yr/no.

This series includes individual analyses on various countries, providing economic data for businesses considering investments abroad. The *FET* is a companion to the *Overseas Business Reports.* It is abstracted in *American Statistics Index.*

International Mail Manual. U.S. Postal Service. Washington, DC: GPO. Irregular, loose-leaf. $14 per year. S/N 939-005-00000-5; SuDoc# P1.10/5:date.

The Postal Service has provided this official listing of regulations and information on postal rates, class of mail, and mailing inquiries for international destinations.

Key Officers of Foreign Service Posts, A Guide for Business Representatives. Department of State. Washington, DC: GPO, 1986. $5. S/N 744–006–00000–7; SuDoc# S1.40/5:date.

This State Department document is the complete directory of missions, consulates general, and consulates, arranged by country. It includes a list of officers for each, including commercial officers when present.

Metric Laws and Practices in International Trade. Washington, DC: GPO, 1982. 113 pp. $4.75. S/N 003–009–00353–9; SuDoc# C1.8/3:M56.

Basic information for exporters on international requirements for imported products.

Official U.S. Sources of Export Assistance for Small Business. International Trade Administration. Washington, DC: GPO, 1985. 17 pp. $1. S/N 003–009–00470–5; SuDoc# C61.2:Of2.

Prepared for small- to medium-sized businesses that may export, this pamphlet describes the programs of eight agencies that can offer assistance.

Overseas Business Reports. International Trade Administration. Washington, DC: GPO. Irregular. $14 per year. S/N 803–007–00000–4; SuDoc# C61.12:yr./no.

Information on the economic outlook trends, trade regulations, and business activities in various countries is included in this companion series to the *Foreign Economic Trends*. Abstracts are included in *American Statistics Index*.

Small Business Incubator: Lessons Learned in Europe. Small Business Administration. Washington, DC: GPO, 1984. 39 pp. $2.25. S/N 045–000–00222–5; SuDoc# SBA1.2:Sm1/14.

How small businesses are supported in Europe is discussed in this aid for U.S. small businesses making trade connections with their European counterparts.

INTERNATIONAL BUSINESS (PERIODICALS)

Business America: The Magazine of International Trade. International Trade Administration. Washington, DC: GPO, 1978–. Biweekly. $40 per year. S/N 703–011–00000–4; SuDoc# C61.18:vol.

Designed to help American exporters penetrate foreign markets, *Business America* gives timely information on opportunities for trade, with hints on doing business in a particular country. Current U.S. trade policy and economic reports from the Foreign Commercial Service are typical topics covered. It is abstracted in *American Statistics Index*.

LEGAL RESOURCES

Government materials on the law are taking on increasing importance with the rise in litigation and bankruptcies, as well as general public interest. Legal resources from the government sit side by side with commercial versions and are generally referred to as the "official" text.

Code of Federal Regulations. Office of the Federal Register. Washington, DC: GPO, 1986/87. Annual. $595 per year. S/N 869-004-00000-6; SuDoc# AE2.106:
The *CFR* is the codification of the general and permanent rules and regulations published in the *Federal Register* by the executive agencies and departments of the U.S. government. The 50 titles are divided by subject areas and are sold individually or as a set.

Code of Federal Regulations, LSA, List of CFR Sections Affected. Washington, DC: GPO, 1987. Monthly. $30. S/N 769-001-00000-9; SuDoc# AE2.106/2.
The *LSA* is a cross-reference guide between the changes and updates published in the *Federal Register* and the various titles of the annual *Code of Federal Regulations.*

Federal Register. Office of the Federal Register. Washington, DC: GPO, 1936-. Daily. $340 per year. S/N 769-004-00000-9; SuDoc# GS4.107: and AE2.106:
This official listing of new and proposed government rules, regulations, and executive orders having legal effect also includes announcements and the closing dates for public comment and committee meetings.

How Our Laws Are Made. U.S. Congress. Washington, DC: 1986. 77 pp. $2.50. S/N 052-071-00697-4; SuDoc# Y1.1/7:99-158.
Basic information on the federal lawmaking process from the legislative proposal through enactment is provided in this handy paperback.

Public Laws. National Archives and Records Administration. Washington, DC: GPO. Irregular. $104 each session. S/N 869-006-00000-9; SuDoc# AE2.110:Cong.-no.
Individual slip laws are printed as soon as possible after the law is enacted and later cumulated into the *U.S. Statutes at Large* (noted above).

Tariff Schedules of the U.S., 1987. International Trade Commission. Washington, DC: GPO, 1987. Loose-leaf subscription, $56. S/N 949-004-00000-7; SuDoc# ITC1.10:987.
This loose-leaf treatment includes the tariff schedules of the United States, along with statistical information. Duties on goods to be imported into the U.S. are also given.

Treaties in Force. Department of State. Washington, DC: GPO, 1987. Annual. $16. S/N 044-000-02183-8; SuDoc# S9.14:987.
Treaties reviewed in this important tool include bilateral and multilateral agreements relating to the United States and in effect as of January 1986.

U.S. Code. U.S. Congress. Washington, DC: GPO, 1982 ed., 25 vols. with annual supplements. S/N and price vary. SuDoc# Y1.2/5:982/vol.
The 1982 edition of the *U.S. Code* provides the laws of the United States in force January 14, 1983. It is arranged in 50 titles, by broad subject areas. Indexes are included.

U.S. Reports. U.S. Supreme Court. Washington, DC: GPO, 1790-. S/N and price vary, $22.00-30.00. SuDoc# Ju6.8:vol.

U.S. Reports contains the official text of U.S. Supreme Court cases. Three major commercial alternatives exist that supplement the "official" source: The *Supreme Court Reporter* (West Publishing Co.), *U.S. Law Week* (Bureau of National Affairs), and the *United States Supreme Court Reports, Lawyers' Edition* (Lawyers Cooperative Publishing Co.).

U.S. Statutes at Large. National Archives and Records Administration. Washington, DC: GPO. 94 vols. S/N and price vary. SuDoc# GS4.111:vol. and AE2.111:vol.
The official text of United States statutes is provided here, along with legislative history notes. The number scheme is by the session of Congress, e.g., 96-113 (96th session, p. 113).

DATABASES

The growing importance of online databases cannot be overstated. A competitive edge in many sectors depends on the factor of currentness provided by databases. New files become available monthly through a multiplicity of vendors such as DIALOG, Mead Data Central (Lexis/Nexus), Westlaw, and BRS. Many files are available directly. The legal field is a good example of one in which a growing percentage of materials required on a day-to-day basis are available in paper, often loose-leaf, as well as online. Most of the major indexes mentioned in the two essays on government resources in this volume are available online, including CIS services such as *American Statistics Index* and the federal *Government Reports Announcements and Index.* The option of downloading improves the prospect of this format. The ability to identify resources that are available in this format is critical. Numerous federal government guides have been referred to previously. In addition, two commercial sources are available:

Computer-Readable Databases: A Directory and Data Sourcebook. Martha E. Williams, ed. New York: Elsevier Science Publishing, Inc., 1988. 4th ed. 2 vols. $139 each.

Directory of Online Databases. New York: Elsevier Science Publishing Inc., 1988. $95.

Both of these services are also available online.

Business Periodicals: A Core Collection for the Smaller Business Library

by Louise S. Sherby and Jane Winland

The premise behind compiling this second edition of a core list of periodicals for the smaller business library remains the same as it was in the first edition. The intention is to provide a list that covers the basic areas of business—general business, economics, management, accounting, finance, and marketing—from which titles can be selected to suit the specific needs of a particular library and its clientele. Journals remain crucial to the subject of business, because patrons will always need the most current information available for the purposes of research, investment, starting new businesses, and career advancement.

Business as a subject has changed somewhat since the first edition of this list appeared. Business has become more international in scope, as consumers and investors begin to relate social and political issues to the corporate arena, and complex corporate activity is characterized by the merger and/or acquisition of one company by another. Other important factors include the emergence of cross-disciplinary business interests (e.g., health and business economics) and the new practice of applying management theory to not-for-profit (e.g., museums, operas, etc.) and public-sector organizations (e.g., hospitals, human-services agencies). The net result is that librarians purchasing journals must even more carefully assess the needs of their particular user communities and select titles accordingly.

The first edition of this list included 49 titles; this edition's recommendations total 67, with two titles from the previous list deleted and 20 new titles added. Each title included is indexed in one or more of the following: *Business Periodicals Index, Public Affairs Information Service Bulletin* (PAIS), and the database ABI/INFORM. The titles

Louise S. Sherby is deputy head for administration, Butler Reference Department, Columbia University Libraries, New York, NY. Jane Winland is acting assistant director, Social Sciences Division, Columbia University Libraries, New York, NY.

selected were checked against the serials holdings of the Columbia University Business Library, the serials list of the Bryant College library (Rhode Island), and the second edition of *Business Information Sources*, by Lorna M. Daniells (2nd ed. Berkeley: University of California Press, 1985). Price (institutional price is noted where appropriate) and publishing information were verified in the most recent issue of the title available at Columbia's Business Library. The total cost for the 67 titles at current subscription rates is $3,506.10—more than double the cost of the 1983 list. Inflation, the added titles, and the added emphasis on foreign titles account for much of the increase in total cost.

Excluded from the list are trade journals relating to specific industries (e.g., computers), regional or city business journals (e.g., *Crain's New York Business*), and journals relating to business in a particular country or continent (e.g., *China Business Review, African Business*). All of these areas provide a rich field for selection and should be reviewed by a small library to find what best meets the needs of its particular user community.

As noted in the essay by Janice Sieburth in this book (pp. 101–142), access to business-related articles has improved tremendously, due to the increased use of technology and the emergence of many important databases like ABI/INFORM. Patrons now have access either directly or through a librarian searcher to databases such as Wilsonline, Datext, Infotrac, etc. It has now become impossible for any business library, large or small, to subscribe to all the titles which appear in these databases and indexing services. Therefore, the most important selection criterion for any journal title must be the particular needs of the patrons being serviced. It may be that, unless the library is academic in nature, the smaller business library may choose to rely more heavily on interlibrary loan and other cooperative arrangements for access to the more scholarly titles, concentrating purchase selections from current trade and business journals. With these caveats, we present the following suggested core list of periodicals for the smaller business collection.

Academy of Management Journal. Mississippi State University. 1957–. Quarterly. ISSN: 0001–4273. $38.00.
Scholarly articles, many of which are based on studies undertaken by universities, are included here. Topics cover social and organizational behavior issues, as well as business, economics, and management.

Accounting Review. American Accounting Association. 1926–. Quarterly. ISSN: 0001–4826. $25.00.
Published by the American Accounting Association, the journal emphasizes articles on accounting education and on current trends in accounting. Regular features include book reviews and research notes on current research projects in accounting.

Across the Board. The Conference Board, Inc. 1976–. Eleven times a year. ISSN: 0147–1554. $30.00.

A wide range of current business, economics, and government-relations topics are covered here, along with book reviews and articles on the impact of technology.

Administration and Society. Sage Publications. 1969–. Quarterly. ISSN: 0095–3997. $65.00.

This journal "seeks to further the understanding of public and human service organizations, their administrative processes, and their effect on society." Emphasis is on empirical research and theoretical articles that contribute to that understanding.

Administrative Management: The Magazine of Office and Automation. Dalton Communications. 1985–. Monthly. ISSN: 0884–5905. $30.00.

Formed by *Office Administration* and *Automation and Information Management*, this independent journal's emphasis is on articles and information for office administrators and systems executives in all fields.

Administrative Science Quarterly. Cornell University. Graduate School of Business and Public Administration. 1956–. Quarterly. ISSN: 0001–8392. $62.00.

"Dedicated to advancing the understanding of administration through empirical investigation and theoretical analysis," this quarterly emphasizes research articles. Each issue contains several lengthy, critical book reviews and a list of current publications received.

Advanced Management Journal. Society for Advancement of Management. 1936–. Quarterly. ISSN: 0036–0805. $24.00.

This official journal for the Society for Advancement of Management focuses on clear, reliable, and practical information in the field of management. Regular features include both national and international issues.

Advertising Age. Crain Communications. 1930–. Weekly. ISSN: 0001–8899. $55.00.

Advertising Age, a weekly newspaper, is one of the most important and influential publications in the advertising and marketing fields. It is issued in two sections: the first covers current advertising campaigns, agency, account, and personnel changes, and new products; the second is devoted to a special report on a single topic of very current interest.

American Economic Review. American Economic Association. 1911–. Quarterly with two supplements. ISSN: 0002–8282. $100.00.

One of the most prestigious economics journals, *American Economic Review* covers all areas of economics. The articles are written primarily by outstanding researchers in the field. The two supplements contain the annual proceedings of the American Economic Association and a directory of its membership.

Barron's National Business and Financial Weekly. Dow Jones. 1921–. Weekly. ISSN: 0005–6073. $82.00.

Barron's weekly review of business and financial information is indispensable for the stock and bond investor. Articles on companies and industries published in this newspaper can have major impact on the performance of a particular stock or bond. Also included are statistics on economic indicators and money rates, as well as stock and bond price quotations.

Black Enterprise. Earl G. Groves Publishing Co. 1970–. Monthly. ISSN: 0006–4165. $10.00.

The purpose of most articles and regular features that appear here is to provide information on how and where to get ahead in the current business world. Each year the magazine includes annual surveys on top black-owned businesses, cities with the best opportunities for blacks, etc.

Business America. U.S. Department of Commerce. International Trade Administration. 1978–. Biweekly. ISSN: 0190–6275. $41.00.

A review of activities relating to private enterprise involved in international business is included in *Business America,* as are articles on current foreign business developments. Special features include a calendar of international business conferences, business outlooks abroad, business opportunities and trade promotions, and foreign market briefs.

Business and Society Review. Warren, Gorham, and Lamont. 1972–. Quarterly. ISSN: 0045–3609. $56.00.

Directed toward the business professional and the public interest group, articles in this forum are wide-ranging in subject matter. Included are a periodic listing of women currently serving on corporate boards and reviews of corporate achievements and failures in the areas of public concern.

Business History Review. Harvard University. Graduate School of Business Administration. 1926–. Quarterly. ISSN: 0007–6805. $22.50.

The focus of this quarterly is business and economic history in the United States and abroad. Several critical and lengthy book reviews are included in each issue.

Business Horizons. Indiana University. School of Business. 1958–. Bimonthly. ISSN: 0007–6813. $24.00.

Written for businesspersons, educators, and advanced students of business administration, each issue normally has a featured topic with two to four related articles, as well as book notes and reviews.

Business Week. McGraw-Hill. 1929–. Weekly. ISSN: 0007–7135. $39.95.

This general business magazine, which covers all areas of interest to the business community worldwide, has weekly departments on such topics as finance, international business, marketing, and technology.

California Management Review. University of California, Berkeley. Graduate School of Business Administration. 1958–. Quarterly. ISSN: 0008–1256. $38.00.

California Management Review is "an authoritative source of information and ideas contributing to the advancement of management science, it is directed to active managers, scholars, teachers, and others concerned with management."

Columbia Journal of World Business. Columbia University. Graduate School of Business. 1965–. Quarterly. ISSN: 0022–5428. $40.00.

Aimed at the business executive, scholar, and government official interested in an international or comparative approach to business, the articles in this journal deal primarily with practical experience or applied theory and include lengthy and critical book reviews.

CPA Journal. New York State Society of Certified Public Accountants. 1972–. Monthly. ISSN: 0732–8435. $28.00.

New trends in taxes, regulations, financial accounting, and auditing are covered in this excellent state society journal.

Dun's Business Month. Dun & Bradstreet. 1893–. Monthly. ISSN: 0279–3040. $27.00.

Written for the business executive, feature articles cover such areas as the economy, management, companies and industries, marketing, technology, and international business. Shorter articles are designed to keep the executive abreast of current trends.

Economist. Economist Newspaper Ltd. 1843–. Weekly. ISSN: 0013–0613. $75.00.

This weekly magazine provides an excellent summary of British and foreign economic and political affairs. Regular features cover world politics, business, finance, science, and current affairs.

Euromoney. Euromoney Publications. 1969–. Monthly. ISSN: 0014–2433. $108.00.

Euromoney is an essential journal for coverage of the world's financial markets. Special features, such as the annual country risk ranking and special supplements on individual countries or current issues, make this journal a valuable retrospective reference tool as well.

Federal Reserve Bulletin. U.S. Board of Governors of the Federal Reserve System. 1915–. Monthly. ISSN: 0014–9209. $20.00.

This Federal Reserve Board publication is an essential source of information and statistics in such areas as interest rates, commercial banking activities, and foreign debt.

Finance and Development. International Monetary Fund. 1964–. Quarterly. ISSN: 0145–1707. Free.

A joint publication of the International Monetary Fund and the World Bank, this periodical is available in several languages and covers international economic developments and activities of the two sponsoring organizations.

Financial Analysts Journal. Financial Analysts Federation. 1945–. Bimonthly. ISSN: 0015–198X. $36.00.

A wide range of topics related to the stock market and investments, including unbiased reporting on corporate and economic outlooks, is covered in this journal.

Financial Times. Financial Times. 1888–. Daily. $365.00.

Financial Times is an essential source for international financial and investment-activity information.

Forbes. Forbes. 1917–. Biweekly. ISSN: 0015–6914. $42.00.

One of the most important general business magazines, *Forbes* is known for its good, concise articles covering a wide range of topics from the point of view of the executive. Special features include personal profiles and case histories.

Fortune. Time. 1930–. Biweekly. ISSN: 0015–8259. $39.00.

Another important general business magazine that covers news from a broad view, *Fortune* is also known for its Fortune 500 listings.

Harvard Business Review. Harvard University. Graduate School of Business Administration. 1922–. Bimonthly. ISSN: 0017–8012. $30.00.

Research covering all aspects of business and related topics is emphasized in this respected journal. Articles attempt to supply solutions to real, everyday business problems.

INC. Inc. Publishing Company. 1979–. Monthly. ISSN: 0162–8968. $18.00.

A popular journal designed to meet the interests of small businesses, this magazine includes success stories about people and companies. Special features include the annual list of the fastest-growing small public companies.

Industrial and Labor Relations Review. Cornell University. New York State School of Labor and Industrial Relations. 1947–. Quarterly. ISSN: 0019–7939. $30.00.

Features in this comprehensive, major journal in the field of industrial and labor relations include recent publications, research in progress, and book reviews.

Industrial Marketing Management. Elsevier Science Publishing Co. 1971–. Quarterly. ISSN: 0019–8501. $106.00.

An international journal of organization marketing, this periodical contains articles aimed at the businessperson and the scholar involved in product and marketing research, planning, problem solving, and buyer characteristic surveys.

Institutional Investor. Institutional Investor, Inc. 1967–. Monthly. ISSN: 0020–3580. $165.00.

Available in both domestic and international editions, this practical journal is designed for the money manager. Articles regularly deal with corporate finance, pension fund management, investor relations, public finance, and portfolio strategies.

International Labour Review. International Labour Office. 1921–. Bimonthly. ISSN: 0020–7780. $31.30.

International Labour Review presents "articles based on recent ILO and other research in economic and social topics of international interest affecting labour."

Journal of Accountancy. American Institute of Certified Public Accountants. 1905–. Monthly. ISSN: 0021–8448. $20.00.

This major journal in the field of accounting focuses primarily on the information needs of certified public accountants. Although the journal is at times technical, the current information on new accounting releases and professional notes is essential to the practitioner.

Journal of Business. University of Chicago. Graduate School of Business. 1928–. Quarterly. ISSN: 0021–9398. $35.00.

A joint publication of the school of business and the department of economics, this journal is a leading scholarly title. In each January issue doctoral dissertations accepted the previous year are listed by general subject categories. Grants, leaves, and faculty appointments are also included in this issue.

Journal of Finance. American Finance Association. 1946–. Five times a year. ISSN: 0022–1082. $50.00.

The official publication of the American Finance Association, the *Journal of Finance* includes technical and scholarly articles on all aspects of finance. In the fifth issue are published the papers and proceedings of the annual meeting of the American Finance Association.

Journal of International Business Studies. University of South Carolina. College of Business Administration. 1970–. Three times a year. ISSN: 0047–2506. $35.00.

Articles in the journal are results of studies or applied research in international business written by academics. Book reviews, abstracts of doctoral dissertations, and new books in the field are also included.

Journal of Marketing. American Marketing Association. 1936–. Quarterly. ISSN: 0022–2429. $50.00.

This journal is considered one of the leading marketing journals both for academics and practitioners. All aspects of marketing, consumer behavior, legal developments, and methodology and measurement are covered in this title.

Journal of Marketing Research. American Marketing Association. 1964–. Quarterly. ISSN: 0022–2437. $50.00.

Articles on new techniques for problem solving, clarification of theories of methodology, review of developments, and identification of other concepts, methods, and applications of marketing research are presented in this title.

Journal of Money, Credit and Banking. Ohio State University Press. 1969–. Quarterly. ISSN: 0022–2879. $28.00.

Monetary policy, banking, and fiscal policy are some of the basic topics covered in the scholarly articles included here. A lengthy book review is included in most issues.

Journal of Retailing. New York University. Institute of Retail Management. 1925–. Quarterly. ISSN: 0022–4359. $20.00.

Aimed at those interested in retail trade, this scholarly journal tries to promote new ideas and concepts related to the marketplace. Special issues on specific topics are occasionally published.

Management Accounting. National Association of Accountants. 1919–. Monthly. ISSN: 0025–1690. $60.00.

Directed toward a broader audience than the *Journal of Accountancy* and somewhat less technical, this journal is concerned primarily with the practical aspects of management accounting. Articles are for the most part written by National Association of Accountants members.

Management Review. American Management Association. 1914–. Monthly. ISSN: 0025–1895. $28.00.

Management Review presents short articles on topics of general interest, such as corporate restructuring, pay systems, and financial analysis of private companies. Articles on specific companies and interviews with leading businesspeople are included.

Management Science. The Institute of Management Sciences (TIMS). 1954–. Monthly. ISSN: 0025–1909. $86.00.

Emphasis here is on the theory and applications of management science and operations research.

Marketing and Media Decisions. Decisions Publications, Inc. 1966–. Monthly. ISSN: 0195–4296. $40.00.

Brief, up-to-date articles on media, agencies, companies, and brands are included in this title. Special issues throughout the year provide valuable statistics on brands, products, and cost indexes.

Mergers and Acquisitions. MLR Publishing Company. 1965–. Bimonthly. ISSN: 0026–0010. $159.00.

Mergers and Acquisitions publishes case histories and industry studies as well as general articles on merger/acquisitions/divestiture in such areas as finance, taxes, strategic planning, law, and accounting. The rosters of mergers and acquisitions, as well as foreign investment in the U.S. and U.S. investment in companies abroad, make this journal very useful.

Money. Money. 1972–. Monthly. ISSN: 0149–4953. $31.95.

Written for the layperson, articles in this popular magazine deal mainly with personal and family finance. Rankings of mutual funds, ways to invest for income, and retirement planning are only a few of the major topics regularly examined.

Monthly Labor Review. U.S. Department of Labor. Bureau of Labor Statistics. 1915–. Monthly. ISSN: 0098–1818. $16.00.

Articles on labor in the U.S. and around the world are included in each issue, along with statistics on consumer prices, productivity, wages, and information on collective bargaining and legislation.

National Tax Journal. National Tax Association—Tax Institute of America. 1948–. Quarterly. ISSN: 0028–0283. $30.00.

The encouragement and dissemination of research in government finance are the basic objectives of this journal. National, state, and local government finance are covered in several articles in each issue, along with briefer notes and comments.

Nation's Business. Chamber of Commerce of the United States. 1912–. Monthly. ISSN: 0028–047X. $22.00.

All aspects of commerce and industry, as well as up-to-date information on the Chamber of Commerce, are covered here. Reports on economics, legislation, and politics and their impact on business activities also receive regular coverage.

OECD Observer. Organisation for Economic Cooperation and Development. 1962–. Bimonthly. ISSN: 0029–7054. $11.00.

Concise reports on the activities of the OECD, an annual survey of the economic conditions of member countries, and articles on diverse subjects written by the OECD staff make up this journal.

Operations Research. Operations Research Society of America. 1952–. Bimonthly. ISSN: 0030–364X. $65.00.

A scholarly journal, this aims to publish "quality operations research [OR] and management science work of interest to the OR practitioner and researcher in the three substantive categories: OR methods, data-based operational science, and the practice of OR."

Pension World. Communication Channels, Inc. 1964–. Monthly. ISSN: 0098–1753. $41.00.

Pension World, for "plan sponsors and investment managers," specializes in articles on pension planning, investment strategies, and portfolio management. Many issues include annual surveys of fund performances.

Personnel. AMACOM. 1919–. Bimonthly. ISSN: 0031–5702. $36.00.

The American Management Association provides this publication designed for the personnel specialist. Articles emphasize practical applications of all aspects of personnel administration.

Personnel Journal. A. C. Crofts. 1922–. Monthly. ISSN: 0031–5745. $38.00.

Aimed at the practitioner in the fields of personnel and industrial relations, both scholarly and popular articles are included.

Public Administration Review. American Society for Public Administration. 1940–. Bimonthly. ISSN: 0033–3352. $40.00.

This scholarly journal contributes to the society's goal of disseminating information and identifying common public administration programs and services. International, national, regional, state, and local programs are all covered in this title.

Public Personnel Management. International Personnel Management Association—U.S. 1940–. Quarterly. ISSN: 0091–0260. $30.00.

Directed toward the personnel manager in the public sector, the articles, which tend to be practical in nature, cover all aspects of personnel administration as related to the government employee.

Rand Journal Of Economics. Rand Corporation. 1970–. Quarterly. ISSN: 0741–6261. $80.00. (Formerly the *Bell Journal of Economics.*)

The purpose of this journal is to "support and encourage research in the behavior of regulated industries, the economic analysis of organizations, and more generally, applied microeconomics. Both theoretical and empirical manuscripts in economics and law are encouraged."

Review of Economics and Statistics. Harvard University. Department of Economics. 1919–. Quarterly. ISSN: 0034–6535. $120.00.

In this journal, considered one of the most important in the field of theoretical and applied economics, the emphasis is on econometrics and methodology.

Sales and Marketing Management. Sales Management. 1918–. 16 times a year. ISSN: 0163–7517. $38.00.

Aimed toward all those involved in marketing operations, this is the major journal in its field, covering all aspects of the process of marketing: evaluation, planning, packaging, etc. It is noted for its annual series of surveys on selling, buying, and purchasing power.

Sloan Management Review. Massachusetts Institute of Technology. Alfred P. Sloan School of Management. 1960–. Quarterly. ISSN: 0019–848X. $32.00.

Designed for the practicing manager, this journal provides articles on new techniques, trends, and models for decision making and problem solving. A section on "recent management publications" is included in each issue.

Supervisory Management. AMACOM. 1955–. Monthly. ISSN: 0039–5919. $25.00.

Another publication of the American Management Association this practical journal is designed "for the continuing education of the professional manager." It covers a wide variety of key issues in personnel supervision. A series of case studies of common, difficult management situations is included regularly.

Survey of Current Business. Department of Commerce. Bureau of Economic Analysis. 1921–. Monthly, with weekly supplements. ISSN: 0039–6222. $30.00.

An essential source of current business statistics for any collection, in each issue this title usually contains as well annual compilations of special interest, such as operations of U.S. multinational companies, annual revisions of national income and product accounts, and pollution abatement and control expenditures.

Training and Development Journal. American Society for Training and Development. 1947–. Monthly. ISSN: 0041–0861. $50.00.

This monthly publication features brief articles written for managers and others involved in human-resource development. Articles focus on strategies for bringing about and coping with changes in a corporation, how to teach skills to employees, and how to involve employees in the work of the company. Each issue also includes book reviews, reviews of training tools and techniques, and news of interest to society members.

Venture. Venture Magazine, Inc. 1979–. Monthly. ISSN: 0191–3530. $18.00.

The magazine for "entrepreneurial business owners and investors" includes feature articles on legislative, political, and international issues which influence business opportunities.

Wall Street Journal. Dow Jones. 1889–. Five times a week. ISSN: 0043–0080. $101.00.

This newspaper is perhaps the most important title to be included in any business collection. The daily statistics as well as overall news and business coverage make this essential for all libraries.

The Best Investment Sources

by Carla Martindell Felsted

INVESTMENT ADVISORY SERVICES

The investment field is crowded with several hundred advisory newsletters, charting services and the like. This makes selection a great
challenge for even the most astute investor or librarian. The following
is a representative sampling of services, based on performance ratings
and current holdings in several academic and public libraries of varying sizes.

America's Fastest Growing Companies. 35 Mason St., Greenwich, CT
06830. Monthly. $124 per year. Published since 1958.
    This newsletter provides subscribers with a constantly updated list of over
100 growth stocks, based on rapidly growing sales, and analyzes the potential of
each. It includes statistical data, charts, and graphs as well.

Catalyst: Investing in Social Change. 28 Main St., Montpelier, VT
05602. Bimonthly. $49 per year. Published since 1984.
    Socially concerned investors will welcome this source, which covers
community-based alternative enterprises such as co-ops and worker-owned businesses. The publication also includes news, editorials, and book reviews.

Commodity Trader's Consumer Report. P.O. Box 254480, Sacramento,
CA 95825. Bimonthly. $150 per year. Published since 1983.
    This has a summary of the results of recommendations made by
commodity trading services, and examines their systems and advisors, as well as
advisors for gold, index rates, and stock index futures. It is a useful source for
monitoring the success of these advisors and their newsletters.

CRB Futures Chart Service. 100 Church St., #1850, New York, NY
10007. Weekly. $385 per year. Published since 1956.
    Commodity futures, such as grains, soybean products, cocoa, copper, hides,
sugar, eggs, and pork bellies, are charted in this large-format publication. It also
provides technical interpretations and discusses interest rates, stock index futures, and London markets.

Carla Martindell Felsted operates Southwind Information Services, Wimberley, and is
Reference Librarian/Business Liaison at St. Edward's University, Austin, TX.

Dick Davis Digest. Box 2828, Ocean View Station, Miami Beach, FL 33140. Semimonthly. $95 per year.
This popular source abstracts over 300 advisory newsletters and recommendations from Wall Street leaders. Market trend analysis and company and industry news are also covered.

The Dines Letter. P.O. Box 22, Belvedere, CA 94920. Semimonthly. $195 per year. Published since 1960.
Intended for both novice and seasoned investors, this newsletter provides advice based on fundamentals, charts, and mass psychology. It includes editorials, market analyses, and "Capitalist Book Club Reviews."

Donoghue's Moneyletter. P.O. Box 540, Holliston, MA 01746. Bimonthly. $99 per year. Published since 1980.
One of several publications by the author, it covers money market and no-load mutual funds for the do-it-yourself investor in "clear, easy-to-read terms." Reviews of current economic developments and legislation are included, and there is a column for write-in questions. The Newsletter Association voted it the "best financial advisory newsletter" for 1986.

Elliott Wave Theorist. P.O. Box 1618, Gainesville, GA 30503. Monthly. $233 per year. Published since 1979.
This technical newsletter analyzes Elliott waves, Fibonacci relationships, and fixed-time cycles in addition to momentum, sentiment, and supply-demand factors. Although the approach is somewhat controversial, it achieved good results for the years 1983–86.

Hulbert Financial Digest. 643 S. Carolina Ave., S.E., Washington, DC 20003. Monthly. $135 per year. Published since 1980.
This publication summarizes advice from almost 100 investment newsletters and also provides periodic performance ratings, based on model portfolios constructed according to the advice in each. It also contains a monthly scoreboard, topical articles, and editorial comments.

The Insider's Chronicle. 398 Camino Gardens Blvd., Boca Raton, FL 33432. Weekly. $350 per year. Published since 1976.
Securities and Exchange Commission reports of corporate officers' stock transactions are monitored in this publication on a weekly basis, summarized quarterly, and indexed as well. It also includes corporation profiles and a "Wall Street Summary."

The Outlook. 25 Broadway, New York, NY 10004. Weekly. $219 per year. Published since 1937.
Subtitled "Analyzes and Projects Business and Market Trends," this Standard & Poor's publication includes forecasts, recommendations for the more aggressive investor, economic statistics, and follow-up on previous recommendations. Each issue features one of four model portfolios: long-term gain, promising growth, cyclical/speculative, and income with inflation protection. Comprehensive investment libraries might also subscribe to Standard & Poor's *Credit Week, New Issue Investor* and the entire *Trendline* series below.

The Professional Investor. Lynatrace, Inc. P.O. Box 214, Pompano Beach, FL 33061. Semimonthly. $200 per year. Published since 1971.

The newsletter's motto is "The Financial Magazine Designed to be Better." It has front-page buy and sell recommendations and witty editorial comments and also provides summaries of other newsletter market views, information on switch fund trading and options, and book reviews.

Trendline's Current Market Perspective. 25 Broadway, New York, NY 10004. Monthly. $157 per year. Published since 1962.

Technicians will favor this Standard & Poor's charting service, which covers over 1,000 stocks. For each, 42 months of market action is shown and up to five years of statistical information is displayed in a special table. Stocks are arranged in industry groups, and ranked on the basis of price performance. Other *Trendline* publications include *Daily Action Stock Charts* (published weekly) and the *OTC Chart Manual.*

United & Babson Investment Report. 210 Newbury St. Boston, MA 02116. Weekly. $190 per year. Predecessor letter published since 1919.

A new title created by the merger of two well-known investment advisories, in each issue it looks at general business trends, governmental matters, and developments in the stock market. There is a monthly review of supervised stocks, and favorite investment picks in a specific industry.

Value Line Investment Survey. 711 Third Ave., New York, NY 10017. Weekly. $495 per year. Published since 1937.

Perhaps the best-known investment publication, this loose-leaf service reviews over 1,500 stocks and 91 industries. Information on each company and industry is updated quarterly on a rotating basis. Individual pages for each company include an 11–year statistical history on 22 key investment factors and looks at current developments and future prospects. The weekly "Selection and Opinion Section" reviews economic trends and gives advice on investment strategy. The same publisher also offers series titled *New Issues, Options, Convertibles,* and *Special Situations.*

Weisenberger Investment Companies Service: Investment Companies. 210 South St., Boston, MA 02111. Annual hard-back with updates, $374.

An authoritative source on mutual funds and investment companies, the annual publication explains the different types of funds and gives advice on how to select them and monitor performance. It profiles the major investment companies and tracks the performance of individual funds over five-year intervals (for up to 25 years). The service includes the monthly *Current Performance and Dividend Record,* and *Mutual Funds Investment Report,* a quarterly *Management Results,* and *Mutual Funds Panorama.*

Zweig Forecast. P.O. Box 5345, New York, NY 10150. Every three weeks, with occasional special bulletins. $245 per year. Published since 1971.

Each issue includes a "Sentiments Composite" (which estimates the market's liquidity) and other measures of market movements. A general outlook and strategy are included, along with specific stock selections. The *Hulbert Financial Digest* ranks Zweig second in 7–year performance among 102 services.

Comments on selection from the above list:

A conservative approach in a smaller library would be a subscription to *The Outlook* and/or one of the newsletter digests such as those edited by Dick Davis and Mark Hulbert. Two other services that would be most useful are *Value Line* and *Weisenberger Investment Companies Service: Investment Companies.*

For a more comprehensive collection, periodic reviews and ratings of advisory services in *Barron's, Forbes,* the *Wall Street Journal,* and other business publications should be consulted. Select Information Exchange, 2095 Broadway, New York NY 10023, (212) 874–6408, promises a catalog of newsletters from which one may select sample issues, but you will probably need to wait for delivery. Many newsletters also provide trial subscriptions; check their advertisements in the business press. Sources that cover financial newsletters are:

Hulbert Financial Digest Annual Review of Investment Newsletters. Joel B. Wittenberg, ed. Reston, VA: Reston, 1986.

Investment Newsletters. Richard Weiner and Rena Holt, eds. New York: Public Relations Publishing Co., 1987.

Newsletters Directory, 3rd ed. Brigitte T. Darnay and John Nimchuk, eds. Detroit: Gale, 1987.

INVESTMENT PERIODICALS AND STATISTICAL SOURCES

The following periodicals should be considered for inclusion in an investment collection. Although it is assumed that some titles, such as *Business Week,* are in the general business collection, they will be included in this list on the basis of special features of interest to investors. Subscription prices quoted are for one year.

AAII Journal. American Association of Individual Investors, Chicago, IL. 10 times/yr. $45.
   Published by the American Association of Individual Investors, this publication features articles on investment instruments and strategies. It also covers technical analysis, tax information, investment news and views, book reviews, association news, and editorial commentary.

Bank and Quotation Record. National News Service, Inc., New York. Monthly. $180.
   A companion piece to the *Commercial and Financial Chronicle,* this is a monthly compendium of price ranges for stocks and bonds listed on the American and New York, as well as regional, exchanges and NASDAQ OTC securities. Also included are data on U.S. government securities; municipal, foreign, and corporate bonds; mutual funds; commercial paper; and foreign exchange rates.

Barron's. Dow Jones, New York, NY. Weekly. $86.
   Published since 1921, this well-respected tabloid is written for investors. Although there are excellent feature articles on various subjects, it is also known for its detailed financial tables. Its easy-to-read format has weekly, rather than daily, stock prices (high, low, and closing), as well as coverage for bonds,

NASDAQ stocks, regional and Canadian exchanges, and stock options. Also useful are its "Market Laboratory" section and reports from other sources, such as "The Lipper Mutual Fund Performance Averages."

Business Week. McGraw-Hill, New York, NY. Weekly. $39.95.

In addition to its excellent articles, this publication has many special lists of interest to investors. They include: "Bank Scoreboard," "Corporate Scoreboard," "International Corporate Scoreboard," and "Investment Outlook Scoreboard."

Capital Changes Report. Commerce Clearing House, Chicago, IL. 6 vols. $645 on a renewal basis or $710 for one time. Updated weekly.

This Commerce Clearing House service tracks the capital histories of corporations. In alphabetical arrangement, it provides chronological information on each company, including date of incorporation, stock rights, stock splits, dividends, recapitalization, reorganization, mergers and consolidation. Volume 6 includes historical tables on dividend taxability, lists of worthless securities, and a tax guide.

Commercial and Financial Chronicle. National News Service, Inc., Arlington, MA. Weekly. $450.

Strictly a statistical source, with no editorial or news content, serious investors may like this for its easier-to-read tables of securities quotations. It contains daily prices for the New York, American, and Toronto exchanges, bid/ask prices for NASDAQ stocks and mutual funds, weekly listings of fixed unit investment trusts, and declared dividend announcements.

Financial Analysts Journal. Financial Analysts Federation, New York, NY. Bimonthly. $48.

Published by the non-profit Financial Analysts Federation, this publication has authoritative articles written from both theoretical and practical standpoints. It reviews current developments with various investment instruments, and includes pertinent changes in regulations.

Financial World. Macro Communications, New York, NY. Biweekly. $44.95.

As a magazine for "financial service professionals," this reviews industries and various investment markets, including foreign. Specific industries and companies are analyzed, and there are interesting feature articles such as "The 10 Worst Managed Companies in America." The first issue each month gives "Independent Appraisals" for almost 3,000 stocks.

Forbes. Forbes, New York, NY. Biweekly. $45.

This general business publication has much to recommend it for investment collections. Its "Annual Directory" issue ranks the 500 largest corporations (industrial or service) by sales, profits, assets, stock market value, and employees; the "Annual Report on American Industry" ranks within industry groups according to profitability and growth. There are also a "Special Report on International Business," an "Annual Mutual Funds Survey," and the "Annual Forbes 400" list of the wealthiest Americans.

Fortune. Time, Inc., New York, NY. Biweekly. $44.50

The "Fortune 500" (a ranking of the largest U.S. industrial corporations) is the best known of the many business lists. The "Service 500" consists of separate rankings in the areas of diversified service, banking, diversified financial, life insurance, retailing, transportation, and utility companies. Companies on both lists are ranked by sales, assets, net income/stockholders' equity, earnings per share, and total return to investors. The "World Business Directory" covers both industry and banking.

Institutional Investor. Institutional Investor Systems, Inc., New York, NY. Monthly. $165.

Written for the money manager, rather than the individual investor, this covers such topics as corporate financing, pension-fund management, investor relations, and portfolio strategy. New offerings in securities and tax-exempt issues are covered each month, and there are interesting annual features such as "America's biggest brokers" and a ranking of foreign countries by risk potential. An international edition is also published, as well as a quarterly *Journal of Portfolio Management.*

Investor's Daily. Investor's Daily, New York, NY. Five times a week. $84.

Subtitled "America's Business Newspaper," this is an attractive publication that may come to rival the venerable *Wall Street Journal.* Although it lacks the longer feature articles of the latter, it does offer good news coverage of business, economic, national, and world events. Other articles cover specific industries, companies, and names in the news. Its advantages include stock tables that are larger and easier to read than the *Journal's* and statistical measures unique to the O'Neill database.

The Market Chronicle. William B. Dana Co., New York, NY. Weekly. $50.

Written for the financial community, this publication emphasizes the OTC market. Quotes for NASDAQ companies are carried, and it includes two pages of non-NASDAQ stocks, which are seldom seen elsewhere. Prices on tax-exempt trusts are reported, and there are corporate earnings reports, a calendar of future corporate issues, and book reviews. Brief articles cover economic and corporate news.

Media General Financial Weekly. Media General Financial Services, Richmond, VA. Weekly. $108.

This publication is packed full of information on over 4,000 stocks. The main table gives for each of these 29 different indicators of performance; the second groups the stocks into 75 industry categories, allowing the reader to make comparisons within the same industry. Two other groups of tables rank stocks by 12 different criteria and provide a variety of economic barometers. Statistics on mutual funds and some commentary are included.

Money. Time, Inc., New York, NY. 13 times a year. $31.95.

A popular magazine geared to the middle-class individual or family, this provides general money-management advice, case histories, and occasional product reviews. Regular features of interest to investors include its "Wall Street Letter," "Stock of the Month," "Investor's Scorecard" (interest rates), and "Fund Watch." Even the smallest libraries should subscribe.

Wall Street Journal. Dow Jones, New York, NY. Five times a week. $119.

Although this is considered the nation's leading business newspaper, the general reader would find much of interest in its pages as well. For investors, its coverage of business activities is unsurpassed. Its detailed financial tables cover the trading activities of the previous business day, and include stocks, bonds, mutual funds, selected foreign stocks, currency exchange rates, commodities futures, money rates, and economic indicators. It publishes its own index, but can be accessed through other indexing services.

Wall Street Transcript. Wall Street Transcript Corporation, New York, NY. Weekly. $1,440.

Although many libraries cannot afford this publication, major public and academic collections should include it, as much of its information is not available elsewhere. The majority of its content is reproduced from brokerage house reports on corporations and industries. Most valuable are its reprints of executive speeches and interviews—which are often late-breaking—and lengthy roundtable discussions by industry analysts.

MOODY'S AND STANDARD AND POOR'S SERVICES

These two well-known publishers offer "library packages" of certain publications, which are significantly more economical than individual purchase. Moody's Special Library Service package, consisting of four manuals (its *Bond Record, Bond Survey, Dividend Record,* and *Handbook of Common Stocks*) is priced at $1,370. The Standard and Poor's items offered in its Complete Library Reference Shelf for $1,350 include its *Corporation Records, Bond Guide, Stock Guide, Credit Week, Statistical Service,* and *The Outlook* (see "Advisory Services"). For purposes of comparison, similar publications are discussed in pairs below. "Package" items will be denoted with an asterisk; regular prices are also shown for each item. Readers should check with the publishers for other "package" offerings and for details on educational discounts.

*Moody's Bond Record.** Moody's Investors Service, New York, NY. Monthly. $145; *Standard & Poor's Bond Guide.** Monthly. $145.

Both publications provide summary data on corporate bonds listed on the New York and American exchanges. Standard and Poor's tables give information on both the bonds and the companies that issue them; while more information is provided, the disadvantage is that this may be confusing to some readers. Each also assigns ratings to bonds.

*Moody's Bond Survey.** Moody's Investors Service, New York, NY. Weekly. $895.

An advisory service rather than just a statistical source, this publication covers corporate, municipal, and foreign bonds and their issuing sources. Bond indentures are described, along with their purposes and ratings. A weekly review of the bond market in general, with statistics and graphs, is included, and changes in previous ratings are given.

Moody's Dividend Record.* Moody's Investors Service, New York, NY. Weekly. $395; *Standard & Poor's Dividend Record.** Standard & Poor's, New York, NY. Quarterly. $132.
The two publications are virtually identical, with minor variations. Each service provides current information on the stock and mutual fund dividends, indicating amount and date paid. There are annual cumulations for both.

Moody's Handbook of Common Stocks.* Moody's Investors Service, New York, NY. Quarterly. $145.
This is a handy reference to over 900 stocks of high investor interest. A full page of data for each includes stock price history; abbreviated financial data; and a brief description of the firm's business, recent developments, and future prospects. Each issue has a feature article on market trends, list of high and low performers, or index of companies by industry, and other useful data. Their *Handbook of OTC Stocks* ($99/yr.) is comparable in format and content, and can be "packaged" with *Common Stocks* at a lesser price.

Moody's Manuals. Moody's Investors Service, New York, NY.
This service consists of annual hard-back volumes updated by loose-leaf reports with detailed financial information and bond ratings in separate sets according to type of business or government entity. Entries in the volumes vary in length according to the fee paid by the listing entity. A "complete" listing will include five to seven years of financial figures, a brief corporate history, a listing of officers, description of properties, and detailed information about bonds issued. Each volume is arranged according to depth of coverage, and then alphabetically, so the use of indexes is essential. There is also a master index to identify the industry volume in which each of the over 15,000 companies is included. "Special Features" sections in each manual are an invaluable source of comparative data. Individual manuals and their annual "non-package" prices are:

Bank and Finance	$895
Industrial	$895
International	$1,280
Municipal and Government	$1,175
OTC Industrial	$815
OTC Unlisted	$750
Public Utility	$780
Transportation	$750

Standard and Poor's Corporation Records.* Standard & Poor's, New York, NY. $2,136, daily updates; $1,265 quarterly.
Arranged alphabetically in five loose-leaf volumes, with a "Daily News" volume at the higher price, this service is somewhat more accessible than Moody's. Quarterly updates are issued to incorporate the daily news, and the filing information is very specific. As with Moody's, however, users need to know how to use the indexes to locate companies sought. The content is similar, though not always as extensive as in the former; 10–year financial results are offered, however. Fewer companies are included by Standard and Poor's, particularly fewer financial institutions, and there is no coverage of governmental entities or international companies.

Standard and Poor's Credit Week.* Standard & Poor's, New York, NY. Weekly. $1,238.

Like its competitor, this publication reviews bond issues and issuers on a regular basis. It also analyzes trends and the outlook for fixed-income securities and provides weekly opinion and analysis of the economy. Its chief advantage is its inclusion of a "Credit Watch" of companies for which improvements or declines in credit quality have occurred, and rating changes are imminent.

*Standard and Poor's Statistical Service.** Standard & Poor's, New York, NY. $450.

This loose-leaf service contains industry, economic, and investment statistics from both governmental and private sources. The statistics are more comprehensive than Moody's "Special Feature," but a separate subscription is required. Unlike *The Statistical Abstract of the United States*, the data source of origin (agency or association) for each table is identified, but not the specific publication.

*Standard and Poor's Stock Guide.** Standard & Poor's, New York, NY. $88.

This publication is useful not only to investors, but also as a ready-reference guide to such information as a company's ticker symbol, exchanges on which its stocks are traded, and fiscal year dates. Two pages of statistical data for each stock include previous month's price range, historical price range, current dividends, corporate earnings, a rating for preferred stocks or ranking for common stocks, the company's financial position, and its capitalization.

Not included in the library packages mentioned above, but worthy of note are:

Moody's Industry Review. Moody's Investors Service, New York, NY. $325.

Once included with *Investor's Fact Sheets*, this loose-leaf service is now offered separately. A worthy competitor to the titles below, it covers 145 separate industry groups, giving key business ratios, and company-by-company comparisons. Within each industry, companies are ranked by revenues, net income, return on assets, and seven other factors.

Standard and Poor's Industry Surveys. Standard & Poor's, New York, NY. $2,136 loose-leaf; $1,265 quarterly.

Available as either a loose-leaf service updated more frequently, or as quarterly paperback issues, this is a most valuable reference source. Its industry groupings are fewer (22) and much broader than Moody's, making comparisons less precise. Its chief advantage, however, is the narrative portion of each section, which reviews product developments, markets, and regulatory developments affecting each industry.

REFERENCE BOOKSHELF

The larger library might use the list below as a collection checklist. Smaller libraries should at least include a general business or investment dictionary and one of the basic investment handbooks (Barron's, Dow Jones-Irwin, or Dun & Bradstreet), as well as specific items based on the needs of their clientele.

Barron's Finance and Investment Handbook. Woodbury, NY: Barron's Educational Series, 1986. $18.95.

This reasonably priced compendium covers a great deal of material in just under 1,000 pages. Thirty investment vehicles, from annuities and collectibles to real estate, are explored; tips on how to read annual reports and the financial pages are given; and there is a lengthy dictionary. The ready-reference section includes sources of information and assistance, historical economic and investment data, and a list of publicly traded companies.

Commodity Prices: A Sourcebook and Index. Paul Wasserman and Diane Kemmerling, comps. Detroit: Gale, 1974. $48.

Useful for locating sources for commodity prices on more than 5,000 consumer, commercial, agricultural, and industrial products. Entries are alphabetical by commodity and include the title of the periodical where price is found, frequency of price listings, and pertinent market.

Commodity Yearbook. New York: Commodity Research Bureau. Annual. $30.95. Update service (three issues a year) available for $65.

An excellent data source for almost 50 years, this publication covers approximately 100 raw commodities (such as apples, barley, coal) and manufactured products and resources (arsenic, beer, cement). Statistics include prices, production, shipment, and imports. There are also general articles on such topics as commodity price trends and market structures.

Directory of Business and Financial Services. 8th ed. Mary M. Grant and Riva Berleant-Schiller, comps. New York: Special Libraries Association, 1984. $35.

This directory is invaluable for its listings of over 1,000 business, economic, and financial services that are published periodically or have regular supplements. Alphabetical by title, the brief annotations include publisher, price, and frequency. There are indexes by subject, publisher, and geographic area. Over 80 online services are now included as well.

Directory of Obsolete Securities. New York: Financial Information. Annual. $100.

Published since 1927, this is a cumulative list of companies whose identities have been lost due to name change, merger, acquisition, dissolution, reorganization, bankruptcy, charter cancellation, or related capital change. Listings indicate the manner in which the change occurred, the name of the new company (if any), and the year in which the action took place. It would be useful in both a public library that serves investors and an academic library to support research.

Dow Jones Investors Handbook. Phyllis S. Pierce, ed. Homewood, IL: Dow Jones-Irwin. Annual. $10.95.

Thorough coverage of the most widely quoted stock averages is given in this handbook, including a brief explanation of the system, daily closing averages for the most recent year, and monthly closing averages for the last 20 years; transportation and utility stocks are covered in addition to industrials. Other statistics included are quarterly earnings, dividend yields, and price/earnings ratios, as well as Barron's "Confidence Index," and the year's trading data for stocks, bonds, mutual funds and government bonds.

Dow Jones-Irwin Business and Investment Almanac. Summer N. Levine, ed. Princeton, NJ: Dow Jones Books. Annual. $29.95.

This handy compendium of information on business, economics, and investments belongs in all libraries. It provides a summary of the previous year's business activities, reviews of individual industries, and handy economic and business statistics. Well-known lists such as the "Fortune 500" and "America's Most and Least Admired Companies" are included, and there are several chapters on investment vehicles and techniques.

Dun & Bradstreet's Guide to Your Investments. Nancy Dunnan, ed. New York: Harper & Row. Annual. $16.95.

This handy reference guide to the many different types of investments would likely be of greatest interest to the small or beginning investor. Easy-to-use information is given on stocks, bonds, mutual funds, convertibles, options, warrants, and other investment vehicles. Also covered are explanations of investment strategies, tax considerations, and a basic review of the stock market. Other useful sections include computer applications and a guide to industry acronyms.

Encyclopedia of Banking and Finance. Orig. ed. by Glenn G. Munn; 8th ed. rev. and expanded by F. L. Garcia. Boston: Bankers Publishing Co., 1983. $94.

This excellent, one-volume encyclopedia covers the entire area of banking and finance and thus belongs in most business collections. Articles of varying length provide definition, and often discussion, of money, credit, banking practice, history, law, accounting, trusts, foreign exchange, investments, business organization, insurance, and many other topics. Bibliographies and statistics are included, as well as references to laws and regulations.

Handbook for No-Load Investors. Hastings-on-Hudson, NY: No-Load Fund Investor, Inc. Annual. $36; also available with $95 newsletter subscription.

Written for investors in mutual funds, this source includes no-load fund performance tables, a directory, and industry statistics. A case is made for investing in no-load mutual funds, and abundant advice is given on methods of selection and the mechanics of buying and selling.

Handbook of Fixed-Income Securities 2nd ed.. Frank J. Fabozzi and Irving M. Pollack, eds. Homewood, IL: Dow Jones-Irwin, 1986. $55.

Written for both the individual investor and the money manager, this handbook provides an encyclopedic approach to fixed-income securities, investment strategies, and the interest rate environment, with some 50 articles written by subject experts. The book is divided in four parts: general information, securities and instruments, bond investments, and interest rate matter.

The Investment Manager's Handbook. Sumner N. Levine, ed. Homewood, IL: Dow Jones-Irwin, 1980. $65.95.

A handy desk reference for investment managers, with chapters written by both practitioners and academics, its major sections cover basic investment aspects, management strategies, tracking performance, regulation, management by portfolio type, money market, computer applications, and stock market indexes. Bibliographic references are included, as are an index and glossary. The author's *Financial Analyst's Handbook* provides extensive treatment of portfolio management.

Mutual Fund Fact Book. Washington: Investment Company Institute. $5.00.

This basic guide to trends and statistics of the mutual funds industry is a handy reference source. The text section covers basics in the history and development of the industry; the statistical section is divided into three parts: industry totals, long-term funds, and short-term funds.

NASDAQ Handbook. Chicago: Probus, 1987. $24.95.

Subtitled "The Stock Market of Tomorrow—Today," this is a complete guide to the over-the-counter market. It covers types of companies listed on the Automated Quotations system of the National Association of Stock Dealers, strategies for investing in this market, and the services and regulations governing this system.

New York Stock Exchange Investor's Information Kit. New York: NYSE. $12.

Useful items for a pamphlet file are found in this kit. They include: "The Capital Market," "Understanding Stocks and Bonds," "Understanding Financial Statements," "Margin Trading Guide," and "Getting Help When You Invest."

Security Dealers of North America. New York: Standard & Poor's. Semiannual. 2 vols. $348.

This directory lists brokers, dealers, underwriters, securities distributors, and investment banking firms for the U.S. and Canada. Arranged alphabetically, each listing includes names of partners, officers, branch managers, and department heads for each office, as well as its address, telephone number, exchange memberships, specialization, clearing facilities, and wire services. Branch locations are included, and discontinued listings noted.

The VNR Investor's Dictionary. New York: Van Nostrand Reinhold, 1980. $21.95.

Concise definitions are included here, with practical examples of usage and alternate definitions when necessary. Both words and phrases from accounting, banking, business, finance, government, law, real estate, securities, and statistics are covered.

The Wall Street Waltz. Kenneth L. Fisher, ed. Chicago: Contemporary Books, 1987. $30.

A fascinating study of historical trends in the stock market, this book may help students or victims of the 1987 crash have a better perspective. It surveys price/earnings ratios over the years as well as price/cash flow ratios, has special studies of railroad and overseas stocks, and looks at nine major stock market cycles. The infamous "hemline indicator" is included.

INVESTMENT BOOKSHELF

The following titles should be included in a comprehensive collection. Smaller libraries might include a basic text, such as Amling, Engel, or Graham, plus a title or two from popular authors, such as Donoghue, Porter, Quinn, or Tobias.

Amling, Frederick. *Investments: An Introduction to Analysis and Management.* 5th ed. Englewood Cliffs, NJ: Prentice-Hall, 1984. $34.95.

Christy, George A., and John C. Clendenin. *Introduction to Investments.* 8th ed. New York: McGraw-Hill, 1982, $33.95.

Cohen, Jerome B. *Investment Analysis and Portfolio Management.* 4th ed. Homewood, IL: Dow Jones-Irwin, 1982. $35.95.

Darst, David M. *The Handbook of the Bond and Money Markets.* New York: McGraw-Hill, 1981, $48.95.

Donoghue, William E., and Thomas Tilling. *William E. Donoghue's No-Load Mutual Fund Guide.* New York: Bantam, 1984. $4.50.

Edwards, Robert D., and John Magee. *Technical Analysis of Stock Trends.* 5th ed. Boston: John Magee, Inc., 1983. $75.00.

Engel, Louis, and Brendan Boyd. *How to Buy Stocks.* Boston: Little, Brown, 1983. paper. $16.45.

Gastineau, Gary L. *The Stock Options Manual.* 2nd ed. New York: McGraw-Hill, 1979. $31.50.

Graham, Benjamin. *The Intelligent Investor,* 4th rev. ed. New York: Harper & Row, 1986. $18.45.

Huff, Charles, and Barbara Marinacci. *Commodity Speculation for Beginners: A Guide to the Futures Market.* New York: McGraw-Hill, 1982. paper. $5.95.

Little, Jeffrey, and Lucien Rhodes. *Understanding Wall Street.* Cockeysville, MD: Liberty Publishing, 1982. paper. $8.95.

Loll, Leo M., and Julian G. Buckley. *The Over-the-Counter Securities Market.* 4th ed. Englewood Cliffs, NJ: Prentice-Hall, 1981. $30.95.

Porter, Sylvia. *Sylvia Porter's New Money Book for the 80's.* New York: Avon, 1980. paper. $10.95.

Powers, Mark, and David Vogel. *Inside the Financial Futures Market.* 2nd ed. New York: Wiley, 1984. $24.95.

Quinn, Jane Bryant. *Everyone's Money Book.* New York: Delacorte Press, 1979.

Rugg, Donald D., and Norman B. Hale. *The Dow Jones-Irwin Guide to Mutual Funds.* Homewood, IL: Dow Jones-Irwin, 1986. $25.00.

Silk, Leonard. *Economics in Plain English: Updated and Expanded.* New York: Simon & Schuster, 1986. paper. $7.95.

Sokoloff, Kiril. *The Paine-Weber Handbook of Stock and Bond Analysis.* New York: McGraw-Hill, 1979. $52.50.

Stigum, Marcia, and Frank Fabozzi. *The Dow Jones-Irwin Guide to Bond and Money Market Investments.* New York: Dow Jones-Irwin, 1986. $25.00.

Teweles, Richard J., and Edward S. Bradley. *The Stock Market.* 5th ed. New York: Wiley, 1987. $24.95.

Tobias, Andrew. *The Only Investment Guide You'll Ever Need.* New York: Bantam, 1983. paper. $4.50.

United Business Service Co. *Successful Investing: A Complete Guide to Your Financial Future.* New York: Simon & Schuster, 1987. paper. $12.95.

Marketing Considerations for the Business Library

by Christine A. Olson

INTRODUCTION

A key ingredient in a librarian's plans to establish or manage a business information service is marketing. By establishing a strategic marketing plan early in the design and/or development of the business information service, librarians lay the foundation for a dynamic management tool, capable of meeting changing conditions and supporting growth goals.

In library circles, marketing is gaining recognition as an important management tool; it is to be included alongside with personnel, financial, and information-management skills. The purpose of this essay is to alert librarians to the overall scope of marketing as an information-service management tool. The next few pages are not meant to be a comprehensive treatise on marketing. They will, however, present the basic elements of a marketing program including: (1) marketing information systems, and (2) the marketing mix, consisting of the business information service/product offering, pricing strategies, distribution channels, promotion, and public relations.

Many librarians view marketing as a management tool requiring consideration only if their information services carry a price tag or if they are threatened with extinction. It is the author's belief that all libraries are business enterprises. Regardless of whether library services are offered at no cost, cost recovery, or for profit, the library, its services, and products need to be managed as a business operation. Once librarians assume a business orientation to library management, then marketing naturally falls into place along with personnel management, financial management, and administration. All of these management tools apply to a business library and the business information

Christine A. Olson operates an information/marketing resource company, Chris Olson Associates, 857 Twin Harbor Drive, Arnold, MD 21012.

service, whether it operates in a public, academic, medical, legal, or corporate environment.

THERE IS NO FOOLPROOF MARKETING FORMULA

As one of the author's students recently pointed out, "There is no foolproof formula" for marketing programs. Marketing programs require not only workable plans, but also a great deal of both quantitative and qualitative personal analysis skills. Quantitatively, librarians must be able to identify statistics important to the evaluation and control of their library's marketing activities. They also must analyze those statistics in light of marketing goals and objectives, and apply creative thought to how an opportunity can be exploited and how problems can be overcome.

Admittedly, some people are better at marketing than others. It helps if a librarian has an outgoing personality and a creative mind. But more importantly, a good marketer is able to see not only the "forest," but also the "trees." Indeed, if librarians will be carrying out their own marketing plan, then they should be prepared to get down to the level of the "leaves and twigs" as they write press releases and conduct personal sales calls.

If the reader believes that marketing consists of conducting a user survey, writing a brochure, and waiting for the phone to ring (in that order), then they have just fallen into what the author fondly calls the Marketing Trap. Marketing is much more, as evidenced by the American Marketing Association definition:

"Marketing is the process of planning and executing the conception, pricing, promotion, and distribution of ideas, goods, and services to create exchanges that satisfy individual and organizational objectives."[1]

Two basic concepts are evident in this definition. First, marketing is a comprehensive activity, in which all marketing components interact in a coordinated manner. Secondly, marketing is based on exchanges. A library offering business information services appeals to the needs of customers who will exchange money or time to receive those services. If the business information service is not appealing, costs too much, is not available when needed, or remains invisible, then no exchange will take place. Hence, it is very important to understand the business information market and the needs of potential customers.

MARKETING DECISION INFORMATION

The very first step in setting up a marketing program for a library business information service is the establishment of a marketing information system (MKIS). Although it may sound exotic, librarians have been maintaining MKIS's for years with data gathered from reference services, circulation, acquisitions and interlibrary loans. The difference between what was done in the past and what the MKIS librarians need to establish for business information service marketing programs today, lies in how the data is used and generated.

An effective MKIS goes beyond collecting statistics for activity reports. It generates information which identifies market trends, opportunities for service development, and potential strategies for positioning the business information service in the marketplace. Philip Kotler and Paul Bloom, in their book, *Marketing Professional Services* (1984), define an MKIS as:

"...a continuing and interacting structure of people, equipment, and procedures designed to gather, sort, analyze, evaluate and distribute pertinent, timely and accurate information for use by marketing decision makers to improve their marketing planning, execution and control."[2]

A MKIS need not be automated, although it does help. The information needed for a business library will also vary. More importantly, the level of marketing activities being pursued by librarians will have a significant impact on the sophistication of the MKIS and the information it generates. However, some common MKIS components can be presented here.

A MKIS gathers data about the business library's marketing environment. Collecting information on the library's target markets—who they are, their information needs, and if and how they are changing—and tracking competitors—knowing who they are, how and when they offer business information services, and how they affect the library's business information service—are both important to the overall marketing plan of action. Every library service has competition, whether another library, information broker, end-user database system, or a colleague network. A library's MKIS should present, on a regular basis, information on competitors and the relative position the business information service holds to them. Monitoring a library's marketing environment will help keep the library in business.

Other types of information gathered through an MKIS can answer questions such as: the number of new clients and repeat customers in a given time frame, the number of satisfied and dissatisfied customers, the amount of business generated by a promotion effort, or the amount of potential business projected for the coming quarter or year.

Once a librarian has identified the type of information needed to support the library's marketing program (and these needs will change as conditions change), the information-collection mechanisms and frequency rates will need to be implemented. Basically, there are three different mechanisms for collecting information: internal reports, intelligence, and research.

Internal reports can consist of statistical summaries and analyses from circulation, reference, online search, interlibrary loan, acquisitions, and photocopying activities of a library. The operational word in this description is "analyses." It's not enough to just report numbers.

The information in these reports should provide a clear picture of what is happening in the library and business information service. Intelligence data are a variety of information that can help the librarian understand why things are happening: why a service offering is successful, why business has dropped off in recent weeks, or why there is a flood of questions on a specific topic. Everyone on the library staff should be involved in gathering and reporting intelligence data. Whether via marketing contact reports or weekly business meetings, the staff should be aware of the importance of reporting trends, ideas, and observations.

The last mechanism for gathering MKIS information, research, should be most familiar to librarians. In library marketing programs, marketing research is actually part of a MKIS. There are many books and articles on the subject of marketing research and the various techniques available for gathering desired information. If readers are unfamiliar with focus groups, telephone interviews, or stratified sampling, then they are urged to attend educational sessions or read books on market research techniques.

Before leaving this section on MKIS and research, it is critical that librarians understand that market research is conducted with the non-user or potential market in mind as well as current customers. The common library research term "user survey" is a misnomer, leading to ineffective marketing strategies. If librarians have to use a phrase, then "needs assessment" is a better descriptor, although "market research" describes the activity as well or better.

AVOIDING THE "SHOTGUN APPROACH"

Three critical aspects of a library's marketing strategy that evolve from MKIS data are segmentation, targeting, and positioning strategies.

Segmentation refers to the division of the library's market according to specific characteristics. Possible segment variables include geographic (zip code, phone number, regions), demographic (age, life cycle, occupations, education), psychographic (social class, lifestyle), or behavioristic (user status, attitude, loyalty).

Although there is no absolute right or wrong way to segment a market, librarians should be sure their market segments: (1) are large enough to measure for size and purchasing power, (2) can be effectively reached and served through distribution channels, (3) are large enough to support the business information service/product offering, and (4) can be persuaded to act through promotion activities.[3]

When librarians open the doors and announce that business information is available, they are pursuing a "shotgun approach" or "hit-or-miss strategy" for offering of library services. To *effectively* support a marketing program for a business information service, librarians need to identify market segments, groups of individuals and organizations with similar characteristics, so that specific services, products, and messages can be aimed or targeted to specific audiences.

By targeting a market segment, librarians can develop, package, deliver, and promote business information services and products in a manner consistent with the desires and needs of the target market. For example, if a market segment is defined, in behavioristic terms, as Saturday workers, then a marketing strategy targeted to this group would offer 24-hour weekend information services.

The last strategy to emerge from MKIS data is the library's positioning strategy, i.e., what image does the library service hold in the eyes of the target market. Position can be based on a variety of perception factors: price, service quality, convenience, friendliness, responsiveness, and reliability, to name a few. The author has witnessed library staffs who believed their image was one thing, while the actual perception in the marketplace was another. It is therefore recommended that librarians conduct periodic research on the position their business information services and products actually hold in the marketplace. The results of this research will serve to either confirm the library's positioning strategy or identify image problems requiring adjustment.

MARKETING MIX STRATEGIES FOR BUSINESS LIBRARIES

The next phase of a library's marketing program deals with what is commonly referred to as the "four P's" of marketing: product, price, placement, and promotion. These four elements make up the mix of a marketing strategy in which each element is managed in relationship with other elements.

A library that has a superior service, offers it for free, makes it available during business hours, but doesn't make any announcements to the target market, has a marketing-mix strategy that will not yield successful results. The reason? The promotion element of the marketing mix has not been activated in proportion to other elements. A marketing-mix problem in the commercial world exists when a company introduces new products, issues promotion coupons, bombards the airwaves with commercials, but doesn't have the product in the stores. In this case, the placement or distribution element is missing from the marketing mix strategy.

The Product or the Service

The first marketing-mix element of concern is the product or service offered by the business information service. The greatest challenge associated with managing this aspect of the marketing mix is the requirement to create tangible evidence of value for an information service. Because information services are intangible (one cannot inspect the service before use or purchase as one can inspect a fountain pen), every aspect lending solid, visual reference to the information service should be closely managed. The appearance of the library and the staff, the packaging of online searches, and the physical presentation of reference services all present opportunities to attach tangible attributes to a library's business information service.

In many ways, efforts to make tangible an information service are tied directly to a library's positioning strategy. As was discussed earlier, a library's position is the image perceived by the target market. In the attempt to create tangible evidence of the value of a library's service offering, a positioning strategy can be reinforced or even established using tangible evidence. Providing tangible evidence that library services are timely, of high quality, friendly, and reliable all promote positions or images libraries want for their business information services.

Translating images into tangible evidence could also involve publicly noting the date and time when the request was taken, completed and provided to the customer (timeliness); providing service samples and statements attesting to quality from customers (quality); cheerfully answering the telephone and encouraging positive staff personality (friendliness); and publicly documenting timely and effective efforts to provide information to a customer (reliability). Librarians who successfully manage the product/service marketing-mix element and the intangible aspects of information services are those who (1) insert their online searches into handsome pocket folders, (2) pay special attention to the library's design and layout, (3) make sure their communications are on professionally designed and printed stationery, (4) enforce a dress code among staff members, and (5) personally observe the principles of effective interactions with the clientele.

Pricing the Business Information Service

The second element of the library's marketing mix is its pricing strategy. Before setting this strategy, a librarian needs to identify the library's price objectives. In the case of many libraries, the price objective is usage maximization. But increasingly, for some libraries, a secondary price objective is to recover costs. Still another price objective in some libraries is market disincentivization, a pricing objective intended to discourage usage. Academic libraries that charge high fees for filling interlibrary loan requests are pursuing a price objective of disincentivization. By charging a high fee, they hope to encourage requestors to seek alternative resources before turning to the academic library.

Once the price objective has been set, the actual pricing strategy can be determined. It should be noted that different services and products can have different price objectives depending upon the target market segment. At this point a librarian becomes involved in either cost-, demand-, or competition-oriented pricing, and in the various accounting methods used to determine the price elasticity of demand

and break-even analysis, to name a few popular pricing formulas. Whether the business information service charges for its services or not, the librarian needs to understand basic cost accounting principles. If the reader is unfamiliar with how a price is determined or how to set up cost centers, the author recommends attendance at seminars or reading about these principles and their applications to pricing library services.

Lest some readers feel that since they offer their business information services at no charge, they need not learn about pricing formulas, the author hastens to point out that there is no such thing as "free." Somewhere, "someone" is paying for the information service, making it imperative for librarians to know true costs and to tell that "someone," through various marketing strategies, about the value of information service.

Before proceeding onto the next mix element, it should be mentioned that a library's pricing decision is impacted by market perception, i.e., the market is aware of price, has price expectations, and perceives a price-quality relationship. This is true even for libraries offering "free" services. In these cases, instead of money being exchanged, price is perceived as convenience, timeliness, quality, and reliability. Regardless of the library's pricing objectives, a value ratio exists in which the overall value of a product is determined and defined as equal to the ratio of perceived quality to price.

Perceived Quality $\div$ Price = Value

Since quality is considered to be a function of price, when the quality increases, value will increase, and when the price goes up, the value will decrease.[4]

This ratio has a significant impact on a library's marketing program, especially for those libraries struggling to prove the value of their services. Before librarians claim a level of value, it is important to establish perceptions of quality versus the price (monetary or otherwise). This leads back inevitably to the challenge of making library services tangible. Because quality is perceived, the more effectively a librarian can create tangible evidence of the information service, the more easily the customer will "see" the quality and be able to compare it to price, thereby arriving at a value determination.

Placing the Business Information Service

The third element of the library's marketing mix is the actual placement of services and products into the hands of the customer. This element is commonly referred to as distribution channel management, for it involves managing the distribution of the library's services and products through various channels.

The primary channel for a library service is the library itself, to which people either bring in or phone in distribution of their information requests. For a business information service with a geographically centralized target market, the need for sophisticated distribution channels may not be necessary. However, for libraries with geographically dispersed markets, or target segments who typically do not want to walk a flight of stairs to get to the library, the librarian will have to develop a strong distribution strategy to facilitate the placement of services and products into the patron's hands. Examples of such target segments might be patrons located in the manufacturing end of an organization with a research library, field offices, or executives who are too busy to visit the central location.

Public libraries, with their bookmobile routes, have been operating distribution channels for years. Libraries that offer information on CD-ROM or via online database systems off-site from the library have established distribution channels, similar to libraries which operate satellite collections. The key behind any library distribution channel is making the information service accessible and available when and where the market needs it. This definition may have special implications for business information services targeting the business community. As one might guess, when businesspeople need information they want it "yesterday." If a library wishes to assume the position of being able to deliver information when and where a businessperson needs it, then the placement of information services will need careful consideration. Perhaps courier services, facsimile (fax) machines, electronic bulletin boards, or business-reference-collection rentals might be the answer. But it will not be enough to promise information service and not be able to deliver when called upon, unless the librarian wants to emulate the company that failed to have its product on the store shelves.

Promoting the Business Information Service

At last we have arrived at the favorite marketing-mix element of librarians, promotion. In fact, promotion is so favored a topic, many people think marketing is nothing but promotion. Obviously, this is not true. Promotion plays an important role in a library's marketing strategy, but its importance is relative to the other elements of the marketing mix.

A librarian has three major promotion activities from which to select: advertising, sales promotion, and personal sales. It should be parenthetically noted that some marketers include publicity as a promotion tool. The author believes that publicity or public relations is a separate function, to be pursued in coordination with the overall marketing strategy.

Before discussing the three promotion tools, librarians should understand how these tools fit into an overall communications framework. Although different promotion activities involve varying forms of communication, there is a basic communications theory underlying all promotion activities.

Essentially there are two parties in communication, the sender and the receiver. The library (sender) puts a message into symbolic form (encoding). The media represent the paths or vehicles via which the message moves from sender to receiver (the library's target market). The receiver decodes the message and assigns meaning to the symbols transmitted. Based on the decoding process, the receiver transmits a set of reactions or responds to the message, providing feedback to the sender.

The value of understanding this basic communications process becomes apparent to librarians when they conduct open houses and only a few people show up. Here again, market research can contribute immeasurably to successful promotion communications. By understanding what the target market wants to receive, the librarian has a better chance of transmitting a message that will prompt the desired action on the part of the target market.

Essentially, a library's promotion strategy is a combination of advertising, personal sales, and sales promotion. Advertising refers to any paid form of presentation of the library's business information services. Personal sales occur whenever the library staff interacts with the customer. The implication here is that everyone on the library floor is a salesperson, from the reference staff to the person shelving books. Sales promotions, underutilized in library promotion programs, are short-term incentives to encourage the library's target market to try an information service or product. Sales promotions include coupons, trading stamps, premiums, and contests.

The literature reveals a number of promotion ideas utilized by libraries to promote their business information services. Some ideas include:

- Exhibiting at business and industry fairs
- Billboard advertising
- Presentations at business breakfasts, luncheons, and dinners
- Distributing peel-off telephone labels printed with the business information service number
- Providing preprinted telephone Rolodex cards
- Ads in the telephone directory
- Telemarketing campaigns
- Distribution of coupons in paychecks or business magazines
- Display print ads in business periodicals
- Banners outside the library building
- Loudspeaker advertising
- Direct mail campaigns
- Speeches
- Sales presentations and demonstrations
- Free samples of services and products
- Introductory price specials
- Point-of-sale displays

- Sales literature
- Catalogs
- Exhibits in shopping malls

Above all, before readers get carried away with enthusiasm for promotional ideas, it must be remembered that promotion is relative to other marketing-mix elements, and that before a business information service can be promoted, messages, media, and audiences have to be considered in order to yield the greatest return on the promotion dollar.

TYING PUBLIC RELATIONS INTO THE LIBRARY'S MARKETING STRATEGY

As was mentioned earlier, the author believes public relations to be a separate element from promotion and places it as the fifth "P" in the marketing mix. This belief is based on the definition of public relations, as adopted by the 1978 World Assembly of Public Relations Associations:

"Public relations practice is the art and social science of analyzing trends, predicting their consequences, counseling organization leaders and implementing planned programs of action which will serve both the organizations and the public interest."

Simply stated, public relations means two-way communications designed to relate the needs and interests of a library with those of its target audience. A planned program of public relation actions is known as publicity, in which favorable media coverage is obtained of topics important to the library. The difference between promotion and public relations should be evident. Promotion is communications aimed at selling a library service/product, while public relations seeks to foster positive attitudes about a library and its business information service offering. The distinction lies in the general nature of public relations versus the selling services nature of promotion.

The distinction between promotion and public relations is important. Many times librarians combine the two elements, creating confusing messages and producing unmeasurable results. As with promotion, there are various tools and methods to carry the public-relations message. Some include:

- Press releases on new information services, new staff members, the results of a contest, or the announcement of special events
- Participation in radio and TV interviews
- Establishment of a visual identity system for the library's stationery, business cards, and other communications pieces
- Displays highlighting local businesses
- Speakers bureaus
- Lunchtime film programs on topics of interest to small business

- Annual reports
- Presentations on business information services at local schools and colleges
- Brochures and publications describing information services in light of their contribution to the business community
- Sponsorship of contribution of prizes to events such as golf tournaments
- Newsletters
- Public service announcements in print, radio, and TV media

Some libraries have public-relations offices which are prepared to issue press releases and implement the publicity program the library designs. Other librarians, who wear several hats, frequently have to write their own press releases. Getting recognized by the media takes know-how and patience. The author directs the reader to seminars and literature to learn the details of issuing press releases, creating identity systems, and other tools of public relations.

PULLING TOGETHER THE LIBRARY'S MARKETING PROGRAM

The librarian needs to pay close attention to the relationship and interaction of all marketing-mix elements in order to attain stated goals and measurable objectives. Taken separately, each marketing-mix element has its own challenging strategies. Combined, the elements of a marketing mix provide opportunities for growth and creative management. Above all, it should be apparent that marketing is not a one-time activity, to be planned one week and forgotten the next.

It is hoped these few pages describing major marketing tools have sufficiently introduced marketing management concepts to enable readers to begin thinking about their proposed or existing business information service in a marketing context. Omitted from this chapter are the marketing audit and marketing planning processes. Both of these tools require an understanding of the principal marketing concepts presented here, as well as analytical and planning methodologies specific to the individual business information service and its environment.

A number of books and journal articles are available in the business and library literature that can serve to expand concepts introduced in this essay. The few noted below are the author's personal preferences and in no way should be construed to represent the length or breadth of marketing literature.

Aaker, David A., and Day, George S. *Marketing Research.* 2nd ed. New York: John Wiley & Sons, 1983.
  Recommended for librarians who have never been exposed to a comprehensive marketing seminar or literature, this text offers an abundance of interesting examples of marketing concepts, although the examples are not library-related. Contents are arranged in a logical manner, with one of the last chapters devoted to services marketing and its challenges for the marketer.

Assael, Henry. *Marketing Management: Strategy and Action.* Boston: Kent Publishing, 1985.

The best introductory text to marketing research, this is easy reading with many examples. Best of all, it introduces research statistical methods in a painless manner. It is especially recommended for librarians who feel quantitative techniques are not their forte.

Fulz, Jack F. *Overhead: What It Is and How It Works.* Cambridge, MA: Abt Books, 1980.

Recommended to those who have already digested a cost-accounting text or course, this book offers a very concise discussion on cost accounting and overhead elements.

Holechek, James. *Public Relations.* 3rd ed. Jordan-Holechek, Inc., 300 Cathedral St., Baltimore, MD 21201.

Numerous examples of public relations tools and "how-to" advice are presented. Jim Holechek, a public relations practitioner, gives the reader an inside look at how things should be done.

Kotler, Philip, and Andreasen, Alan. *Strategic Marketing for Non-Profit Organizations.* 3rd rev. ed. of *Marketing for Non-Profit Organizations.* Englewood Cliffs, NJ: Prentice-Hall, 1987.

The 660 pages of this text are packed with marketing management theory and illustrations, including examples using library situations. This is the bible for nonprofit marketing managers and contains excellent marketing audit guidelines.

REFERENCES

1. American Marketing Association Board, 1985.

2. Philip Kotler and Paul Bloom, *Marketing Professional Services* (Englewood Cliffs, NJ: Prentice-Hall, 1984), p. 125.

3. "Segmenting Your Library Market," *Marketing Treasures 1* (September 1987): 1.

4. Richard P. Bagozzi, *Principles of Marketing Management* (Chicago: Science Research Associates, 1986), p. 507.

Acquisitions and Collection Development in Business Libraries

by Constance B. Cameron

THE LITERATURE

Although the literature from 1975 through 1987 contains little written about either acquisitions or collection development in business libraries, there is some material worthy of mention.

In the area of acquisitions, Martha Bailey notes in her paper that acquiring library materials is a function performed by 106 of the 108 company libraries responding to a survey. These libraries operated in the areas of aircraft and missiles, chemicals, foods, law, newspapers, office machines, petroleum, and pharmaceuticals.[1] She also notes that 34 of the 108 librarians who answered order personal books and subscriptions for company employees. A brief note on purchasing policies is also found in a pamphlet by Bernhard[2] and Koch and Pask's[3] report on the acquisition of working papers. Bernstein[4] addresses the collection of corporate annual reports. Seventy-five percent of the 335 responding libraries identified these reports as vital for satisfying company interests in career, financial, and historical information. Most libraries maintained one to two years of hard-copy reports, and librarians were admonished to monitor all the financial and selection options of commercial microform vendors for information relevant to annual reports.

Collection-development policy is related to an analysis of reference requests in a paper by Smith,[5] and the general importance of the collection is noted in the pamphlet by Bernhard[6] and a paper by Dermyer.[7] Aids to collection development, for both general and special collections, are discussed in papers by Beeler,[8] DePiesse,[9] Ganly,[10] Haines,[11] Jones,[12] Koch and Pask,[13] Ohlson and Tabuteau,[14] and

Constance B. Cameron is reference librarian, Bryant College Library, Smithfield, RI.

Ternberg.[15] The other papers that relate to collection are concerned with descriptions of various collections.[16-23]

Crucial to the development of a strong collection is the availability of materials evaluating individual components of the collection. Of special interest in this regard are three authors' series, only the latest of each of which is noted below: Balachandran,[24] DiMattia,[25] and the *Library Journal* series.[26] Also worthy of note are the Behles treatment of business periodicals,[27] the Brown materials on Canadian sources,[28] the Bowker volume,[29] the King presentation on U.S. serial publications,[30] and the Hatzfeld material on indexes.[31] For more specific areas of interest, the reader is referred to the collection of abstracts of the literature included as Part 2 of this book.

Another emphasis for this survey of the literature is the impact of electronic technology on collection-development efforts. Bank librarian Marydee Ojala surveyed public librarians and discovered most were ready to accept computerized sources as value-added resources, which have to date caused only a few cancellations of print indexes/abstracts.[32] The concern over the high cost of technology can be seen in the article by Poole and St. Clair, which advocated that online search services be subsidized by the acquisitions budget.[33] These writers provoked a reaction from Dowd, Whaley, and Pankake,[34] who preferred to preserve the more democratic and accessible printed word and defined its allocation in the acquisitions budget. Even the participants of a recent conference sponsored by the database industry felt the change to computerized sources would be an evolutionary, not a revolutionary, one.[35]

PRACTICE IN SELECTED LIBRARIES

To develop a picture of practices in acquisitions and collections development for business libraries in the 1980s, data were collected by the author from six libraries. The six were:

1. A major state university research library, granting both graduate and undergraduate degrees in its business school.
2. A small, private, 4-year business college granting undergraduate and some master's degrees.
3. A small-to-medium-sized, private, 4-year college with undergraduate and master's level programs which focus primarily on business-related areas.
4. A small-to-medium-sized, public library serving an active business community.
5. A small-to-medium-sized, public library serving a small business community.
6. A small, corporate library serving a specialized clientele.

The data were collected from each library in a personal visit with the professional(s) directly responsible for the selection/acquisition of business materials in the facility. Each visit was preceded by an advance mailing of an explanatory cover letter and a list of core questions to be covered. The visits averaged two hours in length.

Although the business-library environments differed, and funding and general procedures varied, some general conclusions can be drawn from this survey. These conclusions are summarized below with additional observations added by the author.

Summaries of Replies

1. *How is the selection of business materials handled? Who initiates the requests for purchase?* The general trend in selection is to have one person be responsible for business reference and a second person responsible for circulating business materials. For the universities, the larger the library, the less direct the involvement of the librarians in selection. In the largest library visited (an academic library), selection was handled by the business faculty in conjunction with purchasing of the total offerings of major business publishers. On the other hand, the smallest academic library approached most closely the ideal model of coordinated business selection in a library/teaching faculty environment. A liaison system that assigned each professional librarian to certain faculty members and their subject areas successfully promoted communication and selection coordination. Although in all cases requests for purchase of materials were encouraged from all active business library users (including students) and professionals, the largest number of requests was initiated by the library professionals.

In her own experience, the author has found it useful, in selecting new materials, to vary the selection procedures according to the price of the item, as described below.

a. For expensive items (those priced at more than $150): Many of these are identified to the selector by a sales representative or by a brochure containing an introductory offer. Even in the largest libraries, in light of limited budgets, one must carefully consider the purchase by:

   (1) Obtaining full information and, if possible, a copy.
   (2) Comparing the tool against comparable tools held by the library or by other libraries in the area. The tool should also be compared with the earlier edition, if there is one, to see if substantive (and valuable) changes have been made. A useful technique is to look up the same, particularly relevant, entries in both earlier editions and in comparable tools.
   (3) Weighing the price against the value, as determined by the comparisons in (2).
   (4) Consulting with colleagues in the library.
   (5) Carefully considering current client demand. Expensive items of this sort may be candidates for resource sharing or for "trial" purchase.
   (6) Investigating the holdings of neighboring libraries.

b. Items of medium expense ($75–$100) are usually identified through the bibliographic tools listed later in this essay. It is helpful to send a simple inquiry form to the publisher, expressing interest in acquiring a copy, and asking for price information and a sample copy. If, on the basis of the preliminary information, the title looks promising, its value should be confirmed by checking for a review, or, if no review is found, by consultation with a colleague, preferably with the tool in hand.

c. Less expensive items (under $75) may be identified from the standard tools or major publishers listed later in this essay. It is important to stay abreast of the brochures of specialized publishers. The client is often helpful here, too; he or she may be on mailing lists not available to the librarian or may notice advertisements in specialty journals. (Close liaison with the patron is always recommended in any case.)

Once an item has been identified, a decision for or against purchase can generally be easily made. Where available, reviews are helpful. And, of course, the decision must always be made on the basis of the value (to the collection and to the user) and the funds available.

In addition to selecting new business materials, the business librarian must remember the ongoing process of business acquisitions, which requires a semiannual review of serials, annuals, and standing orders, all done in some regular, organized form that utilizes all the available staff expertise. The author strongly recommends, in addition, that a regular annual review of interlibrary loan requests be made and considered in collection-development decisions.

2. What are the major selection tools used? Which are used most frequently in actual practice? Reviewing media were the selection tools most prominently mentioned. Advertisements and publishers' brochures, especially from publishers of established quality, were also noted as heavily used.

Generally, the greater the availability of funds, the more likely librarians are to use advertising materials of established publishers in conjunction with reviewing media. The more specialized the library environment, the less likely that general library reviewing media will fill the need; instead, greater dependence will be placed on specialized journal reviews and user requests. Currency and easy availability of recent material are the prime needs of most business users. The stability of the academic environment releases this time pressure to some extent. In the more public and the corporate library environments, the focus is on the ability to mesh funds and on knowledge of both subject and patron to keep selection one jump ahead of the need. In these environments, a more concerted effort is made to order directly from publishers, to ensure currency.

The principal general materials selection and review tools recommended by the author for business materials are :

Book Review Digest. New York: H. W. Wilson, 1905–.

Book Review Index. Detroit: Gale, 1965–.

Booklist. Chicago: American Library Association, 1905–.

Choice. Middleton, CT: Choice, 1964–.

College and Research Libraries. Chicago: Association of College and Research Libraries, 1934–.

Encyclopedia of Associations. Detroit: Gale, 1988.

Encyclopedia of Business Information Sources. Detroit: Gale, 1986.

Harvard Business Review. Boston: Harvard University, 1922–.

Library Journal. New York: R. R. Bowker Co., 1876–.

Management Review. New York: American Management Associations, 1923–.

New Books in Business and Economics: Recent Additions to Baker Library. Boston: Harvard University (10/year).

New York Times Book Review. New York: New York Times, 1896–.

Wall Street Journal. New York: Dow Jones, 1889–.

3. *What major standard catalogs or lists are used as checks for the strength and balance of your collection?* Two major sources were mentioned in almost all cases: *New Books in Business and Economics; Recent Additions to Baker Library, Harvard University* and Lorna M. Daniells's *Business Information Sources (1985).* Daniells was also noted as most useful when basic purchases in a "new" business area are being considered. In addition to these, the author recommends a regular review of:

American Reference Books Annual. Littleton, CO: Libraries Unlimited, 1970–

Library Journal. New York: R. R. Bowker Co., 1876–

Reference Services Review. Ann Arbor, MI: Pierian Press, 1973–

Sheehy, Eugene P. Guide to Reference Books. 10th ed. Chicago: American Library Association, 1986

and a selected list of the business journals appropriate to the particular library. (The core list in Part I of this book should also be checked.)

4. *Are purchases made through a jobber or directly from the publisher? Who are the major jobbers and publishers?* In all cases, the majority of purchases were made through a jobber, with Baker & Taylor listed most frequently. A variety of publishers were listed. Publishers' brochures recommended for routine screening by the author include those of:

American Enterprise Institute for Public Policy Research. 1150 17th St., N. W., Washington, DC 20036.

American Management Associations, Inc. 135 W. 50th St., New York 10020.

Brookings Institution. 1775 Massachusetts Ave., N.W., Washington, DC 20036.

Bureau of National Affairs, Inc. 1231 25th St., N.W., Washington, DC 20037.

Commerce Clearing House, Inc. 4125 W. Peterson Ave., Chicago, IL 60646.

Dow Jones-Irwin. 1818 Ridge Rd., Homewood, IL 60430.

Dun & Bradstreet, Inc. Dun's Marketing Services, 3 Century Dr., Parsippany, NJ 07054.

Lexington Books. 125 Spring St., Lexington, MA 02173.

Matthew Bender and Co., Inc. 11 Penn Plaza, New York 10001.

Moody's Investors Service, Inc. 99 Church St., New York 10007.

National Retail Merchants Association. 100 W. 31st St., New York, 10001.

Prentice-Hall, Inc. Englewood Cliffs, NJ 07632.

Progressive Grocer. 1351 Washington Blvd., Stamford, CT 06902.

Standard and Poor's Corporation. 25 Broadway, New York 10004.

5. *Is there a written selection policy?* Selection policies, although generally in existence, do not seem to be viewed as a major concern in business libraries. Perhaps this is because the principal selection criterion is already established, i.e., meeting a curriculum need of faculty or students, in the case of academic libraries; a project client or organizational need, in the case of special libraries; and a patron need in the public library. In every case, currency is an important consideration.

6. *Are there financial limitations on the purchase of single books?* Generally there are not financial limitations on the purchase of single books as long as the need is demonstrated and funds are available. (The author's additional comments on question (1) above should also be noted in this connection.)

7. *Is the emphasis in your business collection on the purchase of monographs, serials, or periodicals?* The general aim in the majority of the libraries is to strive for a balance between monographs and serials in the allocation of business material funds. Short funding upsets the ratio significantly. The heavy costs involved in maintaining serials (e.g., investment sources and value lines) on occasion does not permit purchases outside of these areas. The smaller business library environments reduce this pressure somewhat and lower costs by alternate-year updating of such services.

8. *How many journals/serials are currently received?* Numbers of current periodical subscriptions range from a low of approximately 80 in the public library to highs of approximately 880 in the larger academic environments. Back issues are held in direct relation to available space for storage and funds for binding. The purchase of back issues on microforms is directly related to funding, and academic libraries are more likely to purchase microforms.

9. **What impact has compact-disk technology or access to online business databases had for your business collection-development efforts? Do you have or anticipate acquiring business information on compact disk in the next three years? Do you anticipate dropping/adding any business periodicals or reference indexes due to electronic technology?** At this writing most of the practitioners interviewed felt the availability of new electronic products had produced marginal effects on their collections. The corporate librarian noticed no change at all.

The librarians for the larger collections were investigating specific products for future purchase and had dropped only an isolated title or two, e.g., *FIND/SVP*, the *Wall Street Journal Index*, the *Magazine Index*. Only the business college had actually acquired two products on compact disk. Discussions with these librarians seemed to bear out the evolutionary nature of the transition from print to electronics espoused by the authors Lancaster and Goldhor.[36]

Newer trends in information delivery are being monitored as well. The author was referred to an article about Datext, as an example, by the university librarian.[37] Kollin and Shea note that such multiple-base products will be helpful to the user, but that their development must be market- rather than technology-controlled.[38] Practitioners can help shape these developments by utilizing one of their traditional assets, i.e., professional cooperation and consultation.

REFERENCES

1. Martha J. Bailey, "Functions of Selected Company Libraries/Information Services," *Special Libraries* 72 (January 1981): 18–30.

2. Genore H. Bernhard, "The Business Firm Library," in her *How to Organize and Operate a Small Library* (Fort Atkinson, WI: Highsmith, 1976), p. 39.

3. Jean E. Koch and Judith M. Pask, "Working Papers in Academic Business Libraries," *College and Research Libraries* 41 (November 1980): 517–23.

4. Judith R. Bernstein, "Corporate Annual Reports in Academic Business Libraries," *College and Research Libraries* 47 (May 1986): 263–73.

5. Gerry M. Smith, "The Demand for Business Information in an Academic Library: An Analysis of the Library Inquiry Service of the City University Business School," *ASLIB Proceedings* 28 (November/December 1976): 392–99.

6. Bernhard, p. 39.

7. Angela Dermyer, "Try on a Company Library," *Industry Week* 194 (August 1, 1977): 56–57.

8. Margery Beeler, "Business Reference Tools for Small or Medium-Sized Library," *Unabashed Librarian* 50 (1984): 15.

9. Larry DePiesse, "Business Basics: a Bibliography for Better Business," *Unabashed Librarian* 46 (1986): 21–26.

10. John Ganly, "Consider the Source: Developing Business Collections," *Collection Building* 5 (Summer 1983): 24–28.

11. Michael Haines, "Company Correspondence: An Important Information Resource," *ASLIB Proceedings* 31 (August 1979): 401–11.

12. H. Jones, "Why the Bookmen Turn to Business," *Director* 22 (December 1976): 33–34.

13. Koch and Pask, pp. 517–23.

14. June Ohlson and Christine Tabuteau, "Microfiche Project on Australian Companies' Annual Reports," *Australian Academic and Research Libraries* 9 (December 1978): 215–18.

15. Milton G. Ternberg, "Business Basics: A Guide to Selection Sources," *Collection Building* 5 (Spring 1983): 22–27.

16. Deborah Abraham and Annette Pelcher, "Information for Tennessee Economic and Community Development," *Tennessee Librarian* 30 (Spring 1978): 24–26.

17. *Illinois Libraries* 62 (March 1980). Entire issue.

18. "Meeting the Need of GM Research Laboratories," *Information Manager* 2 (Spring 1980): 21–25.

19. K. Ruokonen, "Survey of Economic and Business Libraries in Scandinavia," *UNESCO Bulletin for Libraries* 31 (September 1977): 277–85.

20. B. T. Salter, "Economics Libraries in the United States," *INSPEL* 12 (1977): 113–24.

21. J. Spencer, *Business Information in London: A Study of the Demand and Supply of Business Information in the Thirteen London Business Libraries* (London: ASLIB, 1976).

22. Frances K. Wood, "Business and Industrial Needs: Special Libraries Are Willing to Share Resources," *Wisconsin Library Bulletin* 76 (May/June 1980): 109–10.

23. Anne R. Zimmerman, "Library Services for Members: How the FHL Banks Can Help," *Federal Home Loan Bank Board Journal* 11 (September 1978): 21–40.

24. M. Balachandran, *Academic Business Library: A Core Collection* (Monticello, IL: Vance Bibliographies, 1986). 12 vols.

25. Susan S. DiMattia, "Business Books: 1986; A Selected List of Business Titles Published Last Year That Reflect Important Trends in the Literature," *Library Journal* 112 (March 15, 1987): 26–33.

26. "Scientific, Technical, Medical and Business Books," *Library Journal* 111 (November 1, 1986): 58–85.

27. Richard J. Behles, "Business America," *Serials Review* 6 (April/June 1980): 7–8.

28. B. E. Brown, ed., *Canadian Business and Economics: A Guide to Sources of Information* (Ottawa, Ontario: Canadian Library Association, 1976).

29. *Business Books and Serials in Print* (New York: Bowker, 1977).

30. Richard L. King, ed., *Business Serials of the U. S. Government* (Chicago: American Library Association, 1978).

31. Lois A. Hatzfeld, "Business," in her *Periodical Indexes in the Social Sciences and Humanities: A Subject Guide* (Metuchen, NJ: Scarecrow, 1978), pp. 22–26.

32. Marydee Ojala, "Public Library Business Collections and New Reference Technologies," *Special Libraries* 74 (April 1983): 138–49.

33. Jay Martin Poole and Gloriana St. Clair, "Funding Online Services from the Materials Budget," *College & Research Libraries* 47 (May 1986): 225–29.

34. Sheila Dowd, John H. Whaley, Jr., and Marcia Pankake, "Reactions to Funding Online Services from the Materials Budget," *College & Research Libraries* 47 (May 1986): 230–37.

35. Brad Schepp, "NFAIS Explores the Database Revolution," *Datapro Directory of On-Line Services* 6 (April 1987): 1–3.

36. F. W. Lancaster and Herbert Goldhor, "The Impact of Online Services on Subscriptions to Printed Publications," in *Managing Online Reference Services* (New York: Neal-Schuman Publishers, Inc., 1986), pp. 372–84.

37. James Fries and Jonathan Brown, "Business Information on CD-ROM: The Datext Service at Dartmouth College, New Hampshire," *Program* 21 (January 1987): 1–12.

38. Richard P. Kollin and James E. Shea, "New Trends in Information Delivery," reprinted in *Managing Online Reference Services* (New York: Neal-Schuman Publishers, Inc., 1986), pp. 385–88.

Organization of Materials in Business Libraries

by Carol A. Hryciw-Wing

INTRODUCTION

In 1919 Stanley Jast created a definition of a business library that emphasized both the provision of commercial information *and* "the collection, arrangement, and cataloguing of such printed matter so as to render it quickly and conveniently available for enquirers and readers."[1] Despite noting the great importance of organization of business materials, however, the literature related to business libraries over the years has continued to concentrate on the retrieval of information for users and the "servicing of users," rather than on collections. Indeed, a survey taken among head librarians of 54 major corporate libraries in 1976 indicated that, for 25 percent of these librarians, literature searching occupied the major part of their time, while percentages spent organizing material as a separate category were not even mentioned.[2] So, too, over the past decade there has been phenomenal growth in the number of books and articles on online retrieval services and bibliographic databases, some of which are very pertinent to business library needs,[3] and a tendency among authors writing on corporate librarianship to stress the need to utilize technology to access information—but not collections—or face extinction.[4-5]

Yet if a business library or information center maintains any collections at all, the materials in these collections should be organized to be as easily accessed as the information in our online reference databases. The literature of the past 20 years or so recognizes the validity of this assertion, but often overlooks the need to state it explicitly. The citations offered below and the information gathered from a survey of business libraries, presented later in this chapter, as well as a brief discussion of the types of business libraries that exist

Carol A. Hryciw-Wing is head of Technical Services, Rhode Island College Library, Providence, RI.

today, should serve to clarify the role and extent of the organization of materials in business libraries.

TYPES OF BUSINESS LIBRARIES

Myers and Frederick describe three kinds of business libraries: the library of a private organization, the business department or branch of a public library, and the university business library.[6] Lorna Daniells notes these same categories of business libraries, but adds trade and professional association libraries.[7] While neither of these sources speaks of organization of business materials, their views on the differences among the types of business libraries provide valuable background information necessary for an understanding of organizational principles and methods in these libraries. These views may be summarized as follows:

(1) Corporate and trade business libraries exist to serve the information needs of their patrons, and they collect material to reflect those needs. Emphasis is not on maintenance and organization but on getting information for individuals. The librarian is expected in many cases to locate the information needed by the client and to "spoon-feed it, if necessary, to the person who needs it."[8]

(2) The public business library must serve "anyone who needs it, from large corporations and universities with their own libraries to the lone small-businessperson who has nowhere to turn but to the public library."[9] The user's need is still mainly for information, but more often a client is pointed to sources, when extended research is needed. Therefore, logical organization of materials in a manner comprehensible to both the business professional and the layperson is a firm requirement.

(3) Both the university business library and the business school library must support the academic programs, and sometimes the faculty research, of the institution and must develop the collection to meet these needs. Library staff members must instruct students in how to locate materials and should, therefore, provide a variety of access points in their catalogs and other aids which are understandable to these students, as well as to business users.

THE LITERATURE OF ORGANIZATION

In-depth coverage of the topic of organization specifically in business libraries appears in three publications, all three by British authors and all, understandably, from a British perspective and bias. In the first, Malcolm Campbell discusses principles of organization and acquisition of a variety of business materials, including special treatment of all types of directories, periodicals and newspapers, and corporate reports.[10] In the second, A. Leslie Smyth proposes some general principles of arrangement; compares the London City Business Library and the Manchester (England) Commercial Library in their arrangement of directories, periodicals, market product and industrial data, statistics, and vertical file materials; and includes special subject classifications provided by these libraries.[11] In the third, Smyth discusses the objectives, use, and staffing of business libraries; how such libraries should be designed; and how they should be fitted out with furniture and shelving for different types of material (directories, company card services, vertical file materials, maps, microforms, etc.)[12]

Two recent works by American authors provide lengthy discussions of organizational methods suggested for special libraries that are pertinent to the business library. Ferguson and Mohley[13] offer a rudimentary introduction to traditional cataloging and classification, indexing, and records management and include a short section on organizing and handling 16 types of materials (for example, reports, periodicals, standards and specifications, patents, and company records). Ahrensfeld, Christianson, and King,[14] in what has become one of the classic introductions to special-librarianship in this country, address the housing and arrangement of collections; creation of records to identify library holdings; and subject analysis by classification, subject cataloging, and indexing—all in one pithy chapter; and space requirements for the collection in a later chapter. They also suggest that, depending on the resources available, organizing materials may be handled at a minimum, intermediate, or maximum functional level.

Several other publications, though more than 10 years old, offer briefer views on organizational topics that are still noteworthy. Eva Lou Fisher's checklist of questions for planning and evaluating company libraries is helpful when one considers cataloging and classification.[15] K. D. C. Vernon not only covers the use of business and management literature and notes the importance of interlibrary cooperation, but also explains in detail what catalogs are and how they are arranged, and provides a clear outline of the *London Classification of Business Studies* while discussing classification.[16] In his chapter on special libraries, in Lock's *Manual of Library Economy,* Ronald Stavely delineates some of the organizational features of the library at Borden, United Kingdom, and that of the IBM United Kingdom Laboratories.[17] In this same volume, K. G. B. Bakewell offers a chapter that speaks of classification, cataloging, and indexing in special libraries; notes the increase of indexing in preference to classification; and stresses the advantages of maintaining a catalog.[18] The Life Office Management Association, in consultation with Elizabeth Ferguson, suggests techniques for organizing and running either a small-scale information center or a professional library in a company.[19] Simple record-keeping and arrangement is advocated for the former, standard cataloging and classification for the latter. Finally, G. D. L. Peterson, in an article on establishing business information services within companies, states the need to access and organize such nontraditional materials as news wire printouts, radio and TV transcripts, microforms, and cassette tapes.[20]

Contemporary with Peterson's piece is a paper by Carol Tenopir, which was among the earliest to emphasize the need to utilize effective computerized systems for the organization and retrieval of materials.[21] Endorsing the establishment of comprehensive information centers in small and medium-sized companies, she presents a comparison of a computerized and a manual card catalog; elaborates on the flexibility and adaptability of storage space, cataloging procedures, classification schemes and thesauri, subject headings, and maintenance procedures within the company library setting, and concerns herself with the design of all of these features in view of "the unique needs of each individual company."[22]

A handful of articles have appeared that address organizing specific types of material. George Henderson, in Campbell's *Manual of Business Library Practice*, speaks of the optimal arrangement of telephone and city directories and briefly describes the special two-digit classification scheme for specialized directories used by the City Business Library in London and by other business libraries in England.[23] Michael Haines details the objectives and actual classification breakdowns of the company-wide correspondence filing scheme used at the Data Retrieval Unit of the mining company, Charter Consolidated, Ltd., in England.[24] Koch and Pask present the results of a survey of academic business librarians and faculty members on the value and cataloging of working papers.[25] (Interestingly enough, less than half of those libraries which collect such papers catalog them.) Another recent survey by Bernstein, which polled 500 academic business libraries on their treatment of corporate annual reports, shows that most collections of these reports are located in reference departments, are filed in cabinets by company name, and are accessed through simple devices such as check-in cards or on library guide sheets.[26] Some years earlier, Ohlson and Tabuteau also drew attention to corporate annual reports with their description of a microfilming project for approximately 12,200 annual reports of Australian companies, carried out at the Australian Graduate School of Management Library,[27] in which they present an explanation of the layout of the fiche and the plan for organizing the file and for updating and filing a particular company's reports. Blick and Ward's detailing of the policy promoted by the Beecham Pharmaceuticals Research Division libraries, to replace hardcopy journals by microfiche after these journals have been in the libraries for a certain period of time (e.g., three to five years), even covers the matter of the filing of the fiche.[28] These libraries integrate microfilm and hard-copy issues in the same shelving locations—a method viewed positively by the users.

Turning next to the literature on the well-known methods of applying organization to collections—classification, indexing, subject analysis, and cataloging—we see a number of informative publications on the first, with only a few specifically devoted to subject analysis and indexing. So, too, computer-produced catalogs assume a high profile, while the art of cataloging warrants just a passing mention.

On the topic of classification schemes developed particularly for business materials, the literature of the 1960s and 1970s is especially helpful. In an early article, Suzanna Lengyel describes a classification system created for materials in the Union Carbide Corporation Business Library, based on a modified Dewey classification, which allowed for the application of the full Dewey range of numbers (0–999) to the materials and which resulted in a more detailed breakdown of subjects without use of long numbers.[29] A classification and indexing scheme utilized by the American Society for Quality Control (ASQC) for its publications is outlined by Ray Wachniak.[30] This literature classification system was originally adopted by the ASQC in 1959 and revised in 1975. The coding includes the methodology or techniques of quality control described, the normal functions using the method or techniques, and the specific business or industry involved. Additions to the numbers identify the journals and issues numbers of the articles. Still of interest is the first major specialized classification for business literature, the Classification of Business Literature, first published at Baker Library of the Harvard University Graduate School of Business Administration in 1937 and appearing in a revised edition in 1960.[31] Although not used at Baker since 1976, it is probably still being used by some private business libraries in this country. The introduction to the revised edition (pp. xiii-xviii) provides the best explanation of the scheme. The classification was intended to accommodate books, periodicals, manuscripts, maps, prints, broadsides, and reports and used three main elements: (1) subject analysis of business organization and activity, divided into many sections with capital letter notations; (2) an "Industries List," which is a classified arrangement of industries and occupations with numerical notations; and (3) a "Local List," which is a classified arrangement of geographical and political divisions with numerical notations.

The best-known classification for business materials, however, is the London Classification of Business Studies (LCBS), compiled by K. D. C. Vernon and Valerie Lang, and published first in 1970 by the London Business School with a revised version appearing in 1979.[32] There is no record of libraries in the United States using the LCBS, but at least 50 libraries in the United Kingdom and 30 in other countries use it.[33] Two articles provide excellent background information on LCBS. The earlier of the two, by K. G. B. Bakewell, describes the origins, scope, and principles of LCBS, outlines the reasons for a revision, and examines the revision process and the major differences between the first and second editions, with illustrative examples.[34] Bakewell notes that the scheme can also be used as a thesaurus or authority list of terms or "as a source of headings for an alphabetical subject catalogue (precoordinate mode) or a postcoordinate index."[35]

In the second article, K. D. C. Vernon concentrates on the necessity for, revision of, and use of LCBS. He includes evidence concerning the usefulness of the second edition and its increasing popularity among business libraries.[36] Bakewell's introduction to the second edition of LCBS not only best explains the background, principles, and revision of the scheme, but indicates the notation and order of the classes and auxiliary schedules of the system.[37] He presents hints on reclassifying from LCBS1 to LCBS2 and gives a complete list of libraries that are using the system. Differing from the Harvard Classification in that it uses facet analysis, LCBS is broken down into three main categories, which, in turn, are divided into a number of main classes and concepts given capital letter notations. Auxiliary tables can be used to specify form of presentation (e.g., dictionary) or country, and these are given numerical notations.

Subject headings for business materials are treated in the literature of the 1950s and 1960s,[38] but in later years the emphasis seems to have shifted to the related subject of indexing. Bakewell, a perennial author of publications on business libraries, provides us with a look at the indexing used in ANBAR, a documentation service for management offering access to selected articles in over 200 journals through abstracts (monthly) and an index (quarterly).[39] The index is classified and has its own alphabetical subject index. In the same year fellow Britisher John Blagden published a book-length description of his Management Information Retrieval System (MIRS), which is designed to answer inquiries from companies about their files of management information.[40] MIRS employs postcoordinate indexing and has a thesaurus.

While the remainder of the seventies bears witness to no other published works on specific business indexing systems, F. A. Graham's article strongly advocates subject indexing of all materials in industrial libraries and the coordination of individual library efforts as a means of attaining true universal bibliographic control.[41] Finally, in the eighties, Eddison and Lyman published a very handy and useful list of 3,000 terms from a variety of business fields that can be—and have been—used in creating indexes and organizing everyday business reports and memos.[42] The inclusion of scope notes and related terms in the main listing and appended lists (which cover pertinent agencies and organizations, major companies, currencies of the world, and standard subject heading subdivisions) increases the value of this work. Such a listing would be a vital asset to the corporate librarians of the future who, according to Culnan, should broaden their traditional skills and, in the area of organization of materials, for instance, should help companies or individuals in indexing internal documents.[43] Library curricula, she advocates, should include training in indexing and organizing office documents.

Computer-produced and *online catalogs* are the rage of the times in business, as in other libraries, and the literature reflects the growing popularity of these access mechanisms. In 1976 and 1980 articles appeared which spoke of computer-produced microfiche catalogs. In one, G. de Saederleer explains the integration of acquisitions, bibliographic retrieval, and loans at the Central Library of the Belgian

Ministry of Economic Affairs into an automated system,[44] and states that the library has a microfiche catalog, updated on a monthly basis, of books and articles, divided into three sections (author, key word in title, and Universal Decimal Classification number). Copies of this catalog are distributed to interested libraries and are encased in a special cassette-microfiche reader. In a second article, Redfield notes the COM (microfiche) catalog developed by Autographics for the Johns Mansville Company, a mining company in Colorado, that in 1980 covered 1,300 items in the subject areas of mining and geology.[45]

Subsequent conference papers and articles document and endorse the development of in-house computer systems that provide catalogs, most of them online. Karmiggelt suggests employing a company computer to store and retrieve bibliographic data and names four different software approaches that may be used to accomplish this.[46] He advocates what several business libraries had already attempted with success. For instance, in 1968 the Technical Information Center at the Eaton Company had developed computer programs, written in FORTRAN and run on the computer center's IBM 1130, which enabled the development of a database of information on the Information Center's books and in-house research and test reports, classed in Dewey and subject-cataloged by approximately eight subjects, each with the *Thesaurus of Engineering and Scientific Terms* as the authority list.[47] At first the results were batch-produced subject searches, but, then, in 1974, the in-house system went online and now, running on an IBM 370-158, allows the main and branch libraries to edit and search from terminals by author, subject, year, and location.

So, too, Johnstone and Taylor had already managed, using existing computer resources—in this case, a PDP-11/70 with a database management package called The Information System—at the Australian Graduate School of Management, to create a database of bibliographic records that in 1979 represented over 10,000 books and allowed staff access by ISBN, LCCN, call number, and Dewey class number. They had also produced four book catalogs (author, title, subject, and class number).[48] Their positive experience was shared by Rivaz and associates, who established an in-house computer-based system at Smith Kline & French Laboratories, Ltd., (U.K.) Library in 1978 to replace the conventional card catalog and to automate the indexing of literature references, internal reports, samples of research compounds, and staff files.[49] The software package CAIRS (Computer Assisted Information Retrieval System) was run on their DEC PDP 11/60 and led to the development of an online interactive system that generated a library book catalog and author, UDL, and keyword microfiche indexes to the catalog and to the large literature reference file.

Other corporate libraries found STAIRS, the Storage and Information Retrieval/Virtual Storage System, a computer software package developed by IBM, to be very useful in creating bibliographic databases and retrieving information from these databases. Poor describes the features of STAIRS as adapted for use as an online catalog of books, technical reports, business reports, and parts/service/sales literature at the Business and Technical Libraries at Cummins Engine Company, Inc. (Columbus, Indiana).[50] Quinn presents a view of the IBM Santa Teresa Laboratory's Information/Library/Learning Center, in which everything is computerized.[51] Since 1975, the catalog of materials at this center has been available online to users either in terminal rooms or in company offices, utilizing STAIRS. Finally, Selby, Lutz, and Maxwell outline the steps that Texas Instruments followed in installing an automated library system to link nine independent libraries, utilizing an in-house IMS-based circulation and control system and STAIRS as a searchable online catalog.[52] Tapes generated through use of the OCLC Cataloging Subsystem serve as the basis of this catalog.

OCLC-derived records are vital to at least three other corporate computerized bibliographic databases, as noted in the literature. The first, BELLTIP, the book acquisitions and cataloging system at Bell Telephone Laboratories, containing reformatted and edited OCLC data, produced an electronically photocomposed and printed book catalog of the book resources of the 25 libraries in the Bell Library Network. It was slated to be replaced with an online catalog in the third quarter of 1983.[53] Other noteworthy computerized operations within the Bell Library Network are the BELLCALL online call number facility, which allows catalogers to check Dewey numbers before assigning them to titles; the subject-heading authority list; serials control system; BELREL, an online interactive circulation system; and MERCURY, the SDI service for internal technical documents. The second as described by Martin, who briefly sketches the planning behind and the features of the network of four libraries at Molycorp, which has at its heart a common database running on IBM PC's, and CARD DIALOG, Data Trek software.[54] The software was chosen for its potential in downloading the OCLC tapes produced by the libraries. Library staff work with the Molycorp system in an online mode, but computer printouts generated by the same software serve the library users. The third system, at the Kennametal Inc. Technical Information Center in Latrobe, Pennsylvania, uses an AT&T 3B2 to run a UNIX System V and BRS/SEARCH, producing an online catalog derived from OCLC records.[55] James P. O'Connor, the manager of this center, characterizes the automated library facilities as an "open" or "hybrid" system, and also notes that BRS/SEARCH was used to develop an acquisitions system for book purchases and databases for searching vertical files and technical, governmental, and internal report collections; that MININET software aids in the creation of MARC records for uploading into the OCLC database; and that MICROLINX was to be applied shortly as an upgrade to the original LINX serials automation system.

The Monsanto Information Center's successes over the past 25 years should also be noted. The center has combined the holdings of 24 company libraries (first, into a printed, computer-produced catalog, and more recently [1983], into an online catalog, BOOKCAT, based on the software package BASIS and in-house produced programs), and run them on IBM and IBM-compatible equipment. Fitzgerald and associates provide us with a complete picture of the history, design, components, maintenance, and use of this online catalog,[56] while Wilkinson offers a more informal presentation, highlighting the service improvements resulting from the online catalog, the combining of the many company libraries into one central collection, and the commitment to a variety of purchased printed, microfilm, and online services.[57]

One more area remains to be mentioned in this survey of the literature on organization of materials: those publications which concern themselves with describing particular business libraries and which, in so doing, deal with managing and organizing collections in these libraries. Thirteen articles of recent vintage should be noted in this category. Six of these appear in the March 1980 issue of *Illinois Libraries*, which is devoted to the presentation of selected Illinois special libraries. All six have unique features in the realm of managing collections.

The library at Clark, Dietz Engineers, Inc., in Urbana, while traditional in its conventional card catalog approach to a large book and pamphlet collection, houses and controls the collection of 3,000-plus company projects in its archives.[58] Two in-house indexes allow employees to tap into this valuable resource. The library of Deere & Company (Molina), which has been using OCLC since 1978 to catalog its collection of books, serials, and government publications, has an automated serials system; has undertaken a recon project through OCLC; and also controls the company archives.[59] An online interactive database, housed at System Development Corporation in California, indexes and provides access to the thousands of documents in this collection.

Most of the large collection of books, periodicals, reports, and translations in the collection of the Portland Cement Association (Skokie) can be accessed by a special subject/author/source abstract file, on four-by-six-inch cards, that utilizes a locally-devised alpha-numeric classification scheme.[60] Including over 100,000 entries in 1980, this file was not yet computerized, because none of the retrieval systems available filled the needs of this specialized collection of cement/concrete literature. Similarly, all of the books and pamphlets added to the collection of the IAA and Affiliated Companies Library (Bloomington)—which increases by 1,000 titles per year—are cataloged and indexed for in-depth subject retrieval through an unusual coordinate index (uniterm) card system with the use of Termatrex equipment.[61] However, the library does keep track of periodicals through a locally-developed computer-assisted system called FARMBLISS (Farm Bureau Library Service System).

Still another library in the *Illinois Libraries* group is the Caterpillar Tractor Company Technical Information Center (Peoria) which, though still typing catalog cards for published literature in 1980, was anticipating using OCLC beginning in 1981 and was entering records for its large internal report and letter collection (38,500-plus) on diskette through an IBM System 6, Model 6/452 Information Processor.[62] The system was also generating traditional catalog cards, while allowing online recall by a variety of access points. The final library in this group is the Marsteller, Inc. Library (Chicago), whose major collection is a picture file (20,000-plus) which is classified by subject and filed in 12-by-18-inch pocket folders.[63] A manual index also provides access to research reports from the company's marketing research department. This library is not interested in detailed cataloging and does very little subject clipping, but relies heavily on printed and online indexes.

Two other short articles in other journals describe the development of their respective libraries and highlight their use of OCLC for cataloging. The first, on the McDonnell Douglas Automation Company Library in St. Louis, Missouri, indicates that the COM (microfiche) catalog that had been in use since 1981 was due to be replaced by an online catalog in two to three years.[64] The other recounts how the Gulf States Utilities Company Library in Beaumont, Texas, began on a shoestring in 1979 but was saved by using a subscription agency, an approval plan, and OCLC for cataloging and interlibrary loan.[65] Automation continues to provide solutions to a multitude of vexing problems for this small library, allowing utilization of various database systems (SDC, Dialog, etc.) for information retrieval and the Faxon LINX system for serials control.

A series of articles on special libraries and information centers in the *Canadian Library Journal* during 1985 offers profiles of three large Canadian business libraries, all of which are utilizing a variety of online services and, at the time of writing, were either involved with or anticipating the advent of online access to library collections. Merry writes that the Canadian Imperial Bank of Commerce Information Center (Toronto) has at its disposal 12 online services, employs a batch periodicals system, and is exploring packaged library software to handle the data files collection (1,500-plus) and LC records (22,000+).[66] The library of the Pulp and Paper Research Institute of Canada (Pointe-Claire, Quebec), also emphasizes online searching with its ability to access over 200 databases via seven online systems.[67] Its computer-produced book catalog, in existence since 1964, provides lists according to author, title, and classification number, as well as location code. Investigations of an online catalog to run on a microcomputer are ongoing. Reid provides a view of a network of four information centers, a records center, and corporate archives at the Imperial Oil and Esso Petroleum Canada offices in Toronto.[68] In 1974 the information centers implemented an automated indexing system that allowed online input but retrieval only on COM fiche, to the book, press release, journal article, speech, and pamphlet materials collections. This was followed, in 1984, by the Easy-data Library System, an integrated library management package marketed by Sydney Development Corporation, which was chosen to allow access to collections in all of the information centers, as well as the records center and archives.

Finally, the literature affords us a glimpse at two corporate libraries on the West Coast—those at the Collagen Corporation (Palo Alto) and Apple Computer Corporation (Cupertino). McCleary promotes the need for the library to become an "intelligence clearinghouse" for a company and to do this based on automation.[69] He suggests the use of two classes of software programs, file-indexing and retrieval packages, and relational database packages, to accomplish this feat and explains how Collagen applied both types to develop and access in-house current events and patent files and an online card catalog for books, government publications, pamphlets, and reprints (FYI3000); and circulation, records, and competition information (dBASE III). Fischer presents a rosy interview with Monica Ertel, librarian at Apple Computer Corporation, who automated her library using Apple computers and became the founder of the Apple Library Users Group.[70] Ertel and her staff are working with Caspr, a software company, to develop an integrated, automated library system called MLS (Macintosh Library System), and, in addition, are designing a library system around the Macintosh employing the database management program Omnis 3. The popular *Apple Library Users Group Newsletter* provides updates on these ventures.

THE PRACTICE OF ORGANIZATION IN BUSINESS LIBRARIES

Information for this section was derived from two status surveys of 11 business libraries representing the four general categories of such libraries listed by Myers and Frederick and by Daniells, as noted earlier in this chapter. The first survey, taken between 1980 and 1982, was accomplished via personal interviews and telephone conversations with library personnel; the second was mailed in early 1987 to the same libraries and requested corrections or additions to the information gathered in the 1980–82 survey. Telephone follow-ups to this second survey were made to clarify or amplify on certain points. Table 1 charts the information for each library gathered in the surveys. The libraries are not identified by name but are identified in the table and referred to below by their alphanumeric codes. The libraries in both surveys are the same, with the exception of Library A.1. The library represented by this code in the 1980–82 survey was closed just after the survey was completed (1982); a substitute was chosen from the same type of business (insurance) to complete the 1987 survey.

The data from the surveys reported here are compared, where appropriate, with data from a 1968 survey by Maura Klingen of five different types of special libraries in business and industry.[71] Klingen visited libraries representative of five of the six types of business libraries identified by the Special Libraries Association in their published profiles.[72]. Table 2 shows the types of libraries she studied and charts information related to the organization of materials in these libraries. The data are discussed below in four major categories:

collections/files maintained, treatment of materials in the library's main catalog, other locally-developed aids/methods to accessing collections or files, and aids to information access.

Collections/Files Maintained

All of the libraries studied have general (circulating) book collections, and most have reference collections composed largely of books. Other collections and files of materials abound, most containing nonbook material. In fact, more of the collections and files in the company libraries surveyed are made up of nonbook than of book materials. Pamphlets, corporate annual reports, periodicals, telephone directories, trade directories, and clippings are the most frequently found items organized in separate collections or files. Archives are found in only four of the libraries, although two others have access to archives that are not associated with the library: These two are company archives, arranged by archival methods. Moreover, two of the archive collections set up in the libraries surveyed are not organized in any fashion. Clearly, contemporary issues are more important to the users and staff of these libraries.

Treatment of Material in the Library's Main Catalog

Type and Form of Catalog

The 1980–82 survey indicates that the card catalog was the predominant type used, as 10 of the 11 libraries reported still maintaining such a file. In five years the picture has changed, and the 1987 survey demonstrates that more than half of the libraries currently utilize computer-produced (2) or online (4) catalogs. Library A.5 is anticipating moving towards an online catalog, as well. Interestingly, Klingen's Research Library in a chemical manufacturing company (Library 4 in Table 2) provided a machine-produced book catalog—a progressive move for the time. In both the 1980–82 and 1987 surveys all but two of the card and COM catalogs are in dictionary form. The divided catalog approach is found in the academic libraries, which have larger book collections and, thus, larger main catalogs. The online catalogs of the 1987 survey provide several access points to the records therein. At the very least, there are the traditional approaches (author, title, subject) and an additional call number access point. Two libraries are fortunate in having nine or more ways of retrieving bibliographic information through their online catalogs (Libraries A.2 and C.3).

Materials Accessed Through the Catalog

Only in a few instances are materials other than books included in the main catalog, a practice which seems to endorse the general view that full (or even partial) descriptive and subject cataloging according to traditional cataloging codes is not as appropriate for other materials as for book materials. Indeed, in the 1980–82 survey, Libraries A.1 and A.3 were unique in providing access to vertical file materials in their main catalog. The 1987 survey shows that Library A.3 has discontinued this practice. However, Library A.2, now utilizing an online catalog, is finding it possible to add information about selected vertical file items to its catalog, as well as information with respect to selected periodical articles. Library D.1, having maintained a COM catalog for some time, is now including A-V materials in this catalog. Thus, computerization is providing some opportunities for accessing nonbook materials through a main catalog approach that hitherto seemed beyond the capability of library staff to undertake.

Classification Systems

All three surveys indicate that the majority of the libraries employ the Library of Congress (LC) or the Dewey Decimal Classification system, the former being more common in the public and academic libraries and the latter in the company libraries. The lone exception is Library B.1, a professional library in the area of insurance, which developed its own classification system with highly specific insurance categories and notations for these categories in the early 1970s. Staff members at this library are still confident of the usefulness of this system, since very few categories have been outdated, and the schedule accommodates insertion of new categories. On the other hand, Library D.2 changed in 1976 from its own elaborate and effective system to LC in order to take advantage of the MARC cataloging opportunities.

While those libraries using the LC system modify the numbers only slightly, if at all, rigid use of the Dewey system is rare. Sometimes Dewey numbers are modified to avoid the lengthy extensions beyond the decimal point which otherwise result. At other times, new sequences of numbers are developed to accommodate special or new subjects. Although some might criticize this practice, it seems reasonable, if the library's staff is trained in proper application of the changes and if provision is made for proper input of Dewey numbers into the databases in which the library participates. For OCLC, for example, this means utilization of the 19th edition of Dewey at the present time. Among those libraries which reported using Dewey in the 1980–82 and 1987 surveys, most employed Dewey 19, although there has been and is great concern about major changes in the schedules of this edition. Reclassification to conform to these changes has been accomplished only on a limited basis.

Aids to and Codes for Cataloging

Contrary to the results of the 1980–82 survey, which indicated that joining a bibliographic utility was not seen to be a practical option for most of the libraries, the 1987 survey records the fact that eight of the 11 libraries are now using a bibliographic utility (OCLC in seven and UTLAS in one). (The economies of hooking into a large cooperative database seem to have won the day!) In a similar effort at economy, Library C.2, while not enjoying the benefits of a bibliographic utility, does rely on the resources of a regional cooperative database, thereby cutting its costs to a more manageable level. Of the two remaining libraries, Library B.1 alone still has card sets produced by a commercial vendor and the other, Library A.2, has an online catalog with no reported need of cataloging aids. Irrespective of their use of bibliographic utilities and cooperative databases, several of the libraries still reported (1987 survey) consulting such traditional cataloging aids as the *National Union Catalog*, CIP information, MARC printed products, Library of Congress catalogs, *Book Publishing Records*, and others.

While the 1980-82 survey indicated that three non-users of the OCLC system of MARC tapes continued to follow the first edition of the *Anglo-American Cataloguing Rules*, or used no standard code at all and felt that changing to *Anglo-American Cataloging Rules 2nd edition (AACR2)* would be far too costly a venture, all of the libraries in the 1987 survey now use AACR2, with the exception of Library B.1, whose practices are developed locally. OCLC and UTLAS require input of records in AACR2 form, and, thus, all of their cataloging products that represent current cataloging appear in this form. Library of Congress MARC records also appear in AACR2 format, which affects libraries that subscribe to MARC products (Library C.2).

Subject Headings

Results from the three surveys demonstrate that business libraries favor Library of Congress headings over Sears Headings, although specialized headings from other sources (*Business Periodicals Index*, journal literature, corporate reports) are often included as well. The corporate and association libraries tend to make greater use of non-LC subject headings, employing them in their catalogs and other tools for accessing whatever collections and files they maintain. It is also obvious that those libraries employing only LC subject headings for their main catalogs do not necessarily use them for their other files. For instance, *Business Periodicals Index* headings are applied to materials in the Industry & Statistics Index at Library D.2. In general, the company and association libraries want more specific headings to access their files and, even though they may make use of bibliographic utilities, they are willing to spend the time enhancing their bibliographic records with these headings to make them more useful. On the other hand, the public and academic business libraries, bound more by centralized cataloging procedures and cost considerations, use, with few additions or changes, those headings which appear on MARC records.

They do, however, still see the utility of other, more specific, non-LC headings for special collections and files.

Authority Files

Klingen's survey did not address the issue of authority files, but in comparing the 1980-82 survey with the 1987 survey, we find that only three of the libraries in the former and one in the latter did/do not maintain at least one authority file documenting the use of certain names, subject headings, or series. The three in the earlier survey were corporate libraries with smaller main collections, which were just as easily searched for previously used headings as any authority file would be. These libraries could also easily rely on their subject heading sources as their subject authority. The one library currently not keeping an authority file (Library A.1) does use a locally developed thesaurus for subject headings and can look to this for documentation of headings employed.

The most common authority files are those of subject headings taken from non-LC sources (A.2:1987, A.3, A.4:1987, A.5, B.1, C.1, C.2, D.1) and those representing forms of series authorized for bibliographic records (A.5, C.1-C.3, D.1, D.2). Name authority files were (1980-82 and 1987) maintained by four of the five public and academic libraries surveyed, which bears witness to their large main catalog and auxiliary files and the need to discover quickly and efficiently discrepancies between forms of the same name and name changes. For Library A.2, another advantage of going online was the ability to maintain name and subject terms in an interactive online authority file. Previously, this library kept no authority files at all.

Filing Rules

The 1980-82 survey documents the use of locally developed sets of rules in seven of the libraries. Most of these rules were undocumented, and Library D.2 was the only one to have a printed set of rules that could be given to new filers. Three other libraries used the *ALA Filing Rules* published in 1968, and one remaining library employed a standard set of rules for COM catalogs. In the current environment, six of the libraries do not concern themselves with filing in the main catalog, since theirs are computer-produced or online products. Otherwise, local filing systems still are found utilized in the main catalogs of three libraries and ALA rules in the remaining two non-automated main files. In general, filing does not seem to be a major concern. The libraries want to use whatever makes the most sense and is easily understood. It is to be hoped that computer-produced and online arrangements are facilitating retrieval for their users.

Other Locally Developed Aids/Methods to Accessing Collections or Files

The business libraries surveyed employ cross-references in the various catalogs to identify to the user, materials available elsewhere in the library on the same or similar topics, or to guide the user to other subject headings or entries that may be more appropriate or just as useful as the ones consulted. In addition, collections or files of materials not represented in the main catalog are often accessed by many tools developed in-house. These range from Kardex files and more elaborate book and computer-generated catalogs for periodicals collections to simple card files arranged in the same order as the collections/files themselves. Where such tools do not exist, either the collections are organized so that they are self-indexing, or they require no indexing mechanism for ease of access.

Pamphlets and clippings generally are kept in a vertical file arrangement, free-standing or in folders arranged alphabetically by topic. Other materials ordinarily arranged in simple alphabetical order are (1) periodicals, which appear alphabetically by title (in all of the libraries); (2) corporate annual reports, which are arranged by company name or, in some cases, by product, state, or country (Libraries A.1-A.4, B.1, C.3, and D.1-D.2); and (3) telephone directories, which are kept in order alphabetically by state, then by city or town (Libraries A.1:1980-82, A.2, A.4:1987, A.5 and D.1-D.2). Only Library D.2 classifies its periodicals in the reference area by LC, while Library C.2 assigns its telephone directories (and city directories) locally developed classification numbers.

Appearing less frequently in the libraries, map collections tend to be placed in vertical files (Libraries C.1 and C.2) or are not organized to any extent for public use. An example of the latter is at Library B.1, whose collection of Sanborn fire maps lacks a strict shelf arrangement and has only a simple card file as an access tool. However, libraries with access to a bibliographic utility such as OCLC tend to treat maps as part of the book collection. These libraries catalog maps more fully and apply LC or Dewey numbers to them (Library D.2, for example).

Particularly helpful to the user as a finding-aid and as an indication of what of current interest has been added to the collections or files is a new accessions or acquisitions list. Libraries A.1, A.3 and D.1 in the 1980-82 survey provided such lists on a regular basis (monthly or quarterly). The 1987 survey indicates that Libraries A.2, A.3, A.4 and D.1 are publishing these valuable lists at varying frequencies.

Aids to Information Access

A large number of business libraries furnish access to information in their collections/files or in the literature of business at large. The Klingen survey noted the indexing of material by the staff at the research library in an industrial corporation (Library 3 in Table 2) and the daily clipping service at the library for a public utilities firm (Library 5 in Table 2). Similar indexing projects were still pursued by more than half of the libraries in the 1980-82 survey (A.2, A.5, B.1, C.1, C.3, D.1, and D.2), and currently (1987 survey), a similar number (Libraries A.1:1987, A.2, A.5, B.1, C.1, D.1, and D.2) find local indexing worthwhile.

As a supplement to indexing, the business libraries surveyed are learning how best to use technology, both through subscription to a variety of computer-produced and online bibliographic retrieval systems and through creation of their own systems, such as the one developed by Library D.2. Currently, the average number of online services utilized by corporate libraries is five; and the wish, as among other kinds of libraries, is to add as many as is economically possible. Alone in its lack of desire for such a retrieval system is the professional library (B.1), whose needs are so specific (insurance) that anything but an insurance database appears unnecessary.

In summary, organization of materials in business libraries as documented by these surveys remains an exciting, innovative, varied, and challenging responsibility. Above all, it is still dedicated to providing information for users quickly and efficiently.

Table 1. 1980-82 and 1987: Surveys of Business Libraries*

TYPE OF LIBRARY	COLLECTIONS/FILES MAINTAINED	TREATMENT OF MATERIAL IN MAIN CATALOG							OTHER LOCALLY DEVELOPED AIDS/ COLLECTIONS/FILES	AIDS TO INFORMATION ACCESS
		TYPE AND FORM OF CATALOG	MATERIALS ACCESS THROUGH CATALOG	CLASSIFICATION SYSTEM	AIDS TO AND CODES FOR CATALOGING	SUBJECT HEADINGS SOURCE(S)	AUTHORITY FILES MAINTAINED	FILING RULES		
A. CORPORATE										
1. Insurance Company Library. (NOTE: This library closed in 1982.) FOUNDED: 1912 **1973** SIZE OF MAIN COLLECTION: 13,000 volumes (Books) **10,000 volumes** (Books) SPECIALTIES: Accounting; Auditing; Insurance; **Finance; Health care; Insurance**	* Books (General); Archives; Corporate annual reports (alphabetically arranged by company); Old Scottish actuarial files; Old international actuarial files; Periodicals (alphabetically arranged by title); Rate books (other companies; uncataloged); Reference collection; Telephone directories (alphabetically arranged); Old Moody's; Vertical file; Videotapes **• Books (General); Archives; Company services file; Corporate annual reports (alphabetically arranged by company); Periodicals (alphabetically arranged by title); Reference collection; SEC files (fiche); Vertical files (companies, industries in branch library)**	TYPE: Card **Online (BASIS software utilized);** FORM: Dictionary **N/A; accessed by author, title, subject, call number; OCLC number**	All collections except periodicals, rate books, telephone directories, and videotapes. Corporate reports by name card only **Books (General); Reference collection**	Dewey (16th edition, numbers only extended to fourth digit beyond decimal point) **Dewey (19th edition)**	CODE: AACR1 **AACR2** AIDS: Purchased LC card sets **OCLC**	Locally developed from journals and corporate reports **LC; OCLC participating libraries; Locally developed thesaurus**	None **None**	ALA (1968) **Database sorting arrangement**	Accessions list (monthly); Card catalog (divided) for videotapes; Kardex for periodicals; Telephone directory index (alphabetically arranged by state, then city and town) **Index of brokerage house reports (computer-produced, using dBASE); Periodicals list (paper, computer-produced, using dBASE); Inventory list for Archives**	None locally developed **Index of brokerage house reports** ONLINE: None **DIALOG, DOW JONES NEWS/ RETRIEVAL, InfoMaster, NEXIS, OCLC, VUTEXT**
2. Insurance Company Library. FOUNDED: 1949 SIZE OF MAIN COLLECTION: 15,000 volumes (Books) **5,000 volumes** (Books) SPECIALTIES: Business and management; Health & life insurance; Pensions **Employee benefits; Financial services; Health and life insurance; Management**	* Books (General); Archives (uncataloged); Corporate annual reports (alphabetically arranged by company); Insurance histories file (alphabetically arranged by company); Newsletters (alphabetically arranged by title); Periodicals (alphabetically arranged by title); Telephone directories (alphabetically arranged); Vertical (marketing) file (alphabetically arranged by geographic location) **• Books (General); Archives (uncataloged); Corporate annual reports (alphabetically arranged by company); Insurance association file (alphabetically arranged by company); Periodicals (alphabetically arranged by title); Telephone directories (alphabetically arranged by title); Vertical files: market data (alphabetically arranged by geographic location); Subject (arranged by Dewey classification number)**	TYPE: Card **Online (BIB-LIOTECH)** FORM: Dictionary **N/A; accessed by author, title, title words, subject, subject words, series, series words, call number; report number**	Books (General); Reference book collection **Books (General); Insurance association publications; Periodical articles (selected); Reference book collection; Vertical files (selected)**	Dewey (19th edition 200's developed into "Company Library Insurance Classification") **Dewey (19th edition; numbers only extended to third digit beyond decimal point) Financial Services Classification System (locally developed)**	CODE: AACR2 (modified) **AACR2 (modified)** AIDS: Card sets reproduced internally **None**	LC; Locally developed list for collections, files, aids **Locally developed thesaurus, database-controlled, based on: ABI/ INFORM; WORDS THAT MEAN BUSINESS; INSUR-ANCE PE-RIODICALS INDEX thesaurus**	None **Online for authors and subjects**	ALA (1968) **Database sorting arrangement; ALA for manual files**	Catalog of pamphlets and articles (card; subject arrangement); Investment services index (card); Periodicals list (book; generated by word processor, title & subject; Telephone directories index (Kardex; arranged by towns and cities) **Geographic filing scheme (world regions on several levels); NEW BOOKS LIST (computer-generated); Periodicals list (computer-generated; title and/or subject); Telephone directories index (alphabetically arranged by town); various customized, computer-generated reports**	Catalog of pamphlets and articles (card; subject arrangement) **MANAGEMENT UPDATE (bi-monthly; subject arrangement, computer-generated, selected abstracted and indexed articles); BUSINESS INDEX (COM)** ONLINE: BRS, DIALOG, New York Times Information Bank **BRS, DIALOG, MEAD DATA CENTRAL, VUTEXT, others**

*Regular type signifies 1980-82 data; bold type signifies 1987 data.

Table 1. 1980-82 and 1987: Surveys of Business Libraries* (cont.)

TYPE OF LIBRARY	COLLECTIONS/FILES MAINTAINED	TREATMENT OF MATERIAL IN MAIN CATALOG							OTHER LOCALLY DEVELOPED AIDS/ METHODS TO ACCESS COLLECTIONS/FILES	AIDS TO INFORMATION ACCESS
		TYPE AND FORM OF CATALOG	MATERIALS ACCESS THROUGH CATALOG	CLASSIFICATION SYSTEM	AIDS TO AND CODES FOR CATALOGING	SUBJECT HEADINGS SOURCE(S)	AUTHORITY FILES MAINTAINED	FILING RULES		
A. CORPORATE										
3. Insurance Company Library. FOUNDED: 1946 SIZE OF MAIN COLLECTION: 22,000 volumes (Books) **23,000 volumes (Books)** SPECIALTIES: Big business; Fire and liability insurance; Occupational safety; Special hazards **Business; Insurance; Management; Occupational safety and health**	* Books (General); Historical collection; Periodicals; Reference collection; Vertical file (includes corporate annual reports; alphabetically arranged by title) * **Books (General); Company files; Periodicals; Reference collection; Vertical file (no longer updated)**	TYPE: Card **Card** FORM: Dictionary **Dictionary**	Books (General); Historical collection; Reference collection; Vertical file (except corporate annual reports) **Books (General); Reference collection**	Dewey (19th edition) **Dewey (19th edition)**	CODE: AACR1 **AACR2** AIDS: CIP; Card sets produced internally **OCLC (Cataloging done at another branch)**	LC and others locally developed; *Business Periodicals Index* headings for vertical file **LC; List of locally developed headings**	Subject, for locally developed headings **Subject: LC and locally developed headings**	Akers filing rules **ALA (1980)**	Acquisitions list (books; quarterly); Kardex for periodicals **Acquisitions list (books; quarterly); company file list (computer-generated); serials control system (automated)**	None developed locally *Information Bulletin* (quarterly; computer-generated) **ONLINE: BRS, DIALOG, New York Times Information Bank, ORBIT** **DIALOG, DOW JONES NEWS/ RETRIEVAL, MEAD DATA CENTRAL, Pergamon INFO-LINE, VUTEXT**
4. Chemical Company Library. FOUNDED: 1965 SIZE OF MAIN COLLECTION: 5,500 volumes (Books and bound periodicals) **6,000 volumes (Books and bound periodicals)** SPECIALTIES: Chemicals; plastics **Chemicals; plastics**	* Books (General); Corporate annual reports (alphabetically arranged by company); Marketing research reports; Periodicals (alphabetically arranged by title); Reference collection; Vertical file (alphabetically arranged by subject) * **Books (General); Corporate annual reports and 10,000 statements (alphabetically arranged by company); Pamphlets; Periodicals (alphabetically arranged by title); Reference collection; Telephone directories**	TYPE: Card (union, of materials in main catalog of company's 3 libraries) COM (microfiche) FORM: Dictionary **Dictionary**	Books (General); Reference collection **Books (General); Reference collection**	Dewey 17th edition) **Dewey (19th edition; numbers only extended to third digit beyond decimal point)**	CODE: AACR2 **AACR2** AIDS: OCLC (cataloging performed at the main company library) **OCLC (cataloging performed at the main company library)**	LC; locally developed headings for vertical file **LC; OCLC participating libraries**	None **Subject**	Locally developed **COM vendor rules**	Computer-printed list (author and title sections) of holdings; Kardex for periodicals; Marketing research reports catalog (card); Periodicals list (book: subject arranged, computer-generated) ***Bulletin* of acquisitions (computer-printed, bimonthly); Periodicals list (computer-generated, alphabetical by title); Serials check-in, automated**	None developed locally **None developed locally** **ONLINE: BRS, DIALOG, DOW JONES NEWS/ DIALOG, DOW JONES NEWS/ NEXIS, ORBIT** **BRS, DIALOG, DOW JONES NEWS/ RETRIEVAL, LEXIS, NEXIS, NEWSNET, ORBIT, PIERS, VUTEXT**

*Regular type signifies 1980–82 data; bold type signifies 1987 data.

Table 1. 1980-82 and 1987: Surveys of Business Libraries* (cont.)

TYPE OF LIBRARY	COLLECTIONS/FILES MAINTAINED	TREATMENT OF MATERIAL IN MAIN CATALOG							OTHER LOCALLY DEVELOPED AIDS/ METHODS TO ACCESS COLLECTIONS/FILES	AIDS TO INFORMATION ACCESS
		TYPE AND FORM OF CATALOG	MATERIALS ACCESS THROUGH CATALOG	CLASSIFICATION SYSTEM	AIDS TO AND CODES FOR CATALOGING	SUBJECT HEADINGS SOURCE(S)	AUTHORITY FILES MAINTAINED	FILING RULES		
A. CORPORATE										
5. Bank Library. FOUNDED: 1921 SIZE OF MAIN COLLECTION: 45,000 volumes (Books and serials) **53,850 volumes (Books and serials)** (NOTE: No changes are noted in the remaining categories between 1982 and 1987.) SPECIALTIES: Banking; economics; finance	* Books (General); Census materials; Federal Reserve publications (subsection statistical releases); Microforms; Periodicals (alphabetically arranged in oblique files by title; Reference collection; Telephone directories (alphabetically arranged by title); Vertical file (uncataloged)	TYPE: Card (union, of materials in all departments of bank that are cataloged) FORM: Dictionary	Books (General); Census materials; Federal Reserve publications; Reference collection	LC	CODE: AACR2 AIDS: OCLC	LC (and others developed locally or by Federal Reserve banks)	Series; Subject	ALA (1968)	CIS index annotated for microform holdings from 1979 to present; Kardex for periodicals; OCLC Serials Control system (OCLC SC 350)	Reference sources index (cont: arranged by subject, simplified LC) ONLINE: BRS, DIALOG, DRI, Federal Reserve System database, OCLC
B. PROFESSIONAL										
1. Insurance Library. FOUNDED: 1887 SIZE OF MAIN COLLECTION: 6,000 volumes (books) **8,000 volumes (Books)** (NOTE: No changes between 1982 and 1987 were reported for the remaining categories.)	* Books (General); Corporate files (annual reports, house organs, articles; uncataloged; alphabetical by company); Old pamphlet file; Periodicals (alphabetically arranged by title); Reference collection; Sanborn fire maps (uncataloged); Vertical file: pamphlets and clippings (uncataloged, alphabetically arranged by subject)	TYPE: Card FORM: Dictionary	Books (General); Reference collection; Old pamphlet file gradually being added	Locally developed (Uses very specific divisions for various aspects of insurance.)	CODE: None; locally developed practice AIDS: Card sets reproduced by commercial jobber	Locally developed (combining LC *Business Periodicals Index* headings, those of 1974 list of insurance headings from SLA and those used at business branch of the local library)	Subject (for main catalog); Subject (for vertical file); Cross-references file (subject)	Locally developed	Old pamphlet file catalog (card); Periodicals index; Sanborn fire map file (card)	Clippings inserted into vertical file (alphabetically arranged by subject; Subject lists of important articles; Pamphlets (arranged numerically in lists) ONLINE: None

*Regular type signifies 1980–82 data; bold type signifies 1987 data.

Table 1. 1980-82 and 1987: Surveys of Business Libraries* (cont.)

TYPE OF LIBRARY	COLLECTIONS/FILES MAINTAINED	TREATMENT OF MATERIAL IN MAIN CATALOG							OTHER LOCALLY DEVELOPED AIDS/ METHODS TO ACCESS COLLECTIONS/FILES	AIDS TO INFORMATION ACCESS
		TYPE AND FORM OF CATALOG	MATERIALS ACCESS THROUGH CATALOG	CLASSIFICATION SYSTEM	AIDS TO AND CODES FOR CATALOGING	SUBJECT HEADINGS SOURCE(S)	AUTHORITY FILES MAINTAINED	FILING RULES		
C. PUBLIC										
1. Branch specializing in business. FOUNDED: 1944 SIZE OF MAIN COLLECTION: 46,326 volumes (Books) **44,000 volumes (Books)** (NOTE: The few changes between 1982 and 1987 information are noted under the appropriate categories.)	• Books (General); Corporate annual reports (hard-back and fiche; **in 1987 only fiche**) arranged according to Standard & Poor's *Security Owner's Stock Guide*); Import-export books; Investment services; Law collection; Periodicals (alphabetically arranged by title); Reference collection; Taxation collection; Telephone directories; Trade and business directories; Vertical file: Maps and pamphlets (alphabetically arranged by subject)	TYPE: Book (to 1896); Card (1897-1986); **Online (1986-)** FORM: Dictionary (card catalog)	All collections and files except corporate annual reports, periodicals, telephone directories and vertical file materials	Dewey (19th edition, modifications for business focus)	CODE: AACR2 AIDS: OCLC (cataloging performed at main library); BNB, NUC, other LC tools	LC (vertical file has own set of headings developed locally)	Author (personal); Added entry (personal author/ title); Series; Subject (includes corporate names)	Locally developed (based on ALA 1968 card rules); **card catalog; database sorting arrangement for online catalog**	Periodicals file (check-in card); Serials printout (at main library only; Book; Union list of all branches); Statistics catalog (main entry, title, subject access points); Trade and business directory catalog (main entry, title, subject access points)	Statistics catalog, which includes citations to statistics in articles, pamphlets, etc., as well as in books; COM periodical indexes (Information Access); added since 1980-82 survey ONLINE: DIALOG
2. Branch specializing in business. FOUNDED: 1930 SIZE OF MAIN COLLECTION: 41,000 volumes (Books) **40,000 volumes (Books)** (NOTE: Between 1982 and 1987 only one change is noted.)	• Books (General); City directories; Corporate annual reports (fiche) Governmental statistical annuals; Investment services; Periodical indexes; Periodicals (alphabetically arranged by title); Reference collection; Telephone directories; Vertical file (maps, pamphlets)	TYPE: Card FORM: Dictionary	Books (Generally); Nonpublic catalog access); Reference collection	LC (city, telephone directories and investment services have special locally developed classification; reference collection also has locally developed shelf numbering system)	CODE: AACR2 AIDS: Locally developed cooperative database, based on MARC tape use; LC proof-sheets (for non-Roman); (Cataloging performed at main library) ROM Index to MARC database; NUC; LC tools	LC, with modifications made at branch; "Fast Find" files; uses locally developed headings	Name; Series; Subject (name and subject files only for locally developed headings)	Locally developed (based originally on *LC Filing Rules*)	City and telephone directory index (strip listings alphabetically arranged; Kardex for periodicals	"Fast Find" file (card) for important facts and figures frequently sought (arranged by subject) *Business Index* **(COM): added after 1980-82 survey** ONLINE: None

*Regular type signifies 1980-82 data; bold type signifies 1987 data.

Table 1. 1980-82 and 1987: Surveys of Business Libraries* (cont.)

TYPE OF LIBRARY	COLLECTIONS/FILES MAINTAINED	TREATMENT OF MATERIAL IN MAIN CATALOG							OTHER LOCALLY DEVELOPED AIDS/ METHODS TO ACCESS COLLECTIONS/FILES	AIDS TO INFORMATION ACCESS
		TYPE AND FORM OF CATALOG	MATERIALS ACCESS THROUGH CATALOG	CLASSIFICATION SYSTEM	AIDS TO AND CODES FOR CATALOGING	SUBJECT HEADINGS SOURCE(S)	AUTHORITY FILES MAINTAINED	FILING RULES		
C. PUBLIC										
3. Department specializing in business. FOUNDED: 1954	1982 and 1987: 20,000 volumes (Books) * Books (General); Corporate annual reports (paper and fiche; alphabetically arranged by company); Federal and military specifications (chronologically arranged); Government publications (classed by Superintendent of Documents system); Newsletters (alphabetically arranged); Periodicals (alphabetically arranged); Photofact folders; Reference collection; Trade catalogs; Vertical file: Pamphlets and photocopies arranged); **Books (General); Corporate annual reports (paper and fiche; alphabetically arranged by company); Federal and military specifications (chronologically arranged); Government publications (classed by Superintendent of Documents system); Newsletters (alphabetically arranged); Periodicals (alphabetically arranged); Photofact folders; Reference collection; Trade catalogs; Trade directories (alphabetically arranged); U.S. patents 1790- (film depository); Vertical file: pamphlets and photocopies**	TYPE: Card **Card (1954-1985); Online (1986-; only staff access at present); Recon project underway** FORM: Dictionary **Card: Dictionary; Online: many access points (10 different types), including author, title, subject, call number, etc.**	Books (General); Reference collection **Books (General); Reference collection**	Dewey (19th edition, "B" placed before number designates location in this department; 800's for business, rather than 300's) **Dewey (19th edition) for book labels; Online records have both Dewey and LC numbers; Reclassing to LC within two years**	CODE: AACR2 **AACR2** AIDS: MiniMARC, CIP, NUC, Other LC tools, *Book Publishing Record* (cataloging performed centrally for all departments) **UTLAS, CIP, NUC, Other LC tools, Mansell's pre-1956 imprints, *Book Publishing Record* (Cataloging still centrally performed)**	LC (with some additional "popular term" headings) (Vertical file uses locally developed headings.) **Library of Congress (with some additional "popular term" headings) (Vertical file uses locally developed headings.)**	Names; Series; Subject **Online name; Uniform title; Subject files**	*Carnegie Filing Rules* with some local modifications. **Database sorting arrangement**	Corporate annual report file (card; alphabetically arranged by company); Newsletter list; Periodicals list; Selected government publications file (Rolodex; title and subject access); Trade catalog and directory file (Rolodex; title and subject access); Vertical file card index (alphabetically arranged by subject) **Same files as in 1982**	Index local Sunday newspaper for major articles on business None locally developed ONLINE: None **CASSIS (United States Patent and Trademark Office); DIALOG**
D. BUSINESS SCHOOL										
1. College (4-year, undergraduate and graduate programs). FOUNDED: 1919 SIZE OF MAIN COLLECTION: 81,000 volumes (Books) **103,000 volumes (Books)** (NOTE: Changes made between 1982 and 1987 are noted below.)	*Books (General); Archives (uncataloged); Company information file (alphabetically arranged by company); Corporate annual reports (hardbound and fiche); Investment collection; Pamphlet file (alphabetically arranged by subject); Periodicals (alphabetically arranged by title); reference collection; Sir Isaac Newton collection; Special collection for founder of college; Stock reports; Telephone directories (alphabetically arranged by title) **A-V collection** 526,000 volumes (Books) **550,000 volumes (Books)** (NOTE: No changes between 1982 and 1987 were reported for the remaining categories.)	TYPE: COM (film) FORM: Divided (author/title/ subject)	Books (General, post-1982 addition); Archives [10%]; A-V collection (post-1982 addition); Reference collection; Sir Isaac Newton collection (partial)	LC	CODE: AACR2 AIDS: OCLC	LC	Series; Subject (for pamphlet file)	COM vendor (Autographics) rules	Accession list (monthly); Company information file authority file (alphabetically arranged by company); Corporate annual reports check-in file; Kardex for periodicals; Periodicals listing (includes investment collection and stock reports)	Local company information file (card; information taken from selected unindexed journals) ONLINE: DIALOG, OCLC BRS, CD, Disclosure, VUTEXT

*Regular type signifies 1980-82 data; bold type signifies 1987 data.

Table 1. 1980-82 and 1987: Surveys of Business Libraries* (cont.)

TYPE OF LIBRARY	COLLECTIONS/FILES MAINTAINED	TREATMENT OF MATERIAL IN MAIN CATALOG							OTHER LOCALLY DEVELOPED AIDS/ METHODS TO ACCESS COLLECTIONS/FILES	AIDS TO INFORMATION ACCESS
		TYPE AND FORM OF CATALOG	MATERIALS ACCESS THROUGH CATALOG	CLASSIFICATION SYSTEM	AIDS TO AND CODES FOR CATALOGING	SUBJECT HEADINGS SOURCE(S)	AUTHORITY FILES MAINTAINED	FILING RULES		
D. BUSINESS SCHOOL										
2. Graduate school. FOUNDED: 1908	* Books (General); Career Resources Center, core collection (3,500 recent titles in business and related fields); Corporate annual reports (hardbound and fiche, alphabetically arranged by company); *Current Industry Reports* file (alphabetically arranged by subject; Manuscripts and archives; Periodicals and serials (alphabetically arranged in stacks; those in reference classed in LC); Recreational reading collection; Reference collection; Special collection; Telephone directories (alphabetically arranged by place)	TYPE: Card: Old (Pre-1971); New (1971-); also book catalog for pre-1971 holdings FORM: Divided (author/title/ subject)	Books (General); Core collection; Periodicals and serials (discontinued titles only); Reference collection	Library of Congress (until 1976 used locally developed system)	CODE: AACR2 AIDS: OCLC, NUC, Other LC tools	LC, *Business Periodicals Index* for industry and statistics index	Name; Series (monographs)	Locally developed	Core collection catalog (book); Corporate annual reports catalog (card); Periodicals and serials catalog (book, with computer updates); Recreational heading catalog (card); Special collection catalog (book)	Industry and statistics index (card, arranged by subject, indexes articles from a variety of journals) ONLINE: BASIS

*Regular type signifies 1980–82 data

Table 2. Survey of Business Libraries (1968)*

TYPE OF LIBRARY	COLLECTIONS/FILES MAINTAINED	TREATMENT OF MATERIAL IN MAIN CATALOG							OTHER LOCALLY DEVELOPED AIDS/ METHODS TO ACCESS COLLECTIONS/FILES	AIDS TO INFORMATION ACCESS
		TYPE AND FORM OF CATALOG	MATERIALS ACCESS THROUGH CATALOG	CLASSIFICATION SYSTEM	AIDS TO AND CODES FOR CATALOGING	SUBJECT HEADINGS SOURCE(S)	AUTHORITY FILES MAINTAINED	FILING RULES		
A. CORPORATE										
1. Research Library in a Manufacturing Company FOUNDED: 1950 SIZE OF MAIN COLLECTION: 2,000 items (Company reports) SPECIALTIES: Aerodynamics; Business management; Electronics; Optics; Physics; Space science	†Company reports Books (General); Pamphlets; Periodicals; Reference collection; Research reports	TYPE: Card FORM: ?	Books (General); Reference collection	Library of Congress	CODE: AACR1? Purchased LC card sets	Library of Congress (*Thesaurus of ASTIA Descriptors* for company and research reports)	?	?	*Indexes to company and research reports	None
2. Bank Library FOUNDED: 1922 SIZE OF MAIN COLLECTION: 10,000 vols. (Books) SPECIALTIES: Central banking; Economics; Federal Reserve System; Finance	†Books (General) Pamphlets; Periodicals	TYPE: Card FORM: ?	Books (General)	Dewey Decimal	CODE: AACR1?	(Headings for pamphlets based on PAIS and *Business Periodicals Index*)	?	?	?	None
3. Research Library in an Industrial Corporation FOUNDED: 1947 SIZE OF MAIN COLLECTION: 100,000 items (Pamphlets) SPECIALTIES: Aeronautical and aerospace engineering; Military science	†Pamphlets (includes government publications, technical reports, annual reports, reprints, specifications); Books (General); Periodicals; Reference collection	TYPE: Card FORM: Divided: author, title, specific model	Books (General); Reference collection	Library of Congress	CODE: AACR1? Purchased LC card sets	Library of Congress (Locally developed headings for reports and other non-book materials)	?	?	Marginal punched card applications for many materials	Abstracts and indexes made for technical content of significant data (Planning for mechanized retrieval system for technical subject content)

* Source: Maura Downey Klingen. *A Study of Special Libraries in Business and Industry.* (MLS thesis, University of Mississippi, 1968).
Regular type signifies 1980–82 data
† signifies main collection.

Table 2. Survey of Business Libraries (1968)* (cont.)

TYPE OF LIBRARY	COLLECTIONS/FILES MAINTAINED	TREATMENT OF MATERIAL IN MAIN CATALOG							OTHER LOCALLY DEVELOPED AIDS/ METHODS TO ACCESS COLLECTIONS/FILES	AIDS TO INFORMATION ACCESS
		TYPE AND FORM OF CATALOG	MATERIALS ACCESS THROUGH CATALOG	CLASSIFICATION SYSTEM	AIDS TO AND CODES FOR CATALOGING	SUBJECT HEADINGS SOURCE(S)	AUTHORITY FILES MAINTAINED	FILING RULES		
A. CORPORATE										
4. Research Library in a Chemical Manufacturing Company FOUNDED: 1961 SIZE OF MAIN COLLECTION: 26,350 vols. (Books) SPECIALTIES: Fibers; Chemicals; Plastics; Electronics; Engineering; Agriculture	†Books (General); Chemical samples & records; Directories; Company reports & reprints; Patents; Internal reports; Pamphlets; Periodicals; Reference collection; Trade catalogs; Translations	TYPE: Book (union) FORM: Divided: author, title, subject	Books (General); Reference collection	Dewey Decimal	CODE: AACR1?	?	?	?	Serials list; Variety of finding lists and indexes produced through IBM Dokument Writer use	Subject bibliographies (through use of IBM Dokument Writer)
5. Library for a Public Utilities Firm FOUNDED: 1941 SIZE OF MAIN COLLECTION: 7,367 vols. (Books) SPECIALTIES: Engineering; Financing; Public and private power; Public utility regulations; Public utilities	†Books (General); Company reports: Pamphlets (including maps, government publications, public utilities regulations, items of local interest, scientific reports); Periodicals	TYPE: Card? FORM: ?	Books (General)	Dewey Decimal	CODE: AACR1?	Library of Congress Also, SLA's *Subject Headings Suggested for Use in Public Utilities Libraries*	?	?	Special bibliographies (prepared upon request) List of acquisitions (monthly)	Library clipping service (citations from area newspapers, NY *Times*, *Wall Street Journal*, about company power industry, electrical service) performed daily and distributed company-wide

* Source: Maura Downey Klingen. *A Study of Special Libraries in Business and Industry*. (MLS thesis, University of Mississippi, 1968).
Regular type signifies 1980–82 data
† signifies main collection.

REFERENCES

1. A. Leslie Smyth, "Organization and Administration: Objectives, Planning and Staffing," in *Manual of Business Library Practice*, edited by Malcolm J. Campbell, 2nd ed. London: Clive Bingley, 1985, p. 23.

2. Cynthia C. Ryans and John K. Ryans, Jr., "The Role and Functions of the Company Librarian," *Research Management* 20 (March 1977): 38–40.

3. An example is Allan Foster's *Which Database? An Evaluative Guide to Online Bibliographic Databases in Business and the Social Sciences* Hartlepool, England: Headland Press, 1981, 102 pp.

4. Catherine Fay, "The Corporate Information Center," in *Online Searching: The Basics, Settings & Management*, edited by Joann H. Lee Littleton, CO: Libraries Unlimited, 1984, pp. 105–13.

5. Joel Misinsky, "The Corporate Library: Gearing for the Late 1980's," in *Festschrift in Honor of Dr. Anulfo D. Trejo*, edited by Christopher F. Grippo, et al. Tucson: University of Arizona Graduate Library School, 1984, pp. 75–82.

6. Mildred S. Myers and William C. Frederick, "Business Libraries: Role and Function in Industrial America," *Journal of Education for Librarianship* 15 (Summer 1974): 41–52.

7. Lorna M. Daniells, *Business Information Sources* Berkeley, CA.: University of California Press, 1985, pp. 1–4.

8. Myers and Frederick, p. 49.

9. Myers and Frederick, p. 49.

10. Malcolm J. Campbell, *Business Information Sources: Some Aspects of Structure, Organisation and Problems*, 2nd ed. London: Clive Bingley, 1981, pp. 69–88.

11. A. Leslie Smyth, "Organisation and Administration: Classification, Cataloguing, and Arrangement," in *Manual of Business Library Practice*, edited by Malcolm J. Campbell, 2nd ed. London: Clive Bingley, 1985, pp. 41–49.

12. Smyth, "Organisation and Administration: Objectives, Planning and Staffing," pp. 23–29.

13. Elizabeth Ferguson and Emily R. Mobley, *Special Libraries at Work* Hamden, CT: Library Professional Publications, 1984, pp. 59–71.

14. Janet L. Ahrensfeld, Elin B. Christianson, and David E. King, *Special Libraries: A Guide for Management*, 2nd rev. ed., New York: Special Libraries Association, 1986, pp. 9–10, 18–23 especially.

15. Eva Lou Fisher, *A Checklist for the Organization, Operation, and Evaluation of a Company Library*, 2nd rev. ed. New York: Special Libraries Association, 1966, p. 21.

16. Kenneth Denis Cecil Vernon, "Using Libraries as Information Resources," in his *Use of Management and Business Literature* London: Butterworths, 1975, pp. 61–80.

17. Ronald Stavely, "Special Libraries," in *Manual of Library Economy: A Conspectus of Professional Librarianship for Students and Practitioners*, edited by Reginald Northwood Lock London: Clive Bingley, 1977, pp. 74–95.

18. K. G. B. Bakewell, "The Special Library," in *Manual of Library Economy: A Conspectus of Professional Librarianship for Students and Practitioners*, edited by Reginald Northwood Lock London: Clive Bingley, 1977, pp. 320–343.

19. "A Guide to Organizing and Maintaining a Company Information Center or Library," *Best's Review (Life/Health)* 78 (December 1977): 86–90.

20. G. D. L. Peterson, "Designing Business Information Services for Top Management," *ASLIB Proceedings* 30 (April 1978): 142–44.

21. Carol Tenopir, *Total Information Centers* Arlington, VA: Educational Resources Information Center, 1978, (ERIC Report ED 165–738).

22. Tenopir, p. 9.

23. George P. Henderson, "Directories and Company Information Sources," in *Manual of Business Library Practice*, edited by Malcolm J. Campbell, 2nd ed. London: Clive Bingley, 1985, pp. 57–74.

24. Michael Haines, "Company Correspondence: An Important Resource," *ASLIB Proceedings* 31 (August 1979): 401–11.

25. Jean E. Koch and Judith M. Pask, "Working Papers in Academic Business Libraries," *College & Research Libraries* 41 (November 1980): 517–23.

26. Judith R. Bernstein, "Corporate Annual Reports in Academic Business Libraries," *College & Research Libraries* 47 (May 1986): 263–73.

27. June Ohlson and Christine Tabuteau, "Microfiche Project on Australian Companies' Annual Reports," *Australian Academic and Research Libraries* 9 (December 1978): 215–18.

28. A. R. Blick and S. M. Ward, "Microform Policy to Reduce the Physical Growth of Industrial Libraries," *ASLIB Proceedings* 36 (April 1984): 165–76.

29. Suzanna Lengyel, "Modification of Dewey for a Business Library," *Special Libraries* 52 (May 1961): 245.

30. Ray Wachniak, "To Find It, File It Right," *Quality Progress* 8 (July 1975): 8–9.

31. Harvard University. Graduate School of Business Administration. Library, *Classification of Business Literature*, Rev. ed. Hamden, CT: Shoe String Press, 1960.

32. Kenneth Denis Cecil Vernon and Valerie Lang, *The London Classification of Business Studies*, 2nd ed., rev. by K. G. B. Bakewell and David A. Cotton London: ASLIB Publications, 1979.

33. Vernon and Lang, p. 9.

34. K. G. B. Bakewell, "London Classification of Business Studies," *International Classification* 6 (March 1979): 29–35.

35. Bakewell, "London Classification of Business Studies," p. 32.

36. Kenneth Denis Cecil Vernon, "Classification of Business and the Business of Classification," *Catalogue & Index* 59 (Summer 1980): 8–12.

37. Vernon and Lang, pp. 6–24.

38. Special Libraries Association. Financial Division, *Subject Headings for Business and Financial Libraries*. New York: Special Libraries Association, 1952; Special Libraries Association. Financial Division, *Subject Headings for Financial Libraries*. New York: Special Libraries Association, 1954; and Elin B. Christianson and Edward G. Strable, comp., *Subject Headings in Advertising, Marketing and Communications Media*. New York: Special Libraries Association, 1964.

39. K. G. B. Bakewell, "ANBAR Indexing," *Catalogue & Index* 21 (January 1971): 14–15.

40. John Blagden, *Management Information Retrieval: A New Indexing Language*, 2nd ed. London: Management Publications, 1971.

41. F. A. Graham, "The Industrial Librarian and Universal Bibliographic Control," *Industrial Journal of Special Libraries (INSPE)* 9 (1–2) (1974): 16–21.

42. Elizabeth Bole Eddison and Lois B. Lyman, comps., *Words That Mean Business: 3,000 Terms for Access to Business Information* New York: Neal-Schuman, 1981.

43. Mary J. Culnan, "What Corporate Librarians Will Need to Know in the Future," *Special Libraries* 77 (Fall 1986): 213–16.

44. G. de Saederleer, "Automation of the Library, 'Fonds Quetelet'," *Network* 3 (4) (1976): 9–17.

45. Gretchen Redfield, "Automation and Networking," *Colorado Librarian* 6 (June 1980): 29.

46. A. J. Karmiggelt, "Software Alternatives for Corporate IS&R on Microcomputers: Make Use of Facilities Present," in International Conference on the Application of Mini- and Micro-Computers in Information, Documentation, and Libraries (1983: Tel Aviv), *The Application of Mini- and Micro-Computers in Information, Documentation, and Libraries*, edited by Carl Keren and Linda Perlmutter, Contemporary Topics in Information Transfer, v. 3 Amsterdam: North-Holland, 1983, pp. 489–93.

47. Herbert J. Seuss, "In-house Automation at Eaton Corporation: Then and Now," *Wisconsin Library Bulletin* 78 (Summer 1983): 53.

48. I. L. Johnstone and P. Taylor, "In-house Software Development in the AGSM," in National Conference on Library and Bibliographic Applications of Minicomputers (1979: Sydney, N.S.W.), *Proceedings—National Conference on Library and Bibliographic Applications of Minicomputers, Sydney, Australia, August 22–24, 1979*, edited by Michael R. Middleton Kensington, N.S.W.: Unisearch, 1979, pp. 59–68.

49. P. de Rivaz et al., "The Use of CAIRS in an Industrial Library and Information Department," *Journal of Information Science* 4 (August 1982): 193–201.

50. William Poor, "STAIRS: A Storage and Retrieval System Applied in Online Cataloging," *Special Libraries* 73 (January 1982): 52–62.

51. Karen Takle Quinn, "The Information Center—Another Perspective," *ONLINE* 6 (July 1982): 11–23.

52. Karen Selby, Linda Lutz, and Roberta Maxwell, "IMS and STAIRS: An Answer to a Corporate Library's Online system," in American Society for Information Science. Meeting. (46th: 1983: Washington, DC), *Productivity in the Information Age : Proceedings of the 46th ASIS Annual Meeting, Washington, DC, October 2–6, 1983* White Plains, NY: Knowledge Industry Publications, 1983, pp. 217–24.

53. Ann W. Talcott, "Managing Electronic Libraries," in *Managing the Electronic Library: Papers of the 1982 Conference of the Library Management Division of Special Libraries Association*, Michael Koenig, ed. New York: Special Libraries Association, 1983, pp. 46–73.

54. Jean K. Martin, "Planning for and Early Experiences with a Library LAN," in *Local Area Networks and Libraries: The Los Angeles Chapter of ASIS Seminar Proceedings*, edited by Wendy Culotta, Zorona Ercegovac, Danaocs., Inc., 1984, pp. 291–305.

55. James P. O'Connor, "One Happy Hybrid," *American Libraries* 18 (April 1987): 290–92.

56. W. E. Fitzgerald et al., "Monsanto's Company-Wide Online Catalog," in Conference on Integrated Online Library Systems (2nd: 1984: Atlanta, GA), *Proceedings—2nd National Conference on Integrated Online Library*

Systems, edited by David C. Genaway, Canfield, OH: Genaway & Assocs., Inc., 1984, pp. 291–305.

57. W. A. Wilkinson, "Monsanto Company Information Center: Twenty-Five Years of Accelerating Change," *Show-Me Libraries* 37 (January 1986): 5–10.

58. Felicia Rodriguez Bagby, "Clark, Dietz Engineers, Inc.: A Library Profile," *Illinois Libraries* 62 (March 1980): 231–33.

59. Betty S. Hagberg, "Profile of a Library Serving a Corporate Headquarters," *Illinois Libraries* 62 (March 1980): 239–42.

60. Marilyn Macku La Salle, "Portland Cement Association Research and Development/Construction Technology Laboratories Library," *Illinois Libraries* 62 (March 1980): 242–45.

61. Rue E. Olson, "Serving in the Heartland of Illinois," *Illinois Libraries* 62 (March 1980): 260–63.

62. Carol E. Mulvaney, "Technical Information Center: Caterpillar Tractor Company," *Illinois Libraries* 62 (March 1980): 256–58.

63. Ellen Steininger, "An Advertising and Public Relations Agency Library," *Illinois Libraries* 62 (March 1980): 272–74.

64. Jenny Preston, "Starting a Library at McDonnell Douglas Automation Company," *Show-Me Libraries* 32 (July 1981): 14–18.

65. Karen S. McConnell, "Automation [of Gulf States Utilities Company Library]," *Texas Library Journal* 60 (Summer 1984): 52–53.

66. Susan A. Merry, "Inside a Major Banking and Business Library," *Canadian Library Journal* 42 (June 1985): 115–18.

67. Hella Stahl, "Meet PAPRICANS Scientific and Technical Library," *Canadian Library Journal* 42 (December 1985): 375–77.

68. Susan Reid, "An Oil Company's Information Resources," *Canadian Library Journal* 42 (August 1985): 221–24.

69. Hunter McCleary, "A Practical Guide to Establishing a Business Intelligence Clearinghouse," *Database* 9 (June 1986): 40–46.

70. Russell G. Fischer, "Monica Ertel: Librarian Is at Core of Apple Users Group," *American Libraries* 18 (February 1987): 146.

71. Maura Downey Klingen, "A Study of Special Libraries in Business and Industry," (MLS thesis, University of Mississippi, 1968).

72. "Profile of a Library for the GHI Public Utilities Firm," *Special Libraries* 57 (April 1966): 227–29; "Profile of a Library for the JKL Bank," *Special Libraries* 57 (April 1968): 229–31; "Profile of a Library for the Research and Development Division of the DEF Industrial Corporation," *Special Libraries* 57 (March 1966): 182–84; "Profile of a Library for the Research and Development Division of the QRS Chemical Manufacturing Company," *Special Libraries* 57 (May/June 1966): 329–31; and "Profile of a Research Library in the ABC Manufacturing Corporation," *Special Libraries* (March 1966): 180–81.

Reference Service in the Business Area

by John B. Etchingham, Jr.

The key to the provision of good reference service to business clientele is the business reference librarian. The librarian must begin (1) by understanding the subject area of the library collection (business and its related fields), (2) by appreciating the necessity for a collection that meets the needs of clientele and by working toward such a collection, and (3) by providing good reference through application of his/her skills and talents and through the effective use of the reference interview.

TRAINING OF THE BUSINESS LIBRARIAN

In order to accomplish these objectives, the business reference librarian should, ideally, hold academic credentials related to business and should have several years of experience in the field. This is not, however, generally the case. More often, the beginning business librarian is without either significant academic training or experience. Acquiring the necessary experiences requires, first and foremost, a personal commitment over time to pursue them. Once this commitment is present, there are several alternatives to on-the-job experience that should be explored.[1]

1. Business courses offered at local institutions can be invaluable to the beginner. Although business reference courses in library schools are helpful, even more important are introductory courses in the business school. A package of the basic courses in accounting, management, and finance will provide a sound base for the business librarian. One should, however, give careful consideration to the money and time spent in such classes. At least part of

John B. Etchingham, Jr., is business reference librarian, University of Rhode Island, at Kingston.

the costs will likely be covered for academic librarians in institutions where business school course work is offered, but the public library business librarian will probably have to absorb the costs alone. Time, however, will be a critical factor for both. Three basic courses would probably take three semesters for a working librarian. Such an extended (and costly) educational package leads many to consider the other two alternatives.

2. Beginning librarians might explore the availability of training sessions in business and in business librarianship. These are usually no longer than two or three days and take a variety of forms, such as business reference workshops offered by library schools or state library agencies, presentations given by information vendors such as DIALOG and Predicasts in computerized database searching, and short-term noncredit courses given by the continuing education agencies in academic institutions.[2] Keeping abreast of all these activities is not difficult. Information vendors are usually very willing to add the librarian's name to their mailing lists, and a call to the local continuing education agency will accomplish the same for its announcements. Watching the state library journals will help as well, since many carry continuing education listings as a regular feature.

3. Self-education cannot be overlooked. In its broadest sense, this is an all-embracing life-long activity in many subject areas. The narrow context used here refers to becoming as familiar as one can—and as quickly as possible—with the bibliographic materials at hand. This may be done by reading the introductory matter of a set of the popular and high demand business reference sources word for word. As an example, if the librarian had never heard of a financial ratio, a thorough reading of about six pages of the introductory matter in the *RMA Annual Statement Studies*[3] would quickly turn ignorance into knowledge. In the same way, contacting the representatives of business publishers and investment services for their virtually unending flow of announcements of new and old ware—and critically reading the output—would efficiently make the librarian aware of what certain titles provide. Still another method of self-education regarding the basic business sources is to consult the secondary sources. Although they usually provide only a brief overview of the listed materials, they represent an organized and classified collection of many diverse titles. This can afford the librarian a sense of the range of tools in specialized areas of the business spectrum. Three such secondary sources recommended by the author are M. J. Campbell's *Manual of Business Library Practise*, L. M. Daniells' *Business Information Sources*, Oscar Figueroa's *A Business Information Guidebook*.[4]

In recognition not only of the importance of the periodical literature supporting business, but also its great breadth and depth, the business librarian should be familiar with (and in the case of the academic/research librarian have at the ready) David W. E. Cabell's

Cabell's Directory of Publishing Opportunities in Business and Economics.[5] It provides detailed guidance for the person seeking to publish in any of 230 periodicals; in so doing it presents a good deal of information which is of interest to the new librarian as well as the business subject selector. The arrangement is alphabetical by title with a subject index (actually an index by discipline), and the entries include a treatment of the focus of articles desired and detailed manuscript guidelines. *Cabell's,* revised every two to three years, represents an excellent introduction to the business journal literature.

Two additional, helpful titles should be noted: *Materials & Methods for Business Research* by Linda J. Piele, John C. Tyson, and Michael B. Sheffey,[6] and *Business Information: How to Find It, How to Use It* by Michael R. Lavin.[7] The former is made up of a workbook and an instructors manual, and will be especially helpful to any business librarian planning to deliver bibliographic instruction as the preface indicates:

> Intended to guide students through the maze of information sources encountered during their studies, the workbooks are based on the principle that the more students know about the materials and methods required for effective information gathering in their subject discipline, the more productive they will become.

This is equally true for the librarian. Lavin's work is nearly comprehensive in its coverage of sources. The introductory matter for each chapter is invaluable and the descriptive and critical passages on the hundreds of titles are particularly thorough and clearly presented. The selection/acquisition advice is especially noteworthy for business collection selectors.

Finally, it should be emphasized again, in advocating training, that there is no substitute for subject area knowledge. "Winging it," for the business reference librarian, is not a viable method of operation.

APPRECIATION OF THE COLLECTION

The essence of reference work is to match the patron's question with the right answer. Central to this process is the availability of a reference collection that will provide the required information. Especially in academic libraries, a limited number of services/titles can provide answers to a very large number of the business reference questions received at the desk. Such a limited list would include the following.

1. Moody's Investors Service Materials

The seven annual corporate manuals *(Bank and Finance, Industrial, International, OTC [Over the Counter] Industrial, Municipal and Government, Public Utility, Transportation,* and *OTC Unlisted)* present descriptive and tabular data on approximately 22,000 corporations and institutions operating in the national and international sectors, including information on history, subsidiaries, business lines, and plants and properties, as well as management data, income accounts, and balance sheets.[8] Coverage ranges from the comprehensive to the narrowly selective, with retrospective analysis varying with each manual. Beginning dates for the manual range from 1920 for the *Industrial Manual* to 1981 for the *International Manual* and 1986 for the *OTC Unlisted Manual.*

Arrangement in the set varies with each manual. The *Industrial Manual* is organized by coverage (i.e., corporate visibility-plus, corporate visibility-select, corporate visibility-standard) and then alphabetically by corporation/institution name; the *International Manual* is organized first by country then by company name. Indexing provides the additional access needed, a good example being the alphabetical, geographical (state and city), and industry/product access in the *Industrial Manual.* All of the titles are kept current with loose-leaf issues (usually received twice a week) that are usually filed in corresponding *News Reports* binders. The user must be careful of incomplete or broken pagination, such as the gaps of 100 pages or more between some coverage sections in the *Industrial Manual.*

Other Moody titles of special interest to the librarian, researcher, investor, or business student are the *Industry Review, Bond Record* and *Handbook of Common Stocks.*[9] The *Industry Review* provides tabular and graphic presentations of key financial information, operating data, and ratios for 4,000 companies in 145 industries. In addition, comparative industry statistics in company-rank order are displayed. This loose-leaf service is in a constant state of revision, with 10 to 12 industries updated every two weeks. The monthly *Bond Record* covers over 48,000 issues and situations, with the format allowing quick assessment of market position and background statistics. The quarterly *Handbook of Common Stocks* provides financial and business information on over 900 stocks with high investor interest. The data on each company include a long-term price chart, capitalization, earnings, dividend information, company background, and recent developments. The language and tone of the introductory matter in this title make it especially attractive to the new investor.

Moody's Investors Service also offers other products that are worth investigating.

2. Standard and Poor's (S&P) Corporation Materials

A frequent question asked is which company, Moody's or S&P, should be the primary source of business materials, given a limited budget. Which occupies first place as a source of business reference materials is a matter of personal preference. The publications of Dun & Bradstreet might be included in this discussion of preference as well. (Dun & Bradstreet publications are recommended in this essay and elsewhere in this volume.) However, a special word of caution to those contemplating an "every other" acquisition schedule of any of several Dun & Bradstreet annuals: This publisher usually requires the return of these products at subscription year-end, claiming proprietary owner-ship. This situation leaves the library's shelves empty for the succeed-ing and final year of the two-year period. Both Moody's and S&P come free of this stricture. In addition, both offer a comprehensive business collection, with many titles in such close parallel that it is difficult, if not impossible, to choose one over the other. Two S&P titles, however, deserve special consideration for the business reference collection, be-cause of their unique nature.

The *Standard and Poor's Register of Corporations, Directors, and Executives* is an annual publication in three volumes, kept current with three cumulated supplements.[10] Volume 1 is an alphabetical arrange-ment of approximately 45,000 corporations, with information including addresses, names, and titles of officers and directors; primary bank, law firm, and accounting firm; exchange(s) on which the company's stock is traded; annual sales; number of employees; and Standard Industrial Classification (SIC) codes. Volume 2 is a listing of over 70,000 individ-ual directors and executives, with brief biographical and company affiliation data. Volume 3 is the index volume, listing corporations geographically, by SIC code, and by corporate family. The corporate family index is a "Who Owns Whom" directory, identifying subsidiar-ies, divisions, and affiliates. In terms of quantity and quality, the *Register* is unique. Especially noteworthy is that private as well as public firms are listed.

Industry Surveys offers a wide variety of data useful for analysis of an industry.[11] Over 30 major domestic industries are analyzed in two sections, "Basic Analysis" and "Current Analysis," drawing on data from some 1,200 companies. The "Basic Analysis" examines the pros-pects for the industry and presents historical background data. The "Comparative Company Analysis," a regular part of the "Basic Analy-sis," provides tabular data on industry leaders. The "Current Analysis," revised periodically during the year, offers the latest developments and statistics, along with an appraisal of the investment outlook. *Industry Surveys* is available in loose-leaf or bound quarterly format. For high-use environments, the author strongly recommends the bound format.

3. Value Line Investment Survey

Approximately 90 industries embracing some 1,650 companies are covered in this important title for industry and company analysis. *Value Line*[12] is published in three parts. Part I, *Summary and Index*, in addition to its index of companies, contains a screens section that includes a listing of timely, conservative, and high-yield stocks; best and poorest performing stocks; companies with high return on capital; low and high P/E (price/earnings) stocks; and stock market averages. Part I is completely revised every week. Part II, *Selection and Opinion*, a weekly newsletter that offers investment recommendations, includes an important regular feature, the stock highlight column in which an exceptionally high-performing stock is analyzed and strongly recommended to the reader. Part III, *Ratings and Reports*, is organized into 13 editions, consecutively revised on a weekly schedule in such a way that the entire body is revised quarterly. Each industry and its allied companies are given a one- or two-page coverage, providing a statistical, narrative, and graphic overview of historical and projected performance. The newsprint format of Part III causes some problems; in high-use settings, the editions rarely survive their 90-day life.

4. Accounting/Banking/Management Analysis Materials

Three highly specialized titles of interest to the accounting, banking, and management analyst are the *Almanac of Business and Industrial Financial Ratios, Industry Norms and Key Business Financial Ratios: One Year,* and the *RMA Annual Statement Studies.*[13] These are difficult titles to use and their use presumes extensive prior knowledge of financial analysis. For many librarians, their effective use will require a fair measure of self-education. The *Almanac* supplies complete corporate performance facts and figures displayed on an industry basis. The percentages displayed allow one to answer such questions as: How well is the company performing, compared to the industry as a whole, in its ratio of profit to sales? What is its net worth? and What share of sales is going to amortization? *Key Business Ratios* covers over 800 lines of business providing values for 14 financial ratios on each. *Statement Studies* provides composite financial data on manufacturing, wholesaling, retailing, and contracting lines of business. The comparative analytical data, shown for the current year and for the previous four years, are critical for making accurate financial judgments. All are annuals.

5. Statistics Materials

Since few business decisions are not influenced by statistics, a limited business reference collection must contain sources for answering questions in this area. Chief among these sources for U.S. data is the *American Statistics Index* (ASI) and its companion, the *Statistical Reference Index* (SRI).[14] The ASI aims to be a master guide and index to all the statistical publications of the U.S. government. Since there is no single central source of statistical publications published by the federal government, the ASI satisfies a very important need by filling this void. Specifically, it identifies, catalogs, announces, describes, and indexes, on a monthly schedule, federal statistics, the range and depth of which are without parallel. Its companion, the SRI, provides access to statistical information from U.S. sources other than the federal government, including statistics published by trade and business organizations, commercial publishers, research centers, and state government agencies. It does *not* cover municipal and county publications (these are announced in the *Index to Current Urban Documents*).[15] Worthy of special note are the fine abstracts; the cumulation of all loose-leaf monthly issues into annual hard-bound editions; and the availability of microfiche for virtually all of the documents cited in the ASI and for about 90 percent of the material cited in the SRI, which can be provided by subscription, or (in the case of the ASI) on demand as well.

In addition to the ASI and SRI, the author must note two other indispensable publications in the area of statistics: the annual handbook, *Statistical Abstract of the United States*, and the yearly *U.S. Industrial Outlook*.[16] The *Abstract* is a 900–page document of tabular data, citing the primary source for each table and thus providing identification of the source of much federal statistical data. Published for over 100 years, it serves as an excellent tool for retrospective analysis for such diverse areas of interest as state and local government finances; banking, finance, and insurance; business enterprise; and mining and mineral production data. The section on comparative international statistics is especially valuable to those analyzing or considering foreign markets. The *Outlook* is a forecasting publication in which 350 industries are reviewed. Performance projections, extending in some cases to several years, are provided. Much of the data in the *Outlook* come from the U.S. Bureau of the Census.

In this area of statistics, the librarian should further consider acquiring a certain number of census documents, e.g., *Census of Retail Trade, Census of Wholesale Trade, Census of Service Industries, Census of Transportation, Census of Manufacturers*, and *County Business Patterns*.[17] These are available on a state-by-state basis, so that the librarian can select the titles for only his/her state and/or region. For the nondepository library, a subscription service is available from the Superintendent of Documents at a still relatively modest price.

6. Directories

Occupying a prominent place in the business reference section are the directories. In addition to the previously mentioned Standard and Poor's *Register of Corporations, Directors, and Executives*, several other directories should be considered. Heading the list is the *Thomas Register of American Manufacturers*.[18] Its organization into the *Products and Services Volumes*, The *Company Volumes*, and the *Thomcat Catalog Volumes* gives the researcher access to information on who makes what where. Over 100,000 companies—both publicly and privately held—are identified. A strength of company directories like *Thomas Register* is that they provide the job seeker with an extensive listing of companies that may be sources of employment. They are also important to the market analyst and to sales force personnel.

The *Thomas Register* provides a comprehensive national tool. A number of local and regional directories should be made available as well. Examples are the *Directory of New England Manufacturers* and the *Connecticut-Rhode Island Directory of Manufacturers,*[19] both of which are organized into alphabetical, geographical, and product sections. The wide variety of such titles gives the librarian a degree of flexibility in selection, especially when operating under restrictions. In addition to the Polk City Directories and local publishers, the librarian should consult Commerce Register, Inc., of Hohokus, New Jersey, and George D. Hall Company of Boston, Massachusetts.

The user should be aware of the disclaimers found in many directories, i.e., that such works are inherently incomplete, since much of the information is provided voluntarily and nonresponses are inevitable.

THE REFERENCE PROCESS

The patron—the information seeker—and the effectiveness of his/her interaction with the librarian and with the collection are the key elements in the reference process. If there were no patrons, all the available librarians' expertise and all the titles in the reference collection would serve no purpose. That the presence and needs of the patron are paramount in the process is accepted. That the communication of these needs and the understanding of them by the librarian is in many cases difficult to achieve is equally accepted. Human communication is faulty; what we say is easily misunderstood, and what we hear is often only a part of the message. The importance of understanding the patron as well as the patron's needs cannot be overemphasized.

Types of Patrons

No neat scheme of categorizing patrons exists. Some patrons know exactly what information they want and where it is; others know what they want but don't know where to search; still others aren't really sure of the "what" and certainly are less sure of the "where." The librarian has a role to play with each of these patrons, and the involvement varies inversely with the patron's knowledge and self-organization.[20]

For the experienced user, such as the investor in the public library or the researcher in the academic or special library, the librarian's role is to make connections. The opportunity to do so assumes at least two preconditions: that the library holds the appropriate titles, and that the librarian knows where they are and/or how to locate them quickly. Whether the titles are held is a function of collection development; whether they can be found is a function of the librarian's experience and skill. Collection development, practical experience, and skills development take time, but even if all have been diligently pursued, the success of the process is not ensured. There may be other germane and available titles unknown to the librarian which may contain the information sought, or at least part of it. Determining whether the patron has found an answer in the available titles or whether the librarian should intervene and recommend other sources depends on the reference interview, which may be triggered by a formal request or by the briefest of verbal or nonverbal communication.

The author should note that the in-house reference guides in his library, which are readily available and prominently announced, have been very helpful. The kinds and numbers of such guides that should be on hand will depend on the needs of the library clientele. In any case, they should be brief, annotated listings of subject-oriented materials in the library, probably no longer than two pages. Business librarians faced with the task of developing such guides will wish to consult sources available from other libraries with similar clientele, especially the guides used in the libraries of the well-known business schools and in the larger business-oriented public libraries.

For the user who knows what he or she wants but who doesn't know where to start, the role of the librarian goes beyond the basic directional reference encounter, and involves careful and difficult judgments. As one example, let us look at the student who indicates interest in the historical development of a public U.S. company. The librarian would probably start with a Moody's Manual rather than *Value Line*. By the same measure, the "Corporate Section" of the *Wall Street Journal Index* rather than the companion "General Section," would probably be appropriate.[21] But perhaps the student should be referred to the legions of books written on companies, especially the many devoted to the conglomerates and supranational corporations. Or perhaps the periodical literature should be consulted, the *Business Periodicals Index* (BPI) or the *Public Affairs Information Service*, or even, the *Social Sciences Citation Index*.[22] Only the interview can determine the direction taken by the librarian.

A second example of the user who doesn't know where to start may be found every day in the public library, in the person of the beginning investor. The growth of investment clubs and the general interest in small-scale investing have produced a multitude of such patrons. The public library business desk specialist or the reference librarian occupying that role has an obligation to instruct this type of user, first in the mysteries of the simpler tools, such as Moody's *Handbook*, then in the complexities of the more advanced financial services such as *Value Line*, and finally in the intricacies of technical considerations in investing and its associated literature.

One might assume that the user who doesn't know where to start is scarce. However, Pask notes that, in her study 48 percent of the graduate business students surveyed could not list one index or abstract they knew how to use well. In the same source, Pask cites another survey, in which both undergraduate and graduate business students were queried—and 10 percent of the group had never even heard of the *Business Periodicals Index* (BPT).[23] If this is true of the college student who is specializing in the field, it is probably even more true of the general user of the public library, and the librarian should realize that this patron will need considerable help, not only in identifying the applicable primary and secondary sources, but also in hands-on use of the research tools.

For the patron who is uncomfortable with both the what and the where, and who shyly approaches the reference desk (if indeed he or she is aware that the service exists), the reference librarian's role is crucial. The librarian will be called upon not only to render substantial assistance with the bibliographical sources but also to help define and refine the patron's objective: just what it is that is being sought. A typical question from this type of patron might be "Where are the magazines?," generally asked haltingly and apprehensively. The sensitive librarian, in different environments, may discover very different answers are necessary to this seemingly simple question.

The author is familiar with the question "Where are the magazines?" from the college student who, it turns out, has been assigned the first term paper of his/her college career, with the requirement of an eight-citation bibliography, half of journal and half of book citations. Such a student is overwhelmed by the choices and characteristically may select a difficult but attractive topic such as selected legislation controlling the multinational corporation; but he or she may not be able to proceed beyond the choice, because he or she has no idea of where to obtain the necessary information.

For this type of student, the librarian might start with an explanation of the library organization and the different bodies of literature within it (books, serials, microforms, etc.). This might be followed, ideally, by a session on the procedures involved in retrieval of the materials likely to provide the information needed for the paper. Such a session would involve several tasks: an introduction to the card catalog, an overview of the subject classification scheme, and a review of the selection process for the appropriate indexes for the subject periodicals, as well as the methods of searching those indexes.

For specific questions, such as the one noted above on multinational corporations, the author has found it effective to work with students first to see how the subject is treated in the *Sears List of Subject Headings* or the *Library of Congress Subject Headings*.[24] In the latter, for example, the searcher is referred to "International Business Enterprises" under which there are several topical subdivisions, one of which is "Law and Legislation." Analogously, a scan of the organization under "Multinational Corporations" in the latest cumulative volume of the *Business Periodicals Index* shows 13 subdivisions, one of which is "Laws and Regulations."

In another case, patient and sympathetic treatment may introduce a patron seeking information on product research in a particular field to a new world of the *Thomas Register*, the *Moody's Manuals*, the products of the Institute for Scientific Information, and an understanding of the *Chemical Abstracts* and scientific journals.

Finally, public librarians may find in the question, "Where are the magazines?" anything from a request for directions to a request for instruction in the use of popular magazine literature by a town resident and inventor who wants to stay current with the interests of the teenage consumer.

Issues in the Reference Process

1. No matter the level of the patron, the librarian must be careful not to overwhelm him/her. The guidance must be clear and precise, and an attitude of understanding and friendliness must prevail throughout. Any lengthy discourse on the finer points of the bibliographic world will surely fall on impatient, if not deaf, ears and jeopardize the success of the entire process.

2. How much time should a librarian be expected to devote to rendering individual assistance? Given the usual press on the librarian's time, isn't there a better way than a one-to-one encounter? If time and staffing permit, the librarian should render as much help as is needed. Unfortunately, in very few business libraries is there time or staff adequate to meet all the demands placed upon reference service. The reasonable alternative is to enable and encourage the patron to exploit the library independently. The reference interview should reveal the level of independence with which the patron can and desires to operate. With the proper guidance, delivered in a suitably appropriate, warm, and concerned manner, most patrons should welcome and seize upon the opportunities of independent research. Most users simply don't require or like a librarian breathing down their necks. It is incumbent upon the librarian to recognize when the job is done, and to appreciate the rewards to the student of the feeling of accomplishment and satisfaction stemming from self-reliance.

3. What about considering library instruction on a group basis, in light of the economies of such a procedure? The answer to this question depends on whether one is considering public, special, or academic libraries. The opportunities for group instruction in the public or special library are few. Any session should be widely announced, planned at a time convenient to the intended audience, and structured with considerable appeal. In the academic setting, the situation is quite different. The audience can be a captive one and generally is at least minimally motivated. The presentation can be carefully planned to show the clear sequence of steps necessary to retrieve the required information from the applicable bodies of literature. The author has found that a packet of illustrative material reflecting the subject at hand and given to each student at the beginning of the session can be helpful in relating the library resources to the course content and to the

assignment. An added benefit of these hand-out packets is that they may be consulted by the students again and again as a library retrieval directory. The packets should be no longer than 6 or 7 pages and should be readily copiable. The author also should note that it should be emphasized that the session will be more successful if the instructor is present.

4. Should computerized database searching be made available? This form of reference is becoming increasingly popular. (A full discussion of the various business-oriented databases is presented in another essay in this volume.) The point is often made that computerized searching is extremely timely and efficient. With the right array of terms used for the enquiry, one can achieve in a matter of minutes what would take days or even weeks for a researcher working with print indexes and abstracts. Although these points support the desirability of online searching, one must also consider its high price. Despite costs, many public and academic business libraries have initiated computerized searching, usually with a fee schedule for such service,[25] and special libraries have been notable and enthusiastic users of database searching since it first became available.

REFERENCES

1. The reader should consult *Continuing Education for Business People* (Detroit, MI: Gale, 1981).

2. For a model business librarianship course, see Katherine Cveljo's essay in this book titled "Continuing Training of the Business Information Professional," pp. 249–56.

3. Robert Morris Associates, *RMA Annual Statement Studies* (Philadelphia, PA: Robert Morris Associates, Annual).

4. Campbell, Malcolm J., *Manual of Business Library Practise*, 2d ed. (Hamden, CT: Shoe String, 1985); Daniells, Lorna M., *Business Information Sources*, rev. ed. (Berkeley: University of California Press, 1985); and Figueroa, Oscar, *A Business Information Guidebook* (New York: Amacom, 1980).

5. Cabell, David W. E., *Cabell's Directory of Publishing Opportunities in Business and Economics* (Beaumont, TX: Cabell Publishing, 1985).

6. Piele, Linda J., John C. Tyson, and Michael B. Sheffey, *Materials & Methods for Business Research.* (New York, NY: Neal-Schuman Publishers, Inc., 1980).

7. Lavin, Michael R., *Business Information: How to Find It, How to Use It.* (Phoenix, AZ: Oryx Press, 1987).

8. *Moody's Manuals* (New York: Moody's Investors Service. Annuals and Supplements).

9. *Moody Industry Review* (New York: Moody's Investors Service, Biweekly revisions); *Moody's Bond Record Corporates Convertibles, Governments, Municipals* (New York: Moody's Investors Service, Monthly); and

Moody's Handbook of Common Stocks (New York: Moody's Investors Service, Quarterly).

10. *Standard and Poor's Register of Corporations, Directors and Executives* (New York: Standard and Poor's Corporation, Annual and Supplements).

11. *Industry Surveys* (New York: Standard and Poor's Corporation, Quarterly).

12. *Value Line Investment Survey* (New York: Value Line, Inc., Weekly [Parts I and II], and Quarterly [Part III]).

13. Troy, Leo, *Almanac of Business and Industrial Financial Ratios* (Englewood Cliffs, NJ: Prentice-Hall, Annual); Dun & Bradstreet Credit Services, *Industry Norms and Key Business Ratios: One Year* (Murray Hill, NJ: Dun & Bradstreet Credit Services, Annual); and Robert Morris Associates, *RMA Annual Statement Studies* (Philadelphia, PA: Robert Morris Associates, Annual).

14. *American Statistics Index* (Washington, DC: Congressional Information Service, Annual and Monthly); and *Statistical Reference Index* (Washington, DC: Congressional Information Service, Annual and Monthly).

15. *Index to Current Urban Documents* (Westport, CT: Greenwood Press, Quarterly).

16. *U.S. Bureau of the Census, Statistical Abstract of the United States* (Washington, DC: Government Printing Office, Annual); and U.S. Department of Commerce, *U.S. Industrial Outlook* (Washington, DC: Government Printing Office, Annual).

17. U.S. Bureau of the Census, *Census of Retail Trade, Census of Wholesale Trade, Census of Service Industries, Census of Transportation, Census of Manufacturers,* and *County Business Patterns* (All Washington, DC: Government Printing Office).

18. *Thomas Register of American Manufacturers* (New York: Thomas Publishing Co., Annual).

19. *Directory of New England Manufacturers* (Boston: George D. Hall Co., Annual); and *Connecticut-Rhode Island Directory of Manufacturers* (Hohokus, NJ: Commerce Register, Inc., Annual).

20. See Katz, William A., *Introduction to Reference Work*, Vol. 2, (New York: McGraw-Hill, 1982), pp. 44–48, for a discussion of the reference interview.

21. *Wall Street Journal Index* (New York: Dow Jones and Co., Monthly).

22. *Business Periodicals Index* (New York: H. W. Wilson Co., Monthly except July); *Public Affairs Information Service* (New York: PAIS, Semimonthly); and *Social Sciences Citation Index* (SSCI) (Philadelphia, PA: ISI, Triannual).

23. Pask, Judith M., *Special Libraries* 72 (10): 370–78.

24. *Sears List of Subject Headings* (New York: H. W. Wilson, 1986); and *Library of Congress Subject Headings* (Washington, DC: Library of Congress, 1986).

25. Drinan, Helen, *Online* 3 (4): 14–21.

Continuing Training of the Business Information Professional

by Katherine Cveljo

INTRODUCTION

For the purposes of this essay, "continuing training" is defined as the learning process that builds on and updates previously acquired knowledge and skills and helps one to keep up with: (1) new developments in information technology, communications, and principles and techniques of management, and (2) the developments and changes in the areas of librarianship, information science, and business. Continuing training is becoming increasingly important in order for the business professional to survive and prosper in today's competitive, rapidly-changing information world. Information gathering, trend watching, keeping up-to-date and looking ahead have become important career strategies of the business information professional. Professionals who have the capacity to adapt to change will have the chance to prosper; those who do not, on the other hand, will be working with an obsolete knowledge base and will eventually fail. Only a dynamic, forward-looking business information professional, aided by up-to-the-minute information, can provide quality service in the realm of continuously changing specialized business information needs.

In the education essay in the first edition of this work, the author described the content, the instructional objectives, structure and methodology of a basic course covering the information resources and services in the specialized areas of business for students in a school of library and information science. In the appendix to this essay, the reader can find an updated outline of a business information course, and the latest available statistics on offerings of such a course by schools of library and information science. In the present essay, the author concentrates on the topic of

Katherine Cveljo is a professor of library and information science at the North Texas State University in Denton.

continuing training and the various training opportunities available to the business information professional in order to meet:

- the changing aspects of information flows within the parent organization, and between the business library and the parent organization and the external environment;
- the specialized and continuously changing aspects of the management function in business libraries, including training in: (a) the planning process; (b) expanding the range of services in spite of continuous cuts in financial resources; (c) participating in resource sharing; (d) evaluating and utilizing the marketing concept approach in promoting the business library's services;
- the challenge brought about by the expansion of networks, by the increasing provision of services by online bibliographic utilities and vendors, and by the rapid evolution of the microcomputer into a practical tool with an increasing amount of available and relevant software.

THE DEVELOPMENTS AFFECTING THE NEED FOR CONTINUING TRAINING OF THE BUSINESS INFORMATION PROFESSIONAL

The developments of the last 15 to 20 years, including (1) societal change; (2) proliferation of new knowledge; (3) emergence of new forms of materials and documents; (4) impact of newer technologies; (5) growing acceptance of computerized services; and (6) increasing recognition of the value of information and its utilization by all segments of the population, have placed unprecedented demands on services in all types of business information centers. These developments have demanded changes in the technological base, the procedures, the services, and the work patterns of the business information center. At the same time, as noted earlier, they have impacted the whole library and information science profession, forcing a recognition of the urgent need for continuing training. It should also be noted that, in addition to an increased awareness of the need for specialized courses offered in schools of library and information science, the profession has realized that the pace of change has so increased that these courses cannot presume to teach the future professional all he or she will need to know. Establishing and maintaining the procedures for one's own updating, reorientation, and development of new skills and attitudes is more important than ever before.

Before discussing the diverse opportunities for continuing training it is necessary to:

- identify certain assumptions that underlie the varied and complex nature of a business information center, its services and its highly specialized user clientele, and
- define the basic terms and concepts related to the various specialized aspects of business information service.

ASSUMPTIONS AND DEFINITIONS

Under basic assumptions, we should first recognize that the business information center is the fastest growing type of special library, both in numbers and in importance. Second, we should emphasize that the new technologies, which are inducing profound changes in the activities of all types of information centers, are producing even more profound effects in the business information center. Third, business information professionals accept the thesis that there is: (1) a critical need in a business information center for access by patrons to key information for planning in advance of major business decisions, and (2) an increasing reliance upon electronic information acquisition, management, and transfer capabilities in order to utilize the voluminous information demanded by the business world. Finally, the rapid development of information technologies and the emerging variety of employment opportunities have generated a diversity of career goals for the business information professional and a corresponding demand for continuing training. Both continuing training in the skills of the profession and also in interpersonal and interactional skills are called for. Types of training can be broken down into the following:

1. competence in the specialized areas of business;
2. understanding of both the internal and the external operations of the parent organization;
3. familiarity with sources of information;
4. online database searching capability;
5. familiarity with internal information collections and the available external information collections, facilities and services.

It should also be noted that successful interaction between the business information professional and the business user community requires an information system that is designed specifically for specialized user needs. Consequently, the complex nature of the business library as an information center makes its effectiveness dependent on several factors, more or less in order of importance: the support of top management; a significant amount of planning, both before the business information center is launched and on an ongoing basis, to deal with expansion and changing needs; and a great deal of flexibility.

It is also necessary to define certain terms and concepts, especially those that denote different things in different contexts. One key distinction is that between education and training: "education" is taken to mean "the acquisition of organized knowledge of the past and development of critical cognitive abilities, attitudes, and other enduring forms of personally and socially valuable behavior";[1] while "training" refers to "the kind of instruction and training situations in which the goals are clearly determined and their attainment easily demonstrable, and in which skilled mastery is acquired through practice and guided appraisal of learning performance."[2] Education, in terms of these definitions, is the dominant concern of degree programs with structural courses, while training is the province of short courses, workshops, much "continuing education," and so on. Both definitions are part of continuing library education, defined by Elizabeth Stone as education which "consists of all learning activities and efforts, formal and informal, by which individuals seek to upgrade their knowledge, attitudes, competencies, and understanding in their special field (or role) in order to: (1) deliver quality performance in the work setting, and (2) enrich their library careers."[3]

Other terms necessary to redefine, or better still to rename, are the "business library" and the "business librarian." The business library is defined here in its contemporary role as an information center, devoted to meeting specialized information needs, and changing rapidly, particularly under the influence of new information technologies. The term used in this essay is "business information center." Similarly, the "business librarian" is defined here as an information professional whose main responsibilities are to provide information of a specialized and personalized nature; to anticipate the future needs of an increasingly complex and changing user community; and to make every effort to meet the rapidly changing user needs by continually accepting changing concepts and utilizing the newer methods in technology, communications, and the principles and techniques of modern management. The term preferred in this essay is "business information professional."

PROGRAMS FOR CONTINUING TRAINING OF THE BUSINESS INFORMATION PROFESSIONAL

The various avenues that offer opportunities for continuing training of business information professionals, whether designed specifically for their needs or intended for all types of information professionals,[4] include:

1. Participation in conference sessions, seminars, workshops, institutes, and short-term courses. For business information professionals, the most frequently used national organization for continuing training purposes is the Special Libraries Association (SLA) on a national, regional, and local level. Current topics of special interest covered by that organization include technology, fees for service, management skills, marketing, databases, and microcomputer applications.
2. Attendance at sessions offered by state libraries. Representatives of state library activity in this area are recent offerings by the Texas State Library, which covered marketing, planning, management, and budgeting. Similar offerings of interest to business information professionals are available from most state library agencies. Business information professionals should contact their state library agencies for more information.
3. Keeping up with professional literature—both published and unpublished. Professional literature published in journals is supplemented by a great variety of information brochures, news-

letters, announcements, etc., produced and distributed by both library and information science organizations and professional organizations in other subject areas.

4. Participation in informal and formal exchange of experiences and information between information professionals of all types. One form of this exchange is participation in local networks of special libraries organized by SLA chapters and divisions at the regional, state, and local levels. Another mode is offered by sections/columns in newsletters published by business-library-oriented groups.

5. Attendance at a variety of demonstration programs presented by professional organizations and producers of information systems. Related to this is the opportunity to obtain promotional materials providing current awareness of vendor services. Selected publishers/producers that offer frequent workshops of interest to business information professionals include: PREDICASTS, ABI/INFORM, Dialog, BRS, DISCLOSURE Information Group, Industry Data Sources (Harfax), Business Research Corporation, and Institute for Scientific Information.

6. Obtaining packaged programmed instructional continuing training units for improving currentness of expertise and/or gaining new professional skills; Examples of programmed units offered by a variety of producers include Institute of Scientific Information, Inc. (tape/slide presentation on Social Science Citation Index) and ABI/INFORM (manual/tape presentation on ABI Database). Database producers and vendors, including Wilsonline, DIALOG, BRS, etc., also offer instructional packages. (NOTE: It is expected that the availability of instructional units will increase.)

Of the other formats for continuing training, teleconferencing is expected to become increasingly important, especially as a means for the busy business information professional to keep up-to-date. One of the characteristic benefits of this medium is its problem-centered or task-oriented approach in learning. The readiness to learn through teleconferencing is directly related to the immediate potential application of the information gained to business-related information situations.

Finally, in addition to continuing training offered outside of formal library education circles, it should be noted that schools of library and information science can also be important providers of continuing training. Frequently, such training is offered in conjunction with a vendor or producer of computer hardware and/or software or with a vendor or producer of another form of stored information. Such joint ventures most definitely benefit the students of library and information science in professional training beyond their master's degree education.

CONCLUSION

In conclusion, the author emphasizes that it is indeed difficult or even impossible, because of the complex nature of a business information center, to respond to the question, "What does the business information professional of the twenty-first century need to know?" The business world is one of continuously changing opportunities both for the business entrepreneur and the executive: to make a deal, sell an idea, invent and produce a product, and market and sell a product. The business world provides challenges to the professional business information professional to assist in these ventures. There is no doubt that students who are now entering the information profession as well as those already in the profession will have to continuously develop and/or update their knowledge, service skills, and management styles to succeed in this new and continuously changing information age. Continuing training presents a challenge, and perhaps provides a solution to the perplexing problem of obsolescence. Each individual business information professional, indeed any information professional, has a responsibility to continuously expand his/her knowledge and skills well beyond those received in the courses offered and undertaken in the first professional degree.

APPENDIX

Part I: Business Information Course Outline

<u>Unit I</u>
Introduction to:
  (1) The specialized nature of business, finance, management, and other related fields;
  (2) Business and other related libraries—their organization and activities;
  (3) Characteristics of business literature, with references to methods of locating facts, and basic time-saving sources

<u>Unit II</u>
Introduction to:
  (1) Government as Information Source;
  (2) Legislation and Regulation.

<u>Unit III</u>
Introduction to specialized services in business and public affairs, with emphasis on loose-leaf services and their usefulness in providing information in a variety of libraries.

<u>Unit IV</u>
Serials and their use in business and related fields.

<u>Unit V</u>
Locating facts on people, companies, organizations, agencies, etc.

Unit VI
Guides to information sources:
(1) Bibliographies;
(2) Periodical indexing and abstracting services; (special emphasis given to current-awareness tools).

Unit VII
Research organizations as data sources.

Unit VIII
Basic information sources in subject fields selected in accordance with student background and interests.

Unit IX
Selection and acquisition resources in business and related fields (with an introduction to leading publishers).

Unit X
Background information on:
(1) Databases and their producers (with emphasis on numeric databases);
(2) Online suppliers;
(3) Information brokers.

Unit XI
Discussion on the planning and management of different types of business information centers, with emphasis on:
(1) Planning process;
(2) Budgeting and budgets;
(3) Consultants and their usage;
(4) Committees;
(5) Meetings.

Unit XII
Introduction to:
(1) Cooperation, networking, and networks;
(2) Marketing concept approaches in promoting services in different types of business information centers.

Unit XIII
Student discussions of broad problems

Unit XIV
Student discussions of applications.

Part II: Consideration of Offerings of a Business Information Course in Schools of Library and Information Science

A review of the catalogs of accredited schools of library and information science shows that at least 30 schools include a separate, specialized course for business information service. This number represents an increase of 10 schools offering such a course, in comparison to the 20 schools identified in a survey conducted for the education essay in the first edition of this work. While the other schools have no separate course, it is logical to conclude that extensive coverage of the subject can be found within a variety of course titles, including Special Libraries and Information Centers, Information Sources in the Social

Sciences and Socioeconomic Data Resources. The general trend toward an increase in the recognition of the importance of a course in business information service is indeed gratifying.

REFERENCES AND BACKGROUND NOTES

1. Harmon, Glynn. "Information Science Education and Training." In: *Annual Review of Information Science and Technology*, Vol. II, Washington, DC: American Society for Information Science (1976): 345.

2. Ibid, p. 347–48.

3. Stone, Elizabeth. "The Growth of Continuing Education." *Library Trends* Vol. 34, no. 3 (Winter 1986): 489–90.

4. For information on continuing education, the following selected titles are recommended.

(a) Asp, William G., et al. *Continuing Education for the Library Information Professions.* Hamden, CT: Library Professional Publications, 1985.

Provides an overview on the subject in four major chapters, each prepared by an authority in the field. An extensive bibiliography is offered for each chapter.

(b) *Changing Technology and Education for Librarianship and Information Science. (Foundations in Library and Information Science* v. 20) Greenwich, CT: JAI Press, Inc., 1985.

Background information on the topic provided by participants at a conference held June 2–4, 1983, and organized by the School of Librarianship of the University of British Columbia. Interspersed throughout the sections are implications for continuing education as a life-long learning process.

(c) *Continuing Education: Issues and Challenges*: Papers from the Conference held at Moraine Valley Community College, Palos Hills, Illinois, August 13–16, 1985.

Includes papers presented at the first world conference on continuing education for the library and information science professions. This volume represents an important step in developing a world-wide network for library leaders in continuing education.

(d) Durrance, Joan C. "Library Schools and Continuing Professional Education: The De Facto Role and Factors That Influence It." *Library Trends* Vol. 34, no. 4 (Spring 1986): 679–96.

Covers the influence of technology, of social, economic and political pressures, and the programs in library schools as continuing education providers. References include additional readings on the subject for the interested reader.

(e) Stone, Elizabeth. "Continuing Education for Librarians in the United States." In: *Advances in Librarianship*, Vol. 8, New York, NY: Academic Press, (1978): 241–33.

An excellent overview on the subject of continuing education prepared by a noted authority on the subject. Systematically organized with sections on definitions and agencies involved in continuing education and the various aspects of the networking concept pertinent to continuing education. Includes an extensive bibliography of writings on the subject.

Index

Compiled by Pat Fowler, M. Karen Ruddy, and
Bernard S. Schlessinger

All numbers preceded by a 1. refer to numbered entries appearing in
Part I of the book. All numbers preceded by a 2. refer to numbered
entries appearing in Part II. All other numbers refer to page numbers
in the book. Initial-capitalized items in roman typeface indicate
databases or software programs.

Bernard S. Schlessinger is professor and associate dean, School of Library and Information Studies, Texas Woman's University, Denton, TX. He is the author of several books, including *The Basic Business Library: Core Resources* (first edition) and *The Who's Who of Nobel Prize Winners*, both of which were published by Oryx Press. He has published almost 100 journal articles, many of them in the area of business.

Rashelle S. Karp is assistant professor, College of Library Science, Clarion University of Pennsylvania, Clarion. She has served as associate editor for three books, including *The Basic Business Library: Core Resources* (first edition) and has published several journal articles.

Virginia S. Vocelli is director, West Hartford Public Library, West Hartford, CT. She has an extensive background in government documents and business reference and has conducted workshops in business reference across the United States.